THE REFERENCE SHELF

REPRESENTATIVE AMERICAN SPEECHES 1988–1989

edited by Owen Peterson
Professor, Department of Speech Communication
Louisiana State University

THE REFERENCE SHELF

Volume 61 Number 6

THE H. W. WILSON COMPANY

New York 1989

THE REFERENCE SHELF

The books in this series contain reprints of articles, excerpts from books, and addresses on current issues and social trends in the United States and other countries. There are six separately bound numbers in each volume, all of which are generally published in the same calendar year. One number is a collection of recent speeches; each of the others is devoted to a single subject and gives background information and discussion from various points of view, concluding with a comprehensive bibliography that contains books and pamphlets and abstracts of additional articles on the subject. Books in the series may be purchased individually or on subscription.

The Library of Congress has cataloged this serial title as follows:

Representative American speeches. 1937/38-
New York, H. W. Wilson Co.
v. 21 cm. (The Reference shelf)
Annual.
Indexes:
Author index: 1937/38-1959/60, with 1959/60; 1960/61-1969/70, with 1969/70; 1970/71-1979/80, with 1979/80.
Editors: 1937/38-1958/59, A. C. Baird.—1959/60-69/70, L. Thonssen.—1970/71-1979/80, W. W. Braden.—1980/81- O. Peterson.
ISSN 0197-6923=Representative American speeches.
1. Speeches, addresses, etc., American. 2. Speeches, addresses, etc. I. Baird, Albert Craig, 1883- ed. II. Thonssen, Lester, 1904- ed. III. Braden, Waldo Warder, 1911- ed. IV. Peterson, Owen, 1924- ed. V. Series.
PS668.B3 815.5082 38-27962
MARC-S
Library of Congress [8503r85]rev4

Printed in the United States of America

CONTENTS

PREFACE

A national election and a change of presidential administrations dominated public address in 1988–1989. During the year, campaign speech was characterized by both positive and negative features. On the positive side was the large number of preconvention debates—more than 60—among the many candidates in both major parties during the state primaries and caucuses. R. W. Apple, Jr. called these early debates a "dominant event" in the election, noting that one poll showed that 70 percent of the voters from both parties had seen at least one debate on television, and for many that was their main substantive exposure to the candidates. (*New York Times*, April 23, 1988)

On the negative side were two issues. First was the paucity of debates following the convention: there were two debates between George Bush and Michael Dukakis and one between vice presidential candidates Lloyd Bentsen and Dan Quayle. A second and more serious matter was the low level of the campaign rhetoric. Instead of addressing the political issues in a way that the voters could understand, the candidates' campaigns sunk to a contest of mudslinging, photo opportunities, slogans, and sound bites. In the opinion of John B. Oakes, former editorial page editor of the *New York Times*:

> Never in this century has there been such a campaign of personal vilification at the Presidential level. It is all the more sickening because it stems not from a few guttersnipe pols conspiring in a backroom, but from the United States's topmost political elite. . . . What is really frightening . . . is its apparent acceptance by a sizable proportion of the voting public. (*New York Times*, November 5, 1988, p. 17)

Former New York mayor John V. Lindsey called the campaign "the worst in my memory." (*Congressional Record*, February 28, 1989, p. E537) *New York Times* columnist Anthony Lewis wrote, "The 1988 campaign left some reporters who covered it, and their editors and producers, feeling uncomfortable. One said she thought she had been complicit in a fraud on democracy. Another said: 'I feel dirty!'" (see p. 73). Veteran observer James Reston called one candidate's tactics a "cheapshot campaign" of "calculated misrepresentations" orchestrated by "win-at-any-cost hucksters" who are a "disgrace to the democratic process." (*New*

York Times, October 26, 1988, p. 41) While many reporters noted that Americans were disgusted with the campaign, R. W. Apple, Jr. wrote, "But the fault, dear voters, is not in our politicians, but in ourselves. . . . [The] handlers have made this a low, ugly, evasive campaign because that kind of campaign wins American elections." (*New York Times*, December 18, 1988, p. 18)

When the votes were in, only 50.16 per cent of those eligible had voted in the election, making it the lowest turnout in 64 years. Why? No one knows, but Richard L. Berke reported, "Most popular among the assessments of why turnout dropped is that people are growing increasingly frustrated by Presidential campaigns they regard as lacking in substance and at times mean-spirited." (*New York Times*, December 18, 1988, p. 18)

In an attempt to improve the caliber of presidential campaigning, Senator Bob Graham and Representative Edward J. Markey introduced the National Presidential Debates Act in April 1989. Arguing that "democracy requires an informed electorate and debates have proven to be the most popular, useful, and unbiased method of communicating a candidate's views and character in the media age," their bill mandated that presidential candidates participate in four debates and vice presidential nominees in one in order to qualify for federal campaign funds. The compulsory nature of the proposal in qualifying for federal funds may raise serious questions regarding free speech, whether one has a right to remain silent, and "unconstitutional conditions."

One of the most controversial and widely publicized issues in 1988–1989, both in the presidential campaign and elsewhere, was the question of a woman's right to an abortion. Interest in this topic was heightened by the decision of the United States Supreme Court to hear arguments in the summer of 1989 on a Missouri law intended to limit access to abortions. Accordingly, there was much speculation that the Court's deliberations might modify or even overturn its 1973 Roe v. Wade decision, which established a constitutional right to abortion. During the year, anti-abortion—or pro-life—groups regularly picketed abortion clinics in cities throughout the country. In early 1989 they organized a rally that attracted some 67,000 people in Washington. Pro-abortion—or pro-choice—supporters countered with a march and rally in the national capital on April 9, 1989, which attracted a crowd of 250,000 or more.

Several issues concerning free speech surfaced during the year. These included the question of whether limits should be placed on outside speaker fees earned by members of Congress, whether the Federal Communications Commission should be required to reinstate the "fairness doctrine" requiring broadcasters to provide equal time to proponents of both sides on controversial subjects, and whether colleges and universities can prohibit members of their communities from making racial slurs and other speech offensive to minority groups.

Some major problems received scant attention, perhaps because they are difficult and complex and do not lend themselves to sound bites and photo opportunities: the national budget deficit, poverty and the homeless, and the high cost of medical care, to mention only a few.

I am greatly assisted by many people each year in the preparation of this collection. Foremost this year are Barry Cole Poyner and Bill Stone, whose research provided me with important information about the speakers, speeches, audiences, and occasions, and Mary Sue Bainbridge and Patricia Garcia for their help in obtaining information about the speeches and preparing the manuscripts and introductions. I thank Ginger Conrad and Lisa Landry for their cooperation and help.

I also thank my Louisiana State University colleagues and students: Stephen L. Cooper, Gresdna Doty, Mike Futtrell, Mary Frances HopKins, Tommy Karam, Bill Lewis, and Ron Terry.

Others who have provided valuable assistance are Patti Adams, Joshua Bilmes, Martha Boyd, Waldo W. Braden, A. Gilson Brown, Cynthia L. Cooke, Larry B. Dendy, Barbara Hayward, Marjorie Heffron, R. W. Hoaglund, Michael P. Jackson, Robert C. Jeffrey, Judy Johnson, J. Bennett Johnson, Daniel R. Kuehn, Fran Lamb, Murielle Nagl, Joseph O'Rourke, Charlie Owens, Charles B. Rangel, Philip Restifo, Nancy Struckman, Mary V. Wadsworth, Rebecca Wharton, Anthony Wolbarst, and Kimberly Yates.

OWEN PETERSON

Baton Rouge, Louisiana
May 25, 1989

RITES OF PASSAGE

FAREWELL ADDRESS[1]

RONALD W. REAGAN[2]

Following a tradition dating back to George Washington, on January 11, 1989, outgoing President Ronald Reagan delivered a farewell address to the nation. He spoke from the Oval Office in the White House at 9 P.M. EST. All three major television networks carried the address. "It was the 34th and final time that Mr. Reagan, whose mastery of television has been matched by few other politicians, used the medium to speak from the White House to the voters who twice gave him and his conservative agenda decisive electoral victories." (R. W. Apple, Jr., *New York Times*, January 12, 1989, p. 1)

As Reagan prepared to leave office, two-thirds of the American people approved his performance over the eight years of his presidency, the highest rating given any president at the end of his term since World War II. According to a *New York Times*-CBS News poll, 68 per cent of those surveyed approved of his overall job performance, 71 per cent supported his handling of foreign relations, particularly with the Soviet Union, and 62 per cent backed his handling of the economy. (*New York Times*, January 18, 1989, p. 1)

Eight years earlier, Reagan's predecessor, Jimmy Carter, had left office, defeated after one term. At that time, Carter delivered a farewell address described as quiet, low-keyed, and somber, a "reflective", "modest," and "brief but poignant address," "a final I-told-you-so meant for rereading in a decade." (See *Representative American Speeches 1980–1981*, p. 18). By contrast, Reagan's 1989 farewell address was characterized as "ebullient, almost boastful." (Jeff Greenfield, UPS, Baton Rouge *State Times*, January 24, 1989, p. 6B) R. W. Apple Jr. described the tone as "proud, even self-congratulatory at times." (*New York Times*, January 12, 1989, p. 1) Mary McGrory of the *Washington Post* wrote, "Presidential valedictories run heavily to the self-congratulatory, but Reagan's went to the grandiose. 'We have changed a world,' he said to his doting followers." (January 15, 1989, p. 1)

The address was vintage Reagan. It contained the same mix of anecdotes, references, themes, and metaphors to be found in most of Reagan's speeches both as president and before: "Nancy," the unknown or forgotten "little" American, patriotism, military exploits, heroes, religion, and folksy, down-home language ("Children, if your parents haven't been teaching you what it means to be an American, let 'em know and nail 'em on it"). The address reportedly was largely the work of speechwriter Peg-

[1]Delivered from the Oval Office of the White House in Washington, D.C., at 9 P.M. on January 11, 1989.

[2]For biographical note, see Appendix.

gy Noonan, who also wrote speeches for George Bush, including his inaugural address. (R. W. Apple, Jr., *New York Times*, January 12, 1989, p. 1)

Among the responses to President Reagan's address were the following:

> President Reagan paid a sentimental farewell tribute to the American people last night. . . . The speech was the kind Reagan has always felt most comfortable with on formal occasions—a celebration of American values and a denunciation of what he perceives as the excesses of American government. (Lou Cannon, *Washington Post*, January 12, 1989, p.1)

> President Reagan last night offered the vision he hopes will be his legacy—a prosperous, resurgent America. (David Hoffman, *Washington Post*, January 12, 1989, A-8)

> President Reagan's farewell speech to the American people was worthy of both the man and his presidency. . . . It was a speech worthy of the great communicator who delivered it. (*The Sunday Times*, London, January 15, 1989, B-2)

Others were more critical: Hayes Johnson wrote, "President Reagan presented his vision of an American that lives in his mind. It is a land of fables and mythology, of symbols and patriotic dreams, that he evoked Wednesday night." (*Washington Post*, January 13, 1989, A-2)

Mary McGrory explained, "No one anticipated that Reagan of all presidents would touch on any failures of his long spell in office. His style has been to ignore what he could not deny. . . . Reagan was saying . . . what problems? Isn't it great to be an American?" (*Washington Post*, January 15, 1989, p. 1)

Jeff Greenfield asked:

> What kept President Reagan's farewell speech from achieving greatness? The same flaw that kept President Reagan from achieving greatness. Many of the same attributes that made him an immensely popular president were present in his speech: the buoyant optimism, the "aw-shucks" protestations of modesty (did he really tell the leaders of the industrialized world, "My name's Ron"?), the capacity to recount stories that taught moral and political lessons. . . . And then there is the other Ronald Reagan. A great leader might have looked clearly at the work left undone, but that is not who Ronald Reagan is. . . . It is simply not in this remarkable leader's character to demonstrate the authentic attribute of a leader: The willingness to recognize the hard facts, to acknowledge them to the people he leads, and to propose a course of action to deal with them. (Jeff Greenfield, UPS, Baton Rouge *State-Times*, January17, 989, p. 6)

As Reagan departed the White House, observers tried to determine the reasons for his success as a communicator. Early in his presidency, reporters dubbed him "the great communicator." Looking back, over his eight years as president, Washington correspondents offered various explanations for his success. Lou Cannon of the *Washington Post* wrote: "His geniality, optimism, self-depreciating humor commended him to Americans who did not necessarily share his political opinion or his policy prescriptions. As a master communicator with a background in radio, films, and television, he proclaimed old values and new policies in carefully scripted Oval Office television speeches." (January 15, 1989, A-1)

Noting that Reagan was most content when given a schedule to follow and that "even his seemingly off-the-cuff comments were often scripted," Maureen Dowd of the *New York Times* attributed his success to the fact that he "has the romantic, rugged image of an American cowboy and tells sentimental war stories better than anyone else." (*New York Times*, January 15, 1989, 4:1)

Charlotte Saikowski of the *Christian Science Monitor* concluded that Reagan "made masterful use of the bully pulpit and symbols, setting a modern-day standard for presidential communication." (January 12, 1989, p. 1) Saikowski's explanation for Reagan's success was:

> The Reagan White House elevated orchestration of the news to an unparalleled height. President Reagan himself held only 48 formal televised news conferences during eight years. . . . His unfamiliarity with facts and tendency to stumble in public appearances prompted his media handlers to keep to a minimum anything but carefully scripted events. Yet in a tour de force of media manipulation, the White House created and sustained an effective image of presidential presence and leadership. (*Christian Science Monitor*, February 6, 1989, p. 8)

Dissenting from the media's description of Reagan as a "great communicator," syndicated columnist George Will maintained, "A great communicator will communicate complicated ideas, hard choices, and bad news. Reagan had little aptitude and less appetite for those tasks. But, then, communication is not really Reagan's forte. Rhetoric is." (*Newsweek*, January 9, 1989, p. 17)

Ronald W. Reagan's speech: My fellow Americans, this is the 34th time I'll speak to you from the Oval Office, and the last. We have been together eight years now, and soon it will be time for me to go. But before I do, I wanted to share some thoughts, some of which I have been saving for a long time.

It has been the honor of my life to be your President. So many of you have written the past few weeks to say thanks, but I could say as much to you. Nancy and I are grateful for the opportunity you gave us to serve.

One of the things about the Presidency is that you're always somewhat apart. You spend a lot of time going by too fast in a car someone else is driving, and seeing the people through tinted glass, the parents holding up a child, and the wave you saw too late and couldn't return. And so many times I wanted to stop, and reach out from behind the glass, to connect. And maybe I can do a little of that tonight.

People ask how I feel about leaving, and the fact is parting is "such sweet sorrow." The sweet part is California, and the ranch, and freedom. The sorrow? The goodbyes, of course, and leaving this beautiful place.

You know, down the hall and up the stairs from this office is the part of the White House where the President and his family live. There are a few favorite windows I have up there that I like to stand and look out of early in the morning. The view is over the grounds here to the Washington monument, and then the Mall, and the Jefferson memorial. But on mornings when the humidity is low, you can see past the Jefferson to the river, the Potomac, and the Virginia shore. Someone said that's the view Lincoln had when he saw the smoke rising from the battle of Bull Run. I see more prosaic things: The grass on the banks, the morning traffic as people make their way to work, now and then a sailboat on the river.

I have been thinking a bit at that window. I've been reflecting on what the past eight years have meant, and mean. And the image that comes to mind like a refrain is a nautical one, a small story about a big ship, and a refugee, and a sailor.

It was back in the early Eighties, at the height of the boat people, and the sailor was hard at work on the carrier Midway, which was patrolling the South China Sea. The sailor, like most American servicemen, was young, smart and fiercely observant. The crew spied on the horizon a leaky little boat, and crammed inside were refugees from Indochina hoping to get to America. The Midway sent a small launch to being them to the ship, and safety. As the refugees made their way through the choppy seas, one spied the sailor on deck, and stood up and called out to him. He yelled, "Hello American sailor—Hello freedom man."

A small moment with a big meaning, a moment the sailor, who wrote it in a letter, couldn't get out of his mind. And, when I saw it, neither could I.

Because that's what it was to be an American in the 1980s; we stood, again, for freedom. I know we always have but in the past few years the world—again, in a way, we ourselves—rediscovered it.

It has been quite a journey this decade, and we held together through some stormy seas. And at the end, together, we are reaching our destination.

The fact is, from Grenada to the Washington and Moscow summits, from the recession of '81 to '82 to the expansion that began in late'82 and continues to this day, we've made a difference.

The way I see it, there were two great triumphs, two things that I'm proudest of. One is the economic recovery, in which the people of America created, and filled, 19 million new jobs. The other is the recovery of our morale: America is respected again in the world, and looked to for leadership.

Something that happened to me a few years ago reflects some of this. It was back in 1981, and I was attending my first big economic summit, which was held that year in Canada. The meeting place rotates among the member countries. The opening meeting was a formal dinner for the heads of government of the seven industrialized nations. I sat there like the new kid in school and listened, and it was all Francois this and Helmut that. They dropped titles and spoke to one another on a first-name basis. At one point I sort of leaned in and said, "My name's Ron."

In that same year, we began the actions we felt would ignite an economic comeback: cut taxes and regulation, started to cut spending. Soon the recovery began.

Two years later, another economic summit, with pretty much the same cast. At the big opening meeting, we all got together, and all of a sudden just for a moment I saw that everyone was looking at me. Then one of them broke the silence. "Tell us about the American miracle," he said.

Back in 1980, when I was running for President, it was all so different. Some pundits said our programs would result in catastrophe. Our views on foreign affairs would cause war, our plans for the economy would cause inflation to soar and bring about economic collapse. I even remember one highly respected economist saying, back in 1982, that "The engines of economic growth have shut down here and across the globe and they are likely to stay that way for years to come."

Well, he, and the other "opinion leaders," were wrong. The fact is, what they called "radical" was really "right"; what they called "dangerous" was just "desperately needed."

And in all that time I won a nickname—"The Great Communicator." But I never thought it was my style or the words I used that made a difference; it was the content. I wasn't a great communicator, but I communicated great things, and they didn't spring full blown from my brow, they came from the heart of a great nation, from our experience, our wisdom, and our belief in the principles that have guided us for two centuries.

They call it The Reagan Revolution, and I'll accept that, but for me it always seemed more like The Great Rediscovery: a rediscovery of our values and our common sense.

Common sense told us that when you put a big tax on something, the people will produce less of it. So we cut the people's tax rates, and the people produced more than ever before. The economy bloomed like a plant that had been cut back and could now grow quicker and stronger. Our economic program brought about the longest peacetime expansion in our history: real family income up, the poverty rate down, entrepreneurship booming, and an explosion in research and new technology. We are exporting more than ever because American industry became more competitive, and at the same time we summoned the national will to knock down protectionist walls abroad instead of erecting them at home.

Common sense also told us that to preserve the peace we'd have to become strong again after years of weakness and confusion. So we rebuilt our defenses, and this New Year we toasted the new peacefulness around the globe. Not only have the superpowers actually begun to reduce their stockpiles of nuclear weapons, and hope for even more progress is bright, but the regional conflicts that rock the globe are also beginning to cease. The Persian Gulf is no longer a war zone, the Soviets are leaving Afghanistan, the Vietnamese are preparing to pull out of Cambodia, and American-mediated accord will soon send 50,000 Cuban troops home from Angola.

The lesson of all this was, of course, that because we are a great nation, our challenges seem complex. It will always be this way. But as long as we remember our first principles and believe in ourselves, the future will always be ours.

And something else we learned: once you begin a great movement, there's no telling where it will end. We meant to change a nation, and instead, we changed a world.

Countries across the globe are turning to free markets and free speech, and turning away from the ideologies of the past. For them, the Great Rediscovery of the 1980s has been that, lo and behold, the moral way of government is the practical way of government. Democracy, the profoundly good, is also the profoundly productive.

When you've got to the point where you can celebrate the anniversaries of your 39th birthday you can sit back sometimes, review your life and see it flowing before you. For me, there was a fork in the river, and it was right in the middle of my life.

I never meant to go into politics; it wasn't my intention when I was young. But I was raised to believe you had to pay your way for the blessings bestowed on you. I was happy with my career in the entertainment world, but I ultimately went into politics because I wanted to protect something precious.

Ours was the first revolution in the history of mankind that truly reversed the course of government, and with three little words: "We the People."

"We the People" tell the government what to do, it doesn't tell us. "We the People" are the driver, the government is the car. And we decide where it should go, and by what route, and how fast. Almost all the world's constitutions are documents in which governments tell the people what their privileges are. Our Constitution is a document in which "We the People" tell the government what it is allowed to do. "We the People" are free.

This belief has been the underlying basis for everything I have tried to do these past eight years.

But back in the 1960s when I began, it seemed to me that we had begun reversing the order of things, that through more and more rules and regulations and confiscatory taxes, the government was taking more of our money, more of our options, and more of our freedom. I went into politics in part to put up my hand and say, "Stop!" I was a citizen-politician, and it seemed the right thing for a citizen to do.

I think we have stopped a lot of what needed stopping. And I hope we have once again reminded people that man is not free unless government is limited. There's a clear cause and effect here that is as neat and predictable as a law of physics: as government expands, liberty contracts.

Nothing is less free than pure communism, and yet we have, the past few years, forged a satisfying new closeness with the Soviet Union. I've been asked if this isn't a gamble, and my answer is no, because we're basing our actions not on words but deeds.

The detente of the 1970s was based not on actions but promises. They'd promise to treat their own people and the people of the world better, but the gulag was still the gulag, and the state was still expansionist, and they still waged proxy wars in Africa, Asia, and Latin America.

This time, so far, it's different: President Gorbachev has brought about some internal democratic reforms and begun the withdrawal from Afghanistan. He has also freed prisoners whose names I've given him every time we've met.

But life has a way of reminding you of big things through small incidents. Once, during the heady days of the Moscow Summit, Nancy and I decided to break off from the entourage one afternoon to visit the shops on Arbat Street, a little street just off Moscow's main shopping area.

Even though our visit was a surprise, every Russian there immediately recognized us, and called out our names and reached for our hands. We were just about swept away by the warmth; you could almost feel the possibilities in all that joy. But within seconds, a K.G.B. detail pushed their way toward us and began pushing and shoving the people in the crowd. It was an interesting moment. It reminded me that while the man on the street in the Soviet Union yearns for peace, the government is communist—those who run it are communists—and that means we and they view such issues as freedom and human rights very differently.

We must keep up our guard—but we must also continue to work together to lessen and eliminate tension and mistrust.

My view is that President Gorbachev is different from previous Soviet leaders. I think he knows some of the things wrong with his society and is trying to fix them. We wish him well. And we'll continue to work to make sure that the Soviet Union that eventually emerges from this process is a less threatening one.

What it all boils down to is this: I want the new closeness to continue. And it will be as long as we make it clear that we will continue to act in a certain way as long as they continue to act in a helpful manner. If and when they don't, at first pull your punches. If they persist, pull the plug.

It's still trust, but verify.

It's still play, but cut the cards.

It's still watch closely, and don't be afraid to see what you see.

I've been asked if I have any regrets. I do.

The deficit is one. I've been talking a great deal about that lately, but tonight isn't for arguments, and I'm going to hold my tongue.

But an observation: I've had my share of victories in the Congress, but what few people noticed is that I never won anything you didn't win for me. They never saw my troops; they never saw Reagan's regiments, the American people. You won every battle with every call you made and letter you wrote demanding action.

Well, action is still needed. If we're to finish the job, Reagan's regiments will have to become the Bush brigades. Soon he'll be the chief, and he'll need you every bit as much as I did.

Finally, there is a great tradition of warnings in Presidential farewells, and I've got one that's been on my mind for some time.

But oddly enough it starts with one of the things I'm proudest of the past eight years: the resurgence of national pride that I called "the new patriotism." This national feeling is good, but it won't count for much, and it won't last unless it's grounded in thoughtfulness and knowledge.

An informed patriotism is what we want. And are we doing a good enough job teaching our children what America is and what she represents in the long history of the world?

Those of us who are over 35 or so years of age grew up in a different America. We were taught, very directly, what it means to be an American, and we absorbed almost in the air a love of country and an appreciation of its institutions. If you didn't get these things from your family you got them from the neighborhood, from the father down the street who fought in Korea, or the family who lost someone at Anzio. Or you could get a sense of patriotism from school. And if all else failed, you could get a sense of patriotism from the popular culture. The movies celebrated democratic values and implicitly reinforced the idea that America was special. TV was like that, too, through the mid-Sixties.

But now we're about to enter the Nineties, and some things have changed. Younger parents aren't sure that an unambivalent appreciation of America is the right thing to teach modern children. And as for those who create the popular culture, well-grounded patriotism is no longer the style.

Our spirit is back, but we haven't reinstitutionalized it. We've got to do a better job of getting across that America is freedom—freedom of speech, freedom of religion, freedom of enterprise—and freedom is special and rare. It's fragile; it needs protection.

We've got to teach history based not on what's in fashion but what's important: Why the pilgrims came here, who Jimmy Doolittle was, and what those 30 seconds over Tokyo meant. You know, four years ago on the 40th anniversary of D-Day, I read a letter from a young woman writing to her father, who'd fought on Omaha Beach. Her name was Lisa Zanatta Henn, and she said, we will always remember, we will never forget what the boys of Normandy did. Well, let's help her keep her word.

If we forget what we did, we won't know who we are. I am warning of an eradication of the American memory that could result, ultimately, in an erosion of the American spirit.

Let's start with some basics: more attention to American history and a greater emphasis of civic ritual. And let me offer lesson No. 1 about America: All great change in America begins at the dinner table. So tomorrow night in the kitchen I hope the talking begins. And children, if your parents haven't been teaching you what it means to be an American, let 'em know and nail 'em on it. That would be a very American thing to do.

And that's about all I have to say tonight. Except for one thing.

The past few days when I've been at the window upstairs, I've thought a bit of the shining "city upon a hill." The phrase comes from John Winthrop, who wrote it to describe the America he imagined. What he imagined was important, because he was an early Pilgrim, an early "Freedom Man." He journeyed here on what today we'd call a little wooden boat; and, like the other pilgrims, he was looking for a home that would be free.

I've spoken of the shining city all my political life, but I don't know if I ever quite communicated what I saw when I said it. But in my mind, it was a tall proud city built on rocks stronger than oceans, wind swept, God blessed, and teeming with people of all kinds living in harmony and peace, a city with free ports that hummed with commerce and creativity, and if there had to be city walls, the walls had doors, and the doors were open to anyone with the will and the heart to get here.

That's how I saw it, and see it still.

And how stands the city on this winter night? More prosperous, more secure and happier than it was eight years ago. But more than that: after 200 years, two centuries, she still stands strong and true on the granite ridge, and her glow has held steady no matter what storm.

And she's still a beacon, still a magnet for all who must have freedom, for all the pilgrims from all the lost places who are hustling through the darkness, toward home.

We've done our part. And as I "walk off into the city streets," a final word to the men and women of the Reagan revolution, the men and women across America who for eight years did the work that brought America back:

My friends, we did it. We weren't just marking time, we made a difference. We made the city freer, and we left her in good hands.

All in all, not bad. Not bad at all.

And so, goodbye.

God bless you. And God bless the United States of America.

INAUGURAL ADDRESS[1]

GEORGE H. W. BUSH[2]

George Herbert Walker Bush was inaugurated as the 41st President of the United States in a ceremony on the flag-draped west front of the Capitol in Washington, D.C., on January 20, 1989. Bernard Weinraub described the event:

> The inauguration took place on a clear, cold day, the azure sky flecked with white. Barbara Bush, the nation's new First Lady, smiled faintly as Chief Justice William H. Rehnquist administered the presidential oath at 12:03, three minutes after Ronald Reagan's term had officially come to an end under the provisions of the 20th Amendment to the Constitution. Mr. Bush had his left hand on two Bibles held by his wife. One was a family Bible; the other was used by George Washington at his swearing-in 200 years ago.
> Immediately after Mr. Bush had taken the oath, the United States Army Band broke into "Hail to the Chief." A 21-gun salute followed, the sound echoing across the mall. (*New York Times*, January 20, 1989, p. 1)

The new President's day had begun with a private religious service at St. John's Episcopal Church across Lafayette Square from the White House. The soon-to-be President and First Lady then met the Reagans at the White House before traveling down Pennsylvania Avenue to the Capitol to observe Justice Sandra Day O'Connor's swearing-in of former

[1]Delivered at the United States Capitol, Washington, D.C., 12:03 P.M., Friday, January 20, 1989. In the following transcript, because of slips in Mr. Bush's delivery, two sentences—indicated by italics—are taken from his prepared text, though they were not spoken by the President.

[2]For biographical note, see Appendix.

Senator James Danforth Quayle of Indiana as Vice President.

Emerging from the Capitol, Reagan, Quayle, and then Mr. Bush strode down the red-carpeted steps to the inauguration platform, greeted by strong applause from a teeming, cordial crowd whose size was put by *Insight* (February 6, 1989, p. 8) at 150,000, although, of course, the inauguration was viewed by millions more throughout the world on television.

The ceremony began and ended with a prayer by the Rev. Billy Graham, while the Inaugural Address itself was about 20 minutes long. After receiving a standing ovation, the new President and Vice President and their wives walked with the Reagans to the east front of the Capitol, where a helicopter took Ronald and Nancy Reagan to Andrews Air Force Base for their flight to California.

President Bush and his wife then left the Capitol and rode the 1.6-mile route back to the White House, although three times they emerged from their limousine to walk at the head of the vast parade, which was viewed by some 300,000 spectators. That night they attended each of the nine inaugural balls held in their honor in the capital.

> Overall, the inauguration of President Bush was certainly the most expensive and probably the biggest ever. It included five days of public concerts, private dinners, lavish balls, and a nationally televised gala. The new president was wined and dined by the leaders of Congress after his inaugural, then watched a parade that coursed down Pennsylvania Avenue for more than two hours.
>
> There were more than 8,000 military personnel on duty. As many as 35,000 [flags] were handed out to the crowd, and there were 700-plus carried by brass bands and marching groups. (Don McLeod, *Insight*, February 6, 1989, p. 8)

The extravagance of the inauguration was criticized in some quarters. In an editorial, the *New York Times* observed,

> George Bush's lavish Inaugural festivities carry a lavish price tag. By the time the five-day extravaganza ends, a record $30 million will have been spent—almost eight times the tab for Jimmy Carter's 1977 inauguration. Apart from the unseemly extravagance, such extraordinary spending raises serious questions of ethical appearances. For as inaugural costs rise, so does the odor from the big money contributions that help pay the tab. Taxpayers will foot the bill for today's swearing-in ceremony and the luncheon afterward. But all other events are privately funded by the Presidential Inaugural Committee, a non-profit corporation whose members are appointed by the President-elect. Hitting up wealthy friends of the Bush family and major corporations, the committee has collected $20 million in $100,000 interest free loans. (January 20, 1989, p. 26)

Reactions to Bush's address varied.

Bernard Weinraub described Bush's voice as strong and his manner self-assured, the speech as "marked by a theme of harmony and reconciliation," and the inaugural ceremonies "resonant with drama; the melancholy departure of the 77-year old Mr. Reagan . . . and the ascension of the Vice-President who had served faithfully in his shadow for eight years." Throughout the speech, "Barbara Bush beamed; the new President's frail 87-year old mother, Dorothy, watched her son impassively, and Mr. Reagan listened in a manner that appeared reflective." (*New York Times*, January 20, 1989, p. 1)

Charlotte Saikowski described it as "a low-key inaugural address that lacked rhetorical flourish or drum rolls, but conveyed a down-to-earth conviction and simplicity." (*Christian Science Monitor*, January 23, 1989, p. 1)

The *New York Times* editorialized: "George Bush spoke, in measured tones about a new breeze and the age of the offered hand . . . not with alarmed hyperbole but with moral conviction and a realistic agenda." (January 21, 1989, p. 18) It was later written in the *Times* that "President Bush's Inaugural Address contained no specific battle plan, no detailed agenda. . . . But it offered something at least as important; a conciliatory and practical strategy for governing. . . . So, George Bush—the kinder, gentler Bush of the interregnum—wisely used his first few minutes as President to reach out to opponents abroad and at home." (January 22, 1989, p. 24E)

Columnist Jeff Greenfield wrote,

> Anyone who doubts that George Bush means to be a very different kind of president has only to look at the words and the tone of Bush's Inaugural Address. It may have been drafted by Peggy Noonan, who also wrote Reagan's ebullient, almost boastful farewell, but it reflected a very different personality, and a very different approach to government, than offered by Mr. Reagan." (Baton Rouge *State Times*, January 24, 1989, p. 6B)

E. J. Dionne called Bush's address "a conservative one, in the more profound sense of that word" and described the proposed cures as "neither new programs nor structural reforms, but a new commitment by the American citizenry." As a result, Dionne noted, "Some critics were quick to criticize Mr. Bush for offering in his Inaugural Address noble sentiments unsupported by specific proposals." (*New York Times*, January 22, 1989, p. 4:1)

John Cassidy, correspondent for the *Sunday Times* of London, described the address to British readers:

> After Franklin D. Roosevelt's New Deal and John F. Kennedy's New Frontier, comes George Bush's New Breeze. Bush used the phrase four times during his inauguration speech. It was concocted by Roger Ailes, his media advisor, and Peggy Noonan, Ronald Reagan's favorite speechwriter, who wrote the speech Bush gave at last summer's Republican convention in New Orleans, when he promised a "kinder and gentler" America and transformed his reputation overnight. The inauguration speech was meant to be a sequel to that Noonan classic. In the event . . . it was a disappointment. . . . Some Bush aides . . . had been pushing for a harder-hitting, more substantive opening shot, but Noonan's velvet pen prevailed. . . . Despite Noonan's gooey cliches, the inauguration speech was well received by Congress and the American press. (January 22, 1989, B:1)

George H. W. Bush's speech: Mr. Chief Justice, Mr. President, Vice President Quayle, Senator Mitchell, Speaker Wright, Senator Dole, Congressmen Michel and fellow citizens, neighbors and friends.

There is a man here who has earned a lasting place in our hearts and in our history. President Reagan, on behalf of our nation I thank you for the wonderful things that you have done for America.

I've just repeated, word for word, the oath taken by George Washington 200 years ago, and the Bible on which I placed my hand is the Bible on which he placed his. It is right that the memory of Washington be with us today, not only because this is our Bicentennial Inauguration but because Washington remains the father of our country. And he would, I think, be gladdened by this day. For today is the concrete expression of a stunning fact: our continuity these 200 years since our Government began.

We meet on democracy's front porch, a good place to talk as neighbors and as friends. For this is a day when our differences for a moment are suspended. And my first act as President is a prayer—I ask you to bow your heads.

"Heavenly Father, we bow our heads and thank You for Your love. Accept our thanks for the peace that yields this day and the shared faith that makes its continuance likely. Make us strong to do Your work, willing to heed and hear Your will, and write on our hearts these words: 'Use power to help people.' For we are given power not to advance our own purposes nor to make a great show in the world, nor a name. There is but one just use of power and it is to serve people. Help us remember, Lord. Amen."

I come before you and assume the Presidency at a moment rich with promise. We live in a peaceful, prosperous time but we can make it better. For a new breeze is blowing and a world refreshed by freedom seems reborn; for in man's heart, if not in fact, the day of the dictator is over. The totalitarian era is passing, its old ideas blown away like leaves from an ancient, lifeless tree.

A new breeze is blowing, and a nation refreshed by freedom stands ready to push on. There's new ground to be broken and new action to be taken. There are times when the future seems thick as fog; you sit and wait, hoping the mist will lift and reveal the right path.

But this is a time when the future seems a door you can walk right through, into a room called Tomorrow. Great nations of the world are moving toward democracy, through the door to freedom. Men and women of the world move toward free markets, through the door to prosperity. The people of the world agitate for free expression and free thought, through the door to the moral and intellectual satisfactions that only liberty allows.

We know what works: Freedom works. We know what's right: Freedom is right. We know how to secure a more just and prosperous life for man on earth: Through free markets, free speech, free elections and the exercise of free will unhampered by the state.

For the first time in the century, for the first time in perhaps all history, man does not have to invent a system by which to live. We don't have to talk late into the night about which form of government is better. We don't have to wrest justice from the kings, we only have to summon it from within ourselves.

We must act on what we know. I take as my guide the hope of a saint: In crucial things, unity; in important things, diversity; in all things, generosity.

America today is a proud, free nation, decent and civil, a place we cannot help but love. We know in our hearts, not loudly and proudly but as a simple fact, that this country has meaning beyond what we see, and that our strength is a force for good.

Have we changed as a nation even in our time? Are we enthralled with material things, less appreciative of the nobility of work and sacrifice? My friends, we are not the sum of our possessions. They are not the measure of our lives. In our hearts we know what matters. We cannot hope only to leave our children a bigger car, a bigger bank account. We must hope to give them a sense of what it means to be a loyal friend, a loving parent, a citizen who leaves his home, his neighborhood and town better than he found it.

And what do we want the men and women who work with us to say when we're no longer there? That we were more driven to succeed than anyone around us? Or do we stop to ask if a sick child had gotten better, and stayed a moment there to trade a word of friendship.

No President, not government can teach us to remember what is best in what we are. But if the man you have chosen to lead this government can help make a difference, if he can celebrate the quieter, deeper successes that are made not of gold and silk but of better hearts and finer souls; if he can do these things, then he must.

America is never wholly herself unless she is engaged in high moral principle. We as a people have such a purpose today. It is to make kinder the face of the nation and gentler the face of the world.

My friends, we have work to do. There are the homeless, lost and roaming. There are the children who have nothing: no love, no normalcy. There are those who cannot free themselves of enslavement to whatever addiction—drugs, welfare, the demoralization that rules the slums. There is crime to be conquered, the rough crime of the streets. There are young women to be helped who are about to become mothers of children they can't care for and might not love. They need our care, our guidance and our education, though we bless them for choosing life.

The old solution, the old way, was to think that public money alone could end these problems. But we have learned that that is not so. And in any case, our funds are low. We have a deficit to bring down. We have more will than wallet; but will is what we need.

We will make the hard choices, looking at what we have, perhaps allocating it differently, making our decisions based on honest need and prudent safety. And then we will do the wisest thing of all: We will turn to the only resource we have that in times of need always grows: the goodness and the courage of the American people.

And I am speaking of a new engagement in the lives of others, a new activism, hands-on and involved, that gets the job done. We must bring in the generations, harnessing the unused talent of the elderly and the unfocused energy of the young. For not only leadership is passed from generation to generation, but so is stewardship. And the generation born after the Second World War has come of age.

I've spoken of a thousand points of light, of all the community organizations that are spread like stars throughout the nation doing good. We will work hand in hand, encouraging, sometimes leading, sometimes being led, rewarding. We will work on this in the White House, in the Cabinet agencies. I will go to the people and the programs that are the brighter points of light, and I'll ask every member of my government to become involved. The old ideas are new again because they're not old, they are timeless: duty, sacrifice, commitment, and a patriotism that finds its expression in taking part and pitching in.

And we need a new engagement, too, between the Executive and the Congress. The challenges before us will be thrashed out with . . . the House and the Senate. And we must bring the federal budget into balance. And we must insure that America stands before the world united: strong at peace and fiscally sound. But, of course, things may be difficult.

We need compromise; we've had dissension. We need harmony; we've had a chorus of discordant voices. For Congress, too, has changed in our time. There's grown a certain divisiveness. We've seen the hard looks and heard the statements in which not each other's ideas are challenged, but each other's motives. And our great parties have too often been far apart and untrusting of each other.

It's been this way since Vietnam. That war cleaves us still. *But, friends, that war began in earnest a quarter of a century ago; and surely the statute of limitations has been reached.* This is a fact: The final lesson of Vietnam is that no great nation can long afford to be sundered by a memory.

A new breeze is blowing—and the old bipartisanship must be made new again.

To my friends—and yes, I do mean friends—in the loyal opposition—and yes, I mean loyal—I put out my hand. I'm putting out my hand to you, Mr. Speaker. I'm putting out my hand to you, Mr. Majority Leader. For this is the thing: This is the age of the offered hand. And we can't turn back clocks, and I don't want to. But when our fathers were young, Mr. Speaker, our differences ended at the water's edge. And we don't wish to turn back time, but when our mothers were young, Mr. Majority Leader, the Congress and the Executive were capable of working together to produce a budget on which this nation could live. Let us negotiate soon and hard, but in the end let us produce.

The American people await action. They didn't send us here to bicker. They asked us to rise above the merely partisan. In crucial things, unity, and this, my friends, is crucial.

To the world, too, we offer new engagement and a renewed vow: We will stay strong to protect the peace. *The "offered hand" is a reluctant fist; but the fist, once made, it strong and can be used with great effect.*

There are today Americans who are held against their will in foreign lands, and Americans who are unaccounted for. Assistance can be shown here and will be long remembered. Good will begets good will. Good faith can be a spiral that endlessly moves on.

"Great nations like great men must keep their word." When America says something, America means it, whether a treaty or an agreement or a vow made on marble steps. We will always try to speak clearly, for candor is a compliment. But subtlety, too, is good and has its place.

While keeping our alliances and friendships around the world strong, ever strong, we will continue the new closeness with the Soviet Union, consistent both with our security and with progress. One might say that our new relationship in part reflects the triumph of hope and strength over experience. But hope is good. And so is strength, and vigilance.

Here today are tens of thousands of our citizens who feel the understandable satisfaction of those who have taken part in democracy and seen their hopes fulfilled. But my thoughts have been turning the past few days to those who would be watching at home, to an older fellow who will throw a salute by himself when the flag goes by, and the woman who will tell her sons the words of the battle hymns. I don't mean this to be sentimental. I mean that on days like this we remember that we are all part of a continuum, inescapably connected by the ties that bind.

Our children are watching in schools throughout our great land. And to them I say, thank you for watching democracy's big day. For democracy belongs to us all and freedom is like a beautiful kite that can go higher and higher with the breeze. And to all I say: No matter what your circumstances or where you are, you are part of this day. You are part of the life of our great nation.

A President is neither prince nor pope, and I don't seek "a window on men's souls." In fact, I yearn for a greater tolerance, an easy-goingness about each other's attitudes and way of life.

There are few clear areas in which we as a society must rise up united and express our intolerance and the most obvious now is drugs. And when that first cocaine was smuggled in on a ship, it may as well have been a deadly bacteria, so much has it hurt the body, the sould of our country. And there is much to be done and to be said, but take my word for it: This scourge will stop.

And so, there is much to do; and tomorrow the work begins. And I do not mistrust the future; I do not fear what is ahead. For our problems are large, but our heart is larger. Our challenges are great, but our will is greater. And if our flaws are endless, God's love is truly boundless.

Some see leadership as high drama, and the sound of trumpets calling. And sometimes it is that. But I see history as a book with many pages, and each day we fill a page with acts of hopefulness and meaning.

The new breeze blows, a page turns, the story unfolds, and so today a chapter begins: a small and stately story of unity, diversity and generosity, shared and written together.

Thank you. God bless you and God bless the United States of America.

SOBERING THOUGHTS

A RECLAMATION OF LEADERSHIP[1]

VERNON R. LOUCKS, JR.[2]

In a speech to financial executives, Vernon R. Loucks, Jr., addressed an issue of increasing concern to the business community to government, indeed, to the entire country: American leadership. "More specifically," Loucks said, "it's the leadership role that our nation either will or will not have in the small and competitive and highly interdependent world that's soon going to be orbiting into a new century." "Even more specific than that," he stated, "I've been thinking about some of the things that business people ought to be doing about leadership."

Vernon Loucks, Chairman and CEO of Baxter International, Inc., expressed his concern in a speech to the Chicago branch of the Financial Executives Institute on September 15, 1988. The Financial Executives Institute is a professional organization of corporate financial executives who perform the duties of controller, treasurer, or vice-president of finance. It has 92 local groups with a membership of over 13,000, representing 7,000 leading American companies. The institute sponsors research activities, publishes a newsletter and magazine, and holds an annual national conference.

Loucks delivered his speech at the chapter's first monthly meeting of the 1988-1989 year, held in the Mid-Day Club of the First National Bank Building in Chicago. Approximately 110 business executives attended the dinner meeting and heard Louck's address, which he gave at 6:45 P.M.

Loucks used a problem-solution pattern of organization to develop his subject. He first discussed the problem of American leadership, relying heavily on the opinions of scholars and experts. Having delineated the problem, Loucks dismissed some proposed solutions before setting forth five steps that "we" should take—emphasizing that "we" meant "everybody in this room, in our individual companies and in our positions of responsibility, far more than I mean our political parties, our government policymakers, or our professional associations." In a direct, informal manner, Loucks seemed to want to involve his audience and learn their opinions, saying, for example, "I'm also eager to know what you think," "Your thoughts on the matter are extremely important," "What do you think?" "Well, where does that leave us?" and asking rhetorical questions such as, "So why get so fired up about that?" "Do you like the way things are going?" and "Do you think we're headed the right way?"

President Don Foster of the Chicago chapter of the Financial Execu-

[1]Delivered to the Chicago branch of the Financial Executives Institute at the Mid-Day Club of the First National Bank Building in Chicago at 6:45 P.M., September 15, 1988.

[2]For biographical note, see Appendix.

tives Institute presented a summary of Loucks's speech in the organization's October 1988 *Newsletter*. He pronounced the session as "a very successful first meeting of the 1988–89 year."

Vernon R. Loucks, Jr.'s speech: I really appreciate the opportunity to be with you tonight. I know from Baxter people who belong to your group that the FEI [Financial Executives Institute] has worked hard to create a forum for ideas important not just to business but to our nation as well.

That's why I thought I might take a few minutes tonight to talk about a subject that's been on my mind, and that I think ought to be of concern to all of us. I'm also eager to know what you think, because if what I want to talk about is of any real merit, then your thoughts on the matter are extremely important.

So what is it that's on my mind? It's leadership. More specifically, it's the leadership role that our nation either will or will not have in the small and competitive and highly interdependent world that's soon going to be orbiting into a new century. Even more specific than that, I've been thinking about some of the things that business people ought to be doing about leadership.

But why get so fired up about that? Maybe it's because we're in an election year, although that does not mean that I think George and Mike and Dan and Lloyd are doing a great job of getting at the issues. To the contrary, I wish they were all talking more about real leadership and less about the pledge of allegiance.

I therefore have a more substantial reason for my concern. In part, it has to do with Paul Kennedy's current book, *The Rise and Fall of the Great Powers*, which I read a couple of months ago. Kennedy teaches history at Yale. His thesis in his book is that there's a constant cycle down through history where economic and military powers rise to the top and then, quite inevitably, sink to a point far from their highest level. He talks about imperial Spain, Napoleonic France, 19th-century Britain, and many other examples. He shows very clearly how the great powers, one right after the other, forget what made them great in the first place.

Of course, the question that one rushes to ask is whether the United States' economic and diplomatic power is headed in the same direction. Kennedy thinks it may be. If so, he points out that it could happen fast in the kind of world where a Pacific-Rim nation can move from the second or third economic tier to the top tier in the course of a single generation.

I'm not necessarily buying or selling Kennedy's view. But I do think it warrants serious consideration. Either he's right or he's wrong, and, if he's wrong, we might still benefit by acting as though he's right.

But what if he is right? We need then to ask whether the cycle is inevitable or not. If it is, I suppose we could just sit back and take the big ride. But, if it's not inevitable then there are some steps we ought to start taking.

What do you think? Aren't there some real reasons for concern?

We've all heard, for example, about how the United States stopped being the world's greatest creditor and started being the world's largest debtor in the past few years. But did you know that we're now a net importer of high-technology products, as opposed to a $27-billion net exporter as recently as 1981?

Paul Kennedy talks about how the United States is still the single largest economic entity on the planet, but far from a position where our performance puts us in a class by ourselves. He talks about the growing fluidity of economic power and how there are "no more impregnable geographic bastions of economic strength," as once there were.

Lester Thurow from MIT adds fuel to the fire. He points out that, in 1987, foreign funds financed 22 percent of the gross investments in this country: the tools, the homes, the commercial construction, and so forth. And our trade deficit dragged down 4 percent of our gross national product last year.

At the same time, the standard of living in our country is falling relative to other industrialized nations because their productivity is growing four times as fast. American plant and equipment investments are running at half the rate of those in the Pacific and two-thirds of those in Europe.

Here's one that I find appalling. In the years from 1960 through 1986, the amount of money that Americans had invested in savings bonds roughly doubled, to a level of $93 billion. During those same years, however, our national level of consumer credit debt increased 11 times, to a level of $723 billion.

Not all the reasons for concern are economic, either. It's been pointed out with growing frequency that European kids go to school 220 days a year, Japanese kids go 240 days a year and ours go 180 days a year. But every time anybody suggests a change, the parents and the recreation industry, let alone the kids, are all against it.

Believe me, I'm not trying to hang a bunch of crepe here. But let me ask: Do you like the way things are going? Do you think we're headed the right way? Or do you agree with Paul Kennedy that "the American sense of economic security has given way to a feeling of having lost (our) bearings . . . of not knowing where to compete or how to compete"? Those are my questions, and I'd be very interested to hear how you feel about them. But let me tell you where I'm coming from.

I think the situation is bad enough to warrant real concern. I think we've gotten flabby as competitors. I think too much of our political debate is mandated by the pollsters. I think too many of our hopes and plans and appetites are far too short-term.

But I am not ready to say that the cycle of economic and diplomatic decline is inevitable. With leadership, the cycle can be redirected and the future can be affected by us rather than foisted upon us. In offering that view, I really need to differentiate leadership from management.

I know it's been said that management does things right while leadership does the right things. I know that Mr. Dukakis and Mr. Bush have taken some potshots at each other about the difference between competence and progress. But I see the distinction between management and leadership as more fundamental. The two are not mutually exclusive. In fact, they're complementary. But they're definitely distinct, one from the other.

Borrowing in part from John Kotter at Harvard, I'd suggest that management has to do with all the disciplines of planning, budgeting, organizing, staffing, controlling, and problem solving. I don't diminish it by any means. It's highly significant work and, if it's done well, it produces consistent and generally predictable results.

Leadership, on the other hand, concerns itself with creating a clear sense of direction, with communicating that vision, and with energizing and inspiring people. It challenges people to question the status quo. It forces results. It surmounts or removes bureaucratic obstacles. The fundamental nature of leadership is to produce valuable change.

One keenly developed sense that leaders always seem to have is the sense of priority. They're acutely aware of what needs to be done and what needs not to be done. Ted Levitt came up with a colorful way to describe the nature of leadership. He traced it to some individual attributes. He said:

The history of great . . . accomplishments is always the history of an individual's special qualities. Prime Minister Churchill did not rally Britain by showing pie charts, opinion surveys or grids of competitive analysis.

Levitt went on to say that:

Leaders are effective via the authority conferred on them by those on whom they depend for results. That requires evidence that the leader's vision, purposes and convictions are based on solid contact with the grit and grind of things as they really are.

Well, where does that leave us?

I've suggested that "things as they really are" today create some troubling questions for the United States. I've said that the answers need to come from a reinvigorated force for leadership. But where is that impetus going to come from? Washington? Springfield? The City Council of Chicago? Not hardly. I think instead that we're going to have to look in the mirror.

I think there are some specific steps that we in business should be taking, or at least urging forcefully. I want to suggest first, however, that there are some places where we should not be looking for any sort of definitive guidance, and Washington and Wall Street are among them.

It seems to me that there's some notion among business people in our country today that we'll figure out which way to go just as soon as someone tells us what the tax policy is going to be and what sort of investment incentives will be in place and how much trade protection we can expect to have. In fact, I suppose we could wait until all those answers were available, but not if we want to call ourselves leaders.

Let's not hope for leadership by association, either. The business roundtable, the commercial club and our other associations all have valid reasons for existence. I don't doubt that. But remember, groups like those move only as fast as consensus will allow them to move.

Let's also avoid the temptation to think that leadership means recouping some set of past glories. Let's remember that this is not the same country that won World War II, and it's not the same world either. The rules have changed. The players have changed. We have to change as well.

There are five specific steps that I suggest we take. When I say "we," I mean everybody in this room, in our individual companies and in our positions of responsibility, far more than I mean our political parties, our government policymakers, or our professional associations.

Step one is to refocus our vision.

The one thing that I believe is indispensable to leadership is the quality of vision, and I believe we need a new vision for the economic future of this nation. We won't turn the clock back to 1947. We won't be all things to all people. We won't dictate to the rest of the world.

Recognizing the realities of today, I believe we have to focus clearly on what we do best. And there are some things we do very well, for example, aircraft, medical technology, agriculture, chemicals, office equipment and other leadership industries. So let's round out that list, and let's drive our advantages.

That's a step that every individual company needs to take with some regularity. My own company has been engaged for the past three years in pinpointing and organizing around our unique strengths in a changing health-care market. We're doing that with some very conscious designs on leadership.

But I'm not just talking here about concepts and nations and corporations. I'll go so far as to challenge the finance profession (or any other business profession, for that matter) to make sure your own vision is clear and accurate. Look at it personally if you want: Are you and those around you focusing on what's truly important? Are you applying your professional expertise to the real advancement of your company? Are you concentrating on those things that build competitiveness, or are you coasting?

Step two is to develop a much greater appetite for risk and long-term investment.

I don't think this requires much comment, other than to say that we as business people have been treating it somewhat like a diet. We keep saying we'll start tomorrow. But, if we don't start right now, I think we can be all but certain that Paul Kennedy's cycle will carry us to a plane of pure mediocrity.

Again, I can bring it home to the daily work of the finance profession or law or planning or any other discipline. I exhort you to take more risks. There isn't a CEO anywhere, at least not a candid one, who wouldn't appreciate your added help in judging the steps we have to take today in order to insure the viability of our companies tomorrow. The ability to take the right risks as a company is built on the willingness of managers at all levels to determine what's right and then act confidently on their convictions.

Step three is to significantly increase our growth in productivity.

In the 1970s, people bemoaned the drops in productivity in the United States. By comparison, our modest year-to-year improvements today look fairly good. But others are doing much better, and we have to pick up the pace. It's a function of choosing carefully and acting forcefully on our priorities.

Luckily, we have the potential to do much better. The economic trends over the past decade or so have made the United States the low-cost producer in many industries. The wage differentials that we used to cite as the reason for Japan and Germany's competitive edge are now actually headed our way. We must not fail to act on the advantages at our command. They're ours, to keep or to lose.

Again, to give you a comment specific to your work, I might suggest that some significant productivity gains can be achieved just by cutting out the unnecessary bean-counting, computing, and analysis. I'm among the first to say that managers need to assure that decisions are grounded on facts rather than hopes or wishes. But, once we have the facts, let's not forget to move. Nothing bothers me more than a manager who confuses action with analysis.

Step four. We should put the undisputed top priority on quality.

To me, this goes far beyond things like fit-and-finish on the production line or accurate financial reports, as important as those matters are in a competitive world. What we really have to do is a better job of understanding and specifying customer requirements and then meeting those requirements every single time.

In one specific sense, this means we have to stop investing in acquisitions selected because they'll create a quick fix in our quarterly operating results. We ought to be investing our resources much more heavily in the long-term ability to compete and the long-term ability to meet customer needs.

When it comes to international trade, the United States has a long way to go in understanding customer requirements. We're far too insular. I ran Baxter's international business, so I've seen the needs firsthand. We have to do a much better job of learning other people's languages, appreciating their cultures and studying their techniques, understanding all of their requirements.

The area of quality also happens to be one where you can have an important effect. In my own company and others, I've seen many cases where financial executives can help other managers clarify requirements, and then help move us closer to meeting the requirements. What are the right units of measurement, the ones that really matter? What are the right standards? Where should we set our balances as to cost versus quality versus what the customer is really asking of us?

One thing is certain. Regardless of what business you're in, the standards today are global. We all need management-information systems that recognize reality and help give quality the topmost priority that it must have.

Step five may underscore all the others. We must assure that we have a committed and capable workforce.

How often have U.S. business people said that employees were their most valuable asset? But how often have companies acted as if employees were their most dispensable asset?

This is not a moralistic point. It's purely practical. If you hold every other variable equal but give one company a capable, committed workforce while you give another company a group of ill-trained, ill-treated and discontented people, who wins in the long run?

We have to start at the beginning, too. Business can look to government all we want for a solid base of primary education. But if it's not happening, we'd better see what we can do about it. That, for example, is what's behind the Corporate-Community Schools of America initiative that some of us are involved in on the west side of Chicago.

Remember, too, that our employees tomorrow will need to be more capable, not less, and better educated, not worse. Do we want to act on our own behalf? We need to act as individuals to make those things happen. If we wait for others to show the way, then the best thing we can call ourselves is followers.

I don't think we disagree on the stakes that are involved in what I'll go so far as to call a leadership crisis. The United States cannot go back to the 1950s or the 1890s or any other glorious past era. The world won't stand idle while we try to turn back the clock.

But who says we're not capable of achievements as great, or even greater, in the future?

Of all the steps I've mentioned, this is the one where individual managers can have the most lasting impact. Do your people have the skills they need today? How about tomorrow? Do you see that it's in your own, enlightened self-interest to be developing and growing the people who staff your department today and will be running the place tomorrow?

So these are my suggestions. We need to refocus our vision and develop much greater appetite for risk and long-term investment. We need to significantly increase our growth in productivity and place the highest premium on quality. We need to ensure a committed and capable workforce.

I certainly don't doubt that we are capable of that. What we have to ask is whether we have the will to do it. And I'll tell you this: If we're serious about a reclamation of leadership in U.S. business, and I very much hope we are, then we can also believe that the best is yet to come.

SCIENCE AND THE AMERICAN FUTURE[1]

DONALD KENNEDY[2]

With a new president and Congress about to take over in Washington, thousands of the nation's scientists gathered in San Francisco on January 14, 1989 for five days to debate some of the most critical scientific and technical issues facing the country and to report on major research advances.

The occasion was the 155th meeting of the American Association for the Advancement of Science, the largest general scientific organization in the country, representing all fields of science. Membership includes 138,000 individuals and 285 scientific societies, professional organizations, and state and city academies (many of which sponsor junior academies of science). The objectives of the AAAS are to further the work of scientists and to help focus scientific efforts on the promotion of human welfare.

The meeting included three major evening addresses, more than 250 seminar and discussion sessions, and several events designed to generate public support for the sciences, such as a free science film festival, public lectures by noted scientists, and a "Public Science Day" throughout the

[1]Delivered at the 155th meeting of the American Association for the Advancement of Science in the Continental Ballroom of the San Francisco Hilton at 8:30 P.M. on January 14, 1989.

[2]For biographical note, see Appendix.

San Francisco Bay area. It was reported in *Science* that the meeting attracted the largest turnout in several years, with the attendance estimated at more than 6000, and it described the meeting as "reminiscent in some respects of the big AAAS annual gatherings of the late 1960's and early 1970's—even down to the presence of demonstrators, this year from the annual animal rights movement." (*Science*, January 27, 1989, p. 474) Although no single theme dominated the conference, each of the speakers at the three main evening sessions addressed topics of concern to the attendees: public attitudes toward science, how research and development will fare amid the scramble to cut the federal deficit, and the dismal state of scientific literacy in the nation.

Stanford University President Donald Kennedy kicked off the proceedings with a keynote address that, according to *Science* magazine, "was at times feisty, at times lugubrious. Kennedy spoke of a paradox: 'Despite the stunning success of American science, it finds itself increasingly inhibited by negative public attitudes.'" (January 27, 1989, p. 474) Kennedy delivered his speech to an audience of between 1500 and 2000 conference participants and interested members of the public in the Continental Ballroom of the San Francisco Hilton Hotel at 8:30 P.M. on the first day of the conference. Kennedy, who is a biologist and served as a commissioner for the Federal Drug Administration before becoming President of Stanford University, is an effective and popular speaker. (See the Cumulative Speaker Index for other speeches by him in earlier volumes of *Representative American Speeches*.)

Early in his speech Kennedy addressed the paradox that is of great importance to the future of science, that "despite its stunning successes, American science finds itself increasingly inhibited by negative public attitudes—views of the scientific venture that are full of suspicion and doubt." These views, he contended, are stunting the growth of science and cutting into its capacity to resolve other problems. Kennedy organized his speech around a problem-solution format, which he outlined in the introduction, saying,

> I will begin with an account of our scientific potential, and then move to the perplexing phenomenon of social inhibition. Finally, if you have the patience, I will suggest some way in which we might overcome the latter.

Response to the speech was favorable. Media coverage included reports in *Science*, the *Chronicle of Higher Education*, and the San Francisco press.

Donald Kennedy's speech: We begin the last year of a decade; and the next decade we start will be the last of a century. It is tempting at such times to review the past, but much more important to prepare for the future. So what can the *fin de siècle* of the twentieth century say to us about the twenty-first?

Much of what the future portends for our society will, I think, be determined *first* by the scientific preparations for it that we are undertaking now, and *second* by the public attitudes that will govern the extension of such work as a form of social investment.

In the first domain there is every reason for encouragement. Our accomplishments have been extraordinary, and in dozens of research areas we are poised for a kind of progress of which we would not have dared to dream at the midpoint of this century. Not only have we enriched our knowledge of the natural world at a breathtaking rate; we are also beginning to assault some of the great practical problems that burden society. Yet in the second domain we encounter a paradox: despite its stunning successes, American science finds itself increasingly inhibited by negative public attitudes—views of the scientific venture that are full of suspicion and doubt. These views translate readily into political constraints that are already stunting the growth of our science, and cutting into its capacity to help us resolve our other problems.

That paradox will be my subject this evening. I will begin with an account of our scientific potential, and then move to the perplexing phenomenon of social inhibition. Finally, if you have the patience, I will suggest some ways in which we might overcome the latter.

The good news is that by any intellectual measure our science has never been more vigorous, nor has it ever offered more hope for future advances. Somewhat to my dismay I note that in my own field, loosely defined as behavior and the neurosciences, progress in the ten years since I left it has been much greater than in the previous thirty when I was in it! The recent accomplishments seem remarkable to a lapsed practitioner: one can analyze currents at the level of single ionic channels, molecular probes can be constructed for the major classes of channel proteins, and we are beginning to learn about the molecular basis for plasticity and long-term changes in synaptic efficacy. Perhaps even more dramatic, the signals that guide axons to their proper terminations during development are beginning to be unraveled at the biochemical level, so that at last we may begin to penetrate the fundamental mystery of how the brain becomes connected in the right way. These stunning findings on experimental animals are being complemented by the new ability to analyze the genetic nature of the lesions in human neurological and behavioral disorders, from color blindness and muscular dystrophy to depression and perhaps schizophrenia. Just around the corner lies an interplay between these two different levels of approach, an interplay that may be productive beyond our wildest imaginings.

Such visions are arising not just in one or two fields, but everywhere. A couple of decades ago most of the popular attention given to physics was directed at the exciting world of new particles and high energies. None of that is any less interesting now, but condensed-matter physics and materials research have become hot topics as well. The recent breakthroughs in superconductivity are a striking example. These events are reforming the structure of the physical sciences: at Stanford, for example, "advanced materials research" will be one of the main elements in the new science campus, but it will involve researchers from at least three schools and more than seven academic departments. They will take advantage of all the new tools that permit analysis of materials at the atomic level—synchrotron radiation, tunneling scanning electron microscopy, short-wavelength lasers, and so on—turning these to the analysis of phenomena as diverse as the formation of ore at rock-water interfaces and electron migration to quantum effects in artificially synthesized semiconductors.

It is difficult to know why things are moving so fast. There are more people working in science, and I think they're smarter (although I hope maybe they're only better trained). But also, and perhaps as a result, something else is happening: research is developing new tools or technologies, and these are then being applied more quickly to new research problems. Consider, for example, how rapidly the recombinant DNA techniques were applied to a whole family of analytical challenges in genetics and biochemistry. Their application in the basic sciences, in fact, was much more extensive than their much-heralded application to commercial uses. Similarly, laser technology has transformed physical chemistry by permitting it to operate in a new time dimension—the femto-second scale. We work in a time of tight coupling between the invention of tools and their application to new domains of analysis.

It is an exciting time, and as a result we are in a position to make science work for the betterment of the human condition in a way that is unparalleled in our history. We had better be, because the human condition had never been in greater need of help in *its* history!

Just consider the predictable extensions of what we already know. Genetic engineering techniques not only offer medicine new ways in which to produce pharmaceuticals and to diagnose disease; they also hold out the hope of replacement therapies for a number of congenital conditions. Although most of the popular attention given to recombinant DNA technology has emphasized these medical opportunities, some of us believe that its most dramatic successes will be in the other great area of applied biology, agriculture. There, the new methods are likely to improve crop yields by altering plant responses to environmental factors, or by creating new symbiotic relationships or improving old ones between seed and forage crops and bacteria with engineered nitrogen-fixing capacity. Success in the latter area could relieve us of much of our dependence on commercial chemical fertilizers, the enormous energy cost of their production, and the ecological destructiveness of their use. The same kind of opportunity awaits us through the development of insect-resistant crop strains that could unhook us from the grip of ever-increasing dependence on chemical pesticides.

These last two possibilities illustrate another aspect of the breakthroughs in modern biology. They promise to solve important problems in environmental quality—not to exacerbate them, as many of the technological developments of our century have done. Consider just two prospects:

First: bacteria can be developed to attack many of the compounds that have created toxic waste dumps in the industrial nations. We are finding new and exciting properties in naturally-occurring microorganisms that can transform pesticides, PCB's, chlorinated solvents and other persistent hazardous chemicals into innocuous products. Through gene manipulation it should be possible to "evolve" cost-effective detoxifying schemes.

Second: population biologists are now adducing principles that may contribute to the design of wiser and more effective strategies of conservation and preserve design. New applications of population genetics and advances in the analysis of population viability are being combined with biogeographic theory derived from the study of island populations. The prospect is that we might hold back the wave of extinction that is sweeping our planet of its biological diversity—burning our genetic library, book by book.

I am particularly excited by these prospects, because they represent science in the very mode that attracted many of us to our work in the first place: a humane calling, proffering relief from suffering and a better world in which to live. Most of you, I suspect, would find expressions somewhat like those on your list of motivations for doing scientific work.

And yet, despite an abundance of good will and a truly extraordinary record of contemporary success, science in contemporary America finds itself in the midst of a paradox—a situation in which its work, however emphathetic with public need, finds itself inhibited by public mistrust. What forms does the inhibition take?

The first version you will hear from most scientists involves the level of public support. In real-dollar terms, this has not been a bad decade for the federal support of basic research—if you look at the program side only. But the physical infrastructure is crumbling, and most of us know it. That decay is contributing most of the upward pressure on the indirect cost of doing research; indeed, at my own institution space-related costs constitute over 40% of the indirect cost rate, and have been increasing at least four times as fast as administrative costs. Until this last Congress there had been no significant federal program to fund the facilities needs of universities since the 1960s. Although Congress did take the important step of authorizing a facilities program in the National Science Foundation last year, it is by no means clear that any money will actually be appropriated for that purpose. More disturbingly, the institutions responsible for most of the nation's basic research, the universities, have encountered one blockade after another in their efforts to recover the indirect costs of sponsored research or to develop other funding sources for infrastructure maintenance and improvement. The 1986 tax law revision, meanwhile, exacerbated the situation by reducing the incentive for important kinds of private capital gifts and by restricting the access of private research universities to the tax-exempt bond market. In recent years, our work with the Congress on these and related matters has suggested a growing impatience with the needs of the scientific community. Indeed, there is a suggestion that we are now regarded—whether we approach Washington as university representatives or as groups of investigators represented by discipline—as "just another interest group."

There is another and much more local manifestation. It takes the form of a generalized fear and mistrust of the perceived external costs of scientific work. You have come for this meeting to an unusually beautiful and admired part of the United States, and one that has an exceptional concentration of distinguished research universities. But I can say, speaking for the leadership of all of them, that you are also visiting the nation's capital of activist, single-issue, "not-in-my-backyard" politics when it comes to the externalities of science.

During the past two years, for example, facilities for the housing of research animals have been held up at the University of California at Berkeley and at Stanford by objections on the part of animal rights activists. The delays were accomplished by different means: challenge to a state legislative appropriation and lawsuits in one case, objections to the building permit at the county level in the other. The two together cost the universities in excess of two and a half million dollars. At Stanford the construction of a new animal facility designed to house rodents was held up for over a year by the delayed imposition of an environmental impact report—the first ever required for an academic building on the campus. A similar delay was imposed on the construction of a new biological sciences building. In both the Stanford cases, concerns about recombinant DNA research and toxic waste discharge were brought forward by objecting groups. But it is interesting to note that the leaders who used environmental concerns to force the construction delay of the animal facility were the same ones who had earlier opposed its construction on animal rights grounds. I think it is fair to suggest that the real agenda at work was not the stated one.

Meanwhile, in this city, residents succeeded in blocking the relocation of some University of California research programs from its campus on Parnassus Avenue to new facilities in Laurel Heights. What began with neighborhood concerns about traffic and other routine planning impacts escalated into some of the worst science-bashing and fear-mongering of recent times. Exaggerated and distorted information about hazardous materials and toxic wastes, combined with false rumors of the University's intentions in the neighborhood and the ludicrous charge that germ warfare research would be conducted at Laurel Heights, created an ugly community relations problem that threatened the viability of this splendid university's program.

The controversy eventually found its way into the courts where California's complicated and well-intended environmental quality act received its most thorough test to date with respect to university research facilities. A trial court and the Court of Appeal reached differing conclusions, leaving the matter to be resolved by the California Supreme Court.

Just over a month ago, the California Supreme Court handed down what I think will be a landmark decision. While the Court did find aspects of the University of California's Environmental

Impact Report to be deficient on planning grounds, it gave strong endorsement to the University's research programs and restored reason to the discussion about research safety and risk assessment.

More importantly, the Court arched its judicial eyebrows and delivered some badly needed plain talk about the unreasonable positions taken by objectors to the Laurel Heights project. Scattered through its opinion, one finds the Court employing pithy phrases like these to describe the opponents' arguments on issues related to research safety: "entirely unreasonable," "gross misstatement of the record," "unsupported by the record," "greatly exaggerated," and "clearly untenable." This high court ruling is of enormous importance to research in California; and the welcome, sensible language of the Court will be of help in continuing efforts to educate the public and public officials on issues related to science, research, and the environment.

Although these incidents occurred in a region especially hospitable to special-interest local politics, they bespeak a more general phenomenon: a new and corrosive popular mistrust of scientists and their work. The media popularity of the issue of scientific fraud is a barometer that bears careful watching in this connection. A year ago my friend David Baltimore, a Nobel laureate who is as justly renowned for his personal qualities of scientific leadership as he is for his own pathbreaking work, delivered the address I am privileged to give this evening. Now he is the victim of an unprecedented attack, based on a rather narrow difference of scientific interpretation that has been transmuted—through the alchemy of politics—into allegations of misconduct. This attack, shameful though it is, will probably not in the end damage David Baltimore's career. But it tells us something when the United States Congress is prepared to enact legislation to create fraud-catching offices in Federal agencies that support science—based upon hearings at which the accused persons were not even invited to testify. Taken with the other evidence, it tells us much about the paradox of which I spoke. The American public believes in progress, believes in science, and admires you as its practitioners. It knows what a first-rate scientific enterprise has brought us. It is happy to consume the products—technical, social, economic—of that enterprise. But it is much less confident than it once was about what you and I are up to, and it displays an alarming level of mistrust about our motives.

So much for the paradox. I suspect you already believed, without any prompting from me, in the future science promises us. And I hope I have convinced you that we nevertheless face serious inhibitions in the form of public reservations about the external costs of science and the trustworthiness of scientists. Now let me close with a few thoughts about how we might try to cope with the latter problems.

First, I think we must deal in a straightforward way with some misconceptions about the nature of scientific work and its promised outcomes. If what we do has no chance of matching the expectations of those who support us, we are in for real trouble. A particularly important set of misconceptions has to do with the relationship between science and money. It is widely believed that you can buy good science if you spend enough; the corollary is that it doesn't matter where, or on whom, you spend it. This belief has underlain the dramatic growth of the scientific pork barrel in the recent history of federal appropriations. It is fatally wrong, and we owe Senator Nunn a large debt for his recent performance of liposuction on the defense budget. But I fear he has given us only temporary respite, not permanent relief.

A belief of a different kind is that improvement in basic science will by itself make us more economically competitive with other nations. It can help all right, but recent analyses suggest that our deficit position with respect to Japan, for example, owes much more to such factors as product engineering, production management, the opportunity to form industry consortia, and advantages in the cost of capital than it does to research—even applied research. After all, only about one-tenth of the investment in product creation represents research. Nine-tenths represents product development activities that take place outside university settings.

Second, I think we need to examine some reasons behind the public perception of us as human beings. We are seen, I think, as having become more absorbed in our research, and much less concerned with communicating its meaning and its implication to others who are not scientists. This had led to a gradual erosion in our relationship to the polity in this country, an alienation that we can ill afford in a future that promises severe resource constraints. One aspect of this alienation, and I'm afraid it has gone unrecognized, is the increasingly popular belief that those of us who do science in the universities are neglecting our own undergraduate students. My own faculty colleagues—many of whom are devoted undergraduate teachers whom I hasten to exempt from this charge—point out that it is much harder to get grants, to manage the administrative burdens and the reporting requirements of contemporary research management, and to discharge the increasingly time-consuming burdens of faculty citizenship. There is a good deal of evidence for that view; for example, the average science faculty member at Stanford today has half again as many sources of support for a constant real-dollar research volume as a decade ago. However valid the reasons, though, it will be unacceptably costly if the consequences fall heavily on this extraordinarily capable cohort of bright students. Their disillusionment will spread quickly; worse still, we will not have them around to succeed us when the time comes.

Third, we need a lot more resolve in the face of the special political interests that are hostile to American science. We all recognize, and occasionally do battle with, the creationists, the right-to-life advocates who would ban all forms of research with fetal tissues, the animal liberation crowd. But we don't give it much of our time unless we are especially threatened. Such groups, furthermore, are often easy to identify and to dislike because of their tactics, which are often mean-spirited and sometimes violent. Sometimes it seems harder to oppose those forces hostile to science that arise from sources with which many scientists are naturally sympathetic—the environmental movement, for example. Yet the implacable opposition of some environmental organizations to all recombinant DNA research, and the local no-growth movements that reflexively oppose new research facilities, are no less the enemies of scientific progress. If organized science entered the battle against all these forces with the same invigorated self-interest they annually bring to the appropriation cycle of the National Institutes of Health and the National Science Foundation, we would all be better off.

Finally, I have a few thoughts about how we state our case to our public patrons. To the extent that the 1980s have been kind to science, it has been for the most practical of reasons. International competitiveness has become the research buzz-word of the decade, and it is small wonder that we have been willing to link our own future to the powerful political energy it has provided. Thus we have tended to justify, and sometimes to oversell, our science on utilitarian grounds.

Therein lie several traps for the unwary. First, it is not nice to disappoint people, and it is downright dangerous to disappoint your Congressman. To the extent that we persuade policymakers of the economic utility of our work, we risk being held to account if the federal investment in research doesn't produce tracking responses in the index of leading economic indicators. The political fallout from the failure of the well-advertised "war on cancer" is a recent lesson that we could all ponder with profit. Some years ago when I called that war a biomedical Vietnam, it provoked some objections even from my friends. I wasn't trying to be mean; I was just trying to point out that raised expectations turn to frustration and outrage when they aren't met.

Second, the utilitarian argument encourages a pernicious notion, now circulating widely among our policymakers, that if one appropriates research money geographically, economic prosperity will distribute itself along with it. That is the way to convert science to another form of public works project, with all the propensity for haggling and horse-trading we have come to associate with the appropriations process for rivers and harbors.

Third, we unwittingly encourage our patrons to adopt a procurement model for research when we place it on a utilitarian footing. That is not a model with which most basic scientists are familiar, and certainly not one with which they would be comfortable. It includes intensive monitoring of performance, is guarded and suspicious with respect to the Three Devils of Waste, Fraud and Abuse, requires competitive bidding procedures that consider price and quality as tradable, and generally takes a more regulatory approach. Try it; you *won't* like it.

There is another way, and I think it is better. We should be perfectly willing to point to the economic benefits of science, and to the wonderful opportunities it presents us for improving the quality of human life. But we should say, at the same time, that we do it for love; that is, we are engaged in a search for understanding of the physical world and the nature of living systems because we share a passion to know such things and to teach them to others. We should approach our public patrons with some humility, and a grateful acknowledgement that they have made a society that can afford to subsidize discovery—not because it can make us richer or healthier but because it can make us better for knowing these wonderful and mysterious things. The people who make this possible have shown time and again that they are willing to share in that excitement. To suppose that they are only in it for gain is to underrate them, and to disadvantage ourselves.

TRAGEDY OF AN AGE

THE WAR AGAINST DRUGS: WHERE WE STAND[1]

WILLIAM J. BENNETT[2]

In March, 1988 the Senate approved the appointment of William J. Bennett to be director of the new Office of National Drug Control Policy. The post, although not at cabinet level, was designed to end confusion and splintering among government agencies and to develop a coherent national drug policy.

The appointee was already a well-known figure. Richard L. Berke pointed out:

> As Education Secretary in the Reagan administration for three years, Mr. Bennett gained a reputation for stirring controversy to make a point. That skill could prove more valuable in the new, more important position. "The very thing, in my view, that made him troublesome in education may make him very valuable in this position," Senator Joseph R. Biden said. "He's never afraid to pick a fight." (*New York Times*, February 21, 1989, p. 10)

Although the official title was director of national drug control policy, the press quickly dubbed the new position "drug czar."

Rushworth M. Kidder commented on the selection of Bennett to fill the position, saying,

> At first blush, President Bush's choice of William J. Bennett as "drug czar" might seem a curious one. Mr. Bennett's background, after all, is not in drug programs but in education. . . . Maybe a late 20th-century drug czar must design, construct, and occupy a bully pulpit. If so, Bennett fits the job perfectly. That's exactly what he did at the Department of Education. He did it, in part, by issuing a stream of short reports—on such subjects as kids and drugs, by the way—and using the occasions of their release to harangue the public on the need to shape up and pay attention to education. He thundered and pleaded. He outraged and annoyed. He upset applecarts and scandalized the bourgeosie. And people noticed.
>
> That's what a bully pulpit is for. Drug abuse won't be solved by throwing government resources at it. The problem will be solved only when the public has been galvanized into an inspired intolerance reaching deep into schools, streets, and households. For that task, Bennett's got the right ticket. (*Christian Science Monitor*, January 23, 1989, p. 13)

[1]Delivered at the White House Conference for a Drug-Free America at the Omni Shoreham Hotel in Washington, D.C., on March 2, 1988.

[2]For biographical note, see Appendix.

Newsweek described the new appointee:

> The czar is a beefy, rumpled, scrowling figure. . . . The czar is William John Bennett, 45, Ph.D., J.D., former U.S. secretary of education, former college football player and life-long rock-and-roll fan—an iconoclastic, irreverent neoconservative with an acerbic tongue, a taste for the bully pulpit, and a mission many think is impossible. Bennett is a philosopher by training, a teacher by inclination, and a politician mostly by accident: he fits none of the usual Washington stereotypes and takes not small satisfaction in defying the preconceptions of those who meet him. . . .
>
> Alternately earnest, impatient, humorous, and blunt, Bill Bennett is well aware that he holds the best/worst job in Washington. He is a czar without an empire, a general without troops. He is an ambitious, tough-minded man who may, if he is lucky, turn his present assignment into a brilliant political career or just as easily fall flat on his face. (April 10, 1989, p. 20)

Bennett was familiar with the problem of drug abuse. As Secretary of Education, he had initiated the "Schools Without Drugs" campaign in 1986, and sounded the alarm about the dangers of drug usage in speeches to a variety of groups. One of those speeches was an address delivered at The White House Conference for a Drug-Free America in Washington, D.C., on March 2, 1988. The conference culminated nearly a year of planning and six regional meetings, with more than 2000 persons from across the nation congregating to develop strategies for creating a drug-free America. Bennett addressed the conference at a session featuring executive branch decision-makers in the Omni Shoreham Hotel in Washington, D.C. on March 2, 1988.

William J. Bennett's speech: As Secretary of Education, I have said many times that a society is judged by how well it performs the fundamental task of the nurture and protection of its children. With respect to illegal drugs, we are not doing enough. We are not protecting our children. Let me tell you where this fact leads me, and where perhaps it should lead us as a nation. I realize some may disagree with what I have to say, but this is the way I think it is.

On the one hand, we have seen a fundamental shift in attitudes toward illegal drug use. President and Mrs. Reagan have helped to forge a serious national consensus and commitment against drug use. Many dedicated men and women lay their lives on the line every day in the war against drugs. And this Administration and Congress have worked hard to reduce the drug trade; we have greatly increased the resources devoted to fighting the drug problem; and we have increased seizures, arrests, and prison sentences for those convicted of drug trafficking offenses.

On the other hand, we must face the truth: While we are winning some battles, we are in real danger of losing the war on drugs. While public sentiment has changed profoundly, the drug trade and the drug problem are as serious as they have ever been. What is now needed is a transformation of government policy to match, and build on the transformation of public sentiment. This means that we in government must move beyond the sound but piece-meal and incremental steps that we have so far taken. We cannot win simply by doing more of the same. We must consider a qualitative change in how we conduct our war against drugs.

Today we face bumper crops of many illegal drugs. Powerful, billion-dollar drug-producing cartels threaten the stability of several Latin American governments, and threaten to undermine American foreign policy interests in the region. Furthermore, we are interdicting only a small percentage of all drugs shipped to the United States. The drugs sold on our streets today are generally easier to get, cheaper, and more potent.

To cut down on supply, the war on drugs must be a fundamental part of our foreign policy. As the greatest military and economic power in the world, we can do more to prevent criminals in foreign nations from growing and processing illegal drugs. It is to be hoped we can do this in collaboration with foreign governments—but if need be we must consider doing this by ourselves. And we should consider broader use of military force against both the production and shipment of drugs.

We also need to do what it takes to make the shipment of drugs into this country far more difficult, by increasing our ability to search cargoes and mail entering the U.S., by restricting air traffic to specific, constantly monitored, air lanes, and in general by reasserting control over our own borders. I am for reducing demand but, if the country is awash in drugs, lasting reductions in drug use will be very difficult indeed.

In concert with cutting down on the entry of drugs, we must intensify the attack on drug dealing. Today, despite record numbers of arrests, drug dealing is growing in many metropolitan areas. Particularly in the case of crack, we seem to be facing increasingly powerful drug gangs who are ever more willing to use violence and to involve young children in the sale and distribution of drugs. And while the incidence of first-time drug use may be declining among young people generally, this is not true in many metropolitan areas, and the overall consumption of illegal drugs does not seem to be declining significantly.

Our first priority at home must be this: We must take back our streets from the drug traffickers. Security for law-abiding citizens is the first requirement of any civilized society. We need to commit whatever resources are necessary from all levels of government to secure safety and order for all our neighborhoods. In some cases, the police and courts do not have the legal support and the human and material resources to make real headway against the drug trade. We should pass tougher laws, build more prisons, expand forfeiture laws, and raise fines to cover enforcement, court and jail costs. The costs society imposes on those who try to push drugs should be great and certain. Drug pushers are not paying a high enough price for their crimes.

Law enforcement must proceed against users as well as pushers. We should use fines and forfeiture of users' assets to help pay for law enforcement and court costs. We should extend probationary periods and include regular drug tests of parolees as a condition of staying out of jail or avoiding further fines. We may well also need to spend more on treatment—but if we do so, we must introduce accountability into the funding of treatment programs, providing additional funding only for those that work.

And in our schools, as in our society generally, we have to transmit a clear message to young people. We have to transmit that message through drug education courses and through tough school drug policies. And the message must be this: The use of drugs is wrong and will simply not be tolerated. If you get involved with cocaine or other illegal drugs, you have become a criminal, you are subject to punishment, you may be hooked for life, or you may die.

Above all, it seems to me, we need a strong, coherent national policy that attacks all aspects of the drug problem. This *is* a war. We need to win it.

THE LEGALIZATION OF DRUGS[1]

DAVID BOAZ[2]

In April, 1988 *The Economist* called traffic in illegal drugs the main tragedy of our age. In an editorial the British journal charged:

> The traffic in illegal drugs—partly in mildish marijuana and worse cocaine, but most dreadful in heroin—has become a main tragedy of this age. The trade was created in its present worst-possible form because democratic politicians fell into a well-meant confusion of policy 20 years ago. (April 2, 1988, p. 11)

The "well-meant" policies included long-term prison sentences for suppliers and pushers of illegal drugs, widespread drug testing, greater expenditures for drug enforcement agencies, seizure of property of drug traffickers, calls for use of the military in the war against drugs, and "boot camp" sentences for drug offenders.

President and Mrs. Reagan took a strong anti-drug stance. At a White House Conference for a Drug-Free America, the President said, " . . . our policy today is one of 'zero tolerance.' That means absolutely, positively none—no exceptions." (*Congressional Record*, June 14, 1988, p. E1961) On another occasion he observed, "Illegal drugs are one thing no community in America can, should, or needs to tolerate—in the schools, in workplaces, in the streets, anywhere." (*The Challenge*, U.S. Department of Education, May 1988, vol. 2, no. 5, p. 1)

President Reagan and the First Lady were not alone in supporting increasingly harsh, and expensive to implement, anti-drug measures, or in believing the war against drugs can be won. In the words of Ethan A. Nadelmann, " . . . no war proclaimed by an American leader during the past forty years has garnered such sweeping bipartisan support: on this issue, liberals and conservatives are often indistinguishable." (The Great Drug Debate: The Case for Legalization," *The Public Interest*, Summer 1988, p. 3)

However, frustration over the government's inability to control the drug problem led many Americans, including some elected officials, to propose legalization as a solution to the drug crisis. Peter Kerr wrote in the *New York Times* (May 15, 1988),

> Exasperated by the seemingly endless deaths, crime and corruption generated by the world's illicit drug trade, a growing number of public officials and scholars in recent weeks have begun to call for the debate on what for years was politically unspeakable: making drugs legal.
>
> The mayors of Washington, Baltimore and Minneapolis and several

[1]Delivered to the Drug Policy Forum sponsored by the Cato Institute in a Congressional hearing room in Washington, D.C., at 4:00 P.M. on April 27, 1988.

[2]For biographical note, see Appendix.

> Congressmen have declared in the past three weeks that the nation's prohibition against drugs may have failed. They have called on the Federal Government to consider repealing laws against cocaine, heroin, marijuana, and other drugs. (p. 1)

David D. Boaz, vice president of the Cato Institute, was among those speaking the unspeakable. On April 27, 1988 Boaz addressed a group of Washington policymakers and Congressional staff members at a Drug Policy Forum organized by the Cato Institute in Washington, D.C. The Institute is a public policy research foundation dedicated to promoting debates that might provide a range of options to policymakers, options deemed by the institute to be consistent with traditional American principles of limited government, individual liberty, and peace. The *New York Times* described Boaz, who is the author-editor of four books and a frequent contributor to magazines, as a spokesman for the "baby boom generation," which bears a "disaffection for the Vietnam War, suspicion of government and major political parties, personal economic conservatism, and dedication to civil liberties." (Warren Weaver, May 19, 1987)

Boaz delivered his speech to an audience of approximately 50 Congressional staffers and journalists in a Congressional hearing room at 4:00 P.M. Two other speakers addressed the same issue.

David Boaz's speech: Let me start this discussion of drug prohibition by reading the following quotation:

"For thirteen years federal law enforcement officials fought the illegal traffic. State and local reinforcements were called up to help. The fight was always frustrating and too often futile. The enemy used guerrilla tactics, seldom came into the open to fight, blended easily into the general population, and when finally subdued turned to the United States Constitution for protection. His numbers were legion, his resources unlimited, his tactics imaginative. Men of high resolve and determination were summoned to Washington to direct the federal forces. The enemy was pursued relentlessly on land and sea and in the air. There were an alarming number of casualties on both sides, and, as in all wars, innocent bystanders fell in the crossfire.

Well, you may have guessed that although I read that recently, it wasn't written recently. It was written about the prohibition of alcohol in the 1920s, and it illustrates a very simple thesis of my talk: Alcohol didn't cause the high crime rates of the 1920s, prohibition did. Drugs don't cause today's alarming crime rates, drug prohibition does.

What are the effects of prohibition? (Specifically I'm talking here about drug prohibition, but the analysis applies to almost any prohibition of a substance or activity people want.) The first effect is crime. This is a very simple matter of economics. Drug laws reduce the number of suppliers and therefore reduce the supply of the substance, driving up the price. The danger of arrest for the seller adds a risk premium to the price. The higher price means that users often have to commit crimes to pay for a habit that would be easily affordable if it was legal. Heroin, cocaine, and other drugs would cost much less if they were legal.

Crime also results from another factor, the fact that dealers have no way to settle disputes with each other except by shooting each other. You don't see shoot-outs in the car business, you don't see shoot-outs even in the liquor or the tobacco business. But if you have a dispute with another drug dealer, if he rips you off, you can't sue him, you can't take him to court, you can't do anything except use violence.

And then the very illegality of the drug business draws in criminals. As conservatives always say about guns, if drugs are outlawed, only outlaws will sell drugs. The decent people who would like to be selling drugs the way they might otherwise sell liquor will get squeezed out of an increasingly violent business.

The second effect of prohibition is corruption. Prohibition raises prices, which leads to extraordinary profits, which are an irresistible temptation to policemen, customs officers, Latin American officials, and so on. We should be shocked not that there are Miami policemen on the take, but that there are some Miami policemen not on the take. Policemen make $35,000 a year and have to arrest people who are driving cars worth several times that. Should we be surprised that some of this money trickles down into the pockets of these policemen?

A third effect, and one that is often underestimated, is bringing buyers into contact with criminals. If you buy alcohol you don't have to deal with criminals. If you buy marijuana on a college campus, you may not have to deal with criminals, but maybe the person you bought it from does deal with criminals. And if you are a high school student, there is a very good chance that the people you're buying drugs from—the people who are bringing drugs right to your doorstep, to your housing project, to your schoolyard—are really criminals; not just in the sense that they are selling drugs, but these are really criminal types. One of the strongest arguments for legalization is to divorce the process of using drugs from the process of getting involved in a criminal culture.

A fourth effect is the creation of stronger drugs. Richard Cowan in *National Review* has promulgated what he calls the iron law of prohibition: The more intense the law enforcement, the more potent the drugs will become. If you can only smuggle one suitcase full of drugs into the United States or if you can only drive one car full of drugs into Baltimore, which would you rather be carrying: marijuana, coca leaves, cocaine, or crack? You get more dollars for the bulk if you carry more potent drugs. An early example of that is that a lot of people turned to marijuana when alcohol became more difficult to get during Prohibition. A few years after Prohibition began in the 1920s there began to be pressures for laws against marijuana. When you talk about drug legalization, one of the questions you will get is, "Well, marijuana is one thing, maybe even cocaine, but are you seriously saying you would legalize crack?" And the answer is that crack is almost entirely a product of prohibition. It probably would not have existed under a legalized system.

The fifth effect of prohibition is civil liberties abuses. I think the authorities actually overstepped their bounds recently when they seized a yacht because there was a quarter gram of marijuana on it, and there wasn't even anybody on the yacht except the crew, not one of whom could be connected to the marijuana. After a public uproar they actually had to back off. But I recall a time in this country when the government was only allowed to punish you after you got convicted in a court of law. It now appears that they can punish you by seizing your car or your boat, not even after an indictment—much less a conviction—but after a mere allegation by a police officer.

There is an inherent problem of civil liberties abuses in victimless crimes. Randy Barnett wrote about this in the Pacific Research Institute book *Dealing with Drugs*; the problem is that with victimless crimes like buying drugs there is no complaining witness. In most crimes, say robbery or rape, there is a person who in our legal system is called the complaining witness: the person who was robbed or raped, who goes to the police and complains that somebody has done something to him or her. When you buy drugs, neither party to the transaction complains. Now what does this mean? It means you don't have eyewitnesses complaining about the problem so the police have to get the evidence somewhere else. The policemen have to start going undercover, and that leads to entrapment, wiretapping, and all sorts of things that border on civil liberties abuses and usually end up crossing the border.

The sixth effect of prohibition is futility. The drug war simply isn't working. I was asked the other day by a *Washington Post* reporter, isn't a lot of the support for legalization that we're seeing from politicians and others merely a sign of frustration? And I said, frustration is a rational response to futility. It's quite understandable why people have gotten frustrated with the continuing failure of new enforcement policies.

If you are involved in a war and you're not winning, you have two basic choices. The first is escalation, and we've seen a lot of proposals for that.

New York Mayor Ed Koch has proposed to strip-search every person entering the United States from South America or Southeast Asia. Members of the D.C. City Council have called for the National Guard to occupy the capital city of the United States. Bob Dole has called for the death penalty for drug sellers. George Bush, trying to prove that he's no wimp, has upped the ante: he wants *swift* execution of drug dealers. Bush said, "Due process is fine, but we've got to find a way to speed it up." He was asked, how do you get around the due process problem? He responded, "I don't know the answer to that. I'm not a lawyer." Presumably his attorney general will be one, for a change.

On the other side of the political spectrum, Jesse Jackson wants to bring the troops home from Europe and use them to ring our southern border. The police chief of Los Angeles wants to invade Colombia.

The White House drug adviser and the usually sensible *Wall Street Journal* editorial page have called for arresting small-time users. The *Journal*, with its usual spirit, urged the government to "crush the users"; that's 23 million Americans.

The Justice Department wants to double our prison capacity even though we already have far more people in prison as a percentage of our population than any other industrialized country except South Africa. Ed Meese wants to drug test all workers.

The Customs Service has asked for authorization to "use appropriate force" to compel planes suspected of carrying drugs to land. It has clarified, in case there was any doubt, that yes, it means that if it can't find out what a plane is up to, it wants the authority to shoot the plane down and then find out if it's carrying drugs. These rather frightening ideas represent one response to the futility of the drug war.

The more sensible response, it seems to me, is to decriminalize—to de-escalate, to realize that trying to wage war on 23 million Americans who are obviously very committed to certain recreational activities is not going to be any more successful than Prohibition was. A lot of people use drugs recreationally and peacefully and safely and are not going to go along with this "zero tolerance" idea. They're going to keep trying to get drugs. The problems caused by prohibition are not going to be solved by stepped-up enforcement.

What would be the effects of decriminalization? The first concern that most people have is that there would be more drug users. I'm not sure that's true. There are several factors that point in the other direction. One is the forbidden fruit aspect of drugs: because they're illegal, a lot of young people are tempted to give them a try. It's probably also true that both cultural and personality factors are more important than price or legality in determining whether people are going to use drugs. Similarly, consider how drugs would be sold. There would be only print advertising of legal drugs; we would surely ban television ads, as we do with liquor and tobacco. You would go to, say, a liquor store where you would find these drugs with a warning label on them and available only to adults. That system might well be less effective in getting drugs to young people than schoolyard pushers are—and you wouldn't have schoolyard pushers. Those are a number of reasons why drug use might fall after legalization.

Having said all that, I will say I think it is likely that there would be more users of drugs that are currently illegal. There would be somewhat more users, I suspect, using cleaner, safer drugs and dying less often. And of course to the extent that there is drug switching, it's not at all clear that people switching from alcohol to marijuana are doing anything more dangerous; in fact, the medical evidence is almost overwhelming that if you switch from either alcohol or tobacco to marijuana and probably even to other illegal drugs you are more likely to live a long and healthy life.

Most people use drugs recreationally; they're not abusers. The National Institute of Drug Abuse survey of cocaine users under 25 years old found that 250,000 young people used cocaine weekly. But 2.5 million had used it in the past month, 5.3 million had used it in the past year, and more than 8 million had tried cocaine. Now the key point here is that 8 million young people have tried cocaine of which 250,000 used it weekly. Surely those who use it weekly are the only ones who could be considered to have a cocaine problem; and indeed many of those people don't have a problem that requires any kind of attention.

It is generally estimated that there are 100,000 deaths a year in the United States from alcohol, 300,000 deaths a year from tobacco, and only 3,500 deaths from all illegal drugs—and of those, 80 percent are a result of prohibition, not of the drugs themselves.

It's important to look at what's happening with both illegal and legal drugs right now. Illegal drugs, for the reasons I explained, are getting stronger. Crack is replacing cocaine and so on. But legal drugs are getting weaker. We're seeing increased demand for low-tar cigarettes, a shift away from hard liquor toward beer and wine, a shift from wine to wine coolers. In the long run there is a trend away from dangerous drugs in the United States. Right now, despite all the hysteria, there is probably less usage of marijuana and cocaine, as well as alcohol and tobacco, than there was five years ago. And I don't think that prohibition or legalization will have a whole lot of effect on that, except that possibly under legalization health and safety warnings will be taken more seriously because they will not be viewed as just a way of justifying this political crusade. We'll actually listen to them the way we listen to the surgeon general on tobacco.

In the long run, however, if you ask me what will happen to drug use, I would simply say, as Bernard Baruch said of the stock market, it will fluctuate. And there's not a lot that public policy can do about it one way or the other. There will at some points in our future be more drug use than there is today, there will at other points be less. My guess is that there will be a general downward trend.

Finally, the clearest effect to legalization would be less crime. Estimates are that anywhere from 40 to 70 percent of the violent crime in urban areas—robberies, burglaries, and killings—is related to the prohibition of drugs. A lot of policemen will tell you this off the record. A friend of mine, in a big-city prosecutor's office, told me just the other day that her colleagues had talked a lot about Baltimore Mayor Kurt Schmoke's proposal for decriminalizing drugs. She said that a surprising number of people in the district attorney's office think that he is right—including a lot of the cops on the beat. They say he's right that it 's futile, that it causes more crime, and that there is no way around that problem.

Let me say just a word here about the shift in public opinion. Over the last couple of months we have seen a lot of new interest in legalization. We've seen Mayor Schmoke issue a very stirring call for a national debate on the issue. If you read his reasons for why there should be a national debate, it's very clear that he believes legalization is preferable to continuing the drug war. We've seen D.C. Mayor Marion Barry and Rep. Steny Hoyer (D-Md.) also saying that it's time for a national debate.

Interestingly, a month ago, you would almost have said this was more a conservative issue than a liberal issue. People like William F. Buckley, Jr., and Ernest van den Haag, economists like Milton Friedman and Gary Becker, and the British magazine the *Economist* all had endorsed some kind of decriminalization or legalization. Only in the past month or so have we finally seen liberals—who are supposed to protect individual rights—stepping out on this issue. Mayor Schmoke and Mayor Barry have been joined by Rep. Pete Stark (D-Ca.) and Mayor Donald Fraser of Minneapolis. Now state senator Joseph Galiber, a liberal Democrat from the Bronx, has introduced a bill to legalize drugs in New York. Now we're seeing drug legalization discussed on the front pages of both the *Washington Post* and the *New York Times*, in *Time* and *Newsweek*, on "Nightline," "This Week with David Brinkley," and the "CBS Evening News."

We are approaching the point where we're going to keep passing stricter drug laws until the day that we finally give up and decriminalize drugs. People recognize that what we're doing isn't working. So we're going to keep stepping up enforcement but at the same time, more and more people are going to be recognizing the futility of the drug war. And at some point in the not-too-distant future there will be a critical mass in favor of decriminalization. Not in favor of saying drugs are okay, not necessarily even endorsing the attitude that people have the right to do with their own bodies what they want to do, but recognizing on health and safety and economic grounds that this effort at prohibition is not going to be any more successful than the previous one.

HOW FREE IS FREE?

ETERNAL VIGILANCE IS STILL THE PRICE OF LIBERTY[1]

KASSIAN A. KOVALCHECK, JR.[2]

Endowing a lecture in memory of a distinguished scholar or teacher is an appropriate way of honoring that person, of validating his or her contributions. One such lecture series is The Brigance Forum at Wabash College in Crawfordsville, Indiana.

The Brigance Forum is an annual public lecture or debate in memory of the late William Norwood Brigance, a teacher at Wabash for 38 years who, through the leadership he provided in the Speech Association of America, was also a noted scholar and editor. The Brigance family, his friends and former students, and those who continued the tradition of speech at Wabash after his death endowed the forum as an ongoing memorial to him.

As part of this series, on April 7, 1988, Dr. Kassian A. Kovalcheck, Jr., delivered a lecture entitled "Eternal Vigilance Is Still the Price of Liberty." A Wabash graduate, Kovalcheck is associate professor of Speech and director of Forensics at Vanderbilt University and author of scholarly articles in the field of argumentation and debate. He spoke to approximately 130 students, faculty, and townspeople in the Lovell Lecture Hall on the campus of the small all-male liberal arts college at 8:00 P.M.

Dr. Joseph O'Rourke, chairman of the Speech Department and the speaker's former teacher and forensics coach, introduced Kovalcheck. Kovalcheck responded to his former professor's humorous introduction in kind before turning to his topic: the question of freedom of the public platform. More specifically, he explained, "It is the ability of our State Department to control freedom of speech by visa denial that I wish to discuss this evening."

The lecture subsequently was printed and distributed to Wabash alumni and members of the Speech Communication Association. Regarding the published version of the speech, Dr. O'Rourke reported, "We have received favorable responses from all parts of the U.S. and John Crook, Wabash '69, now head of the treaty division in the State Department, made sure it was circulated to those concerned with granting visas."

Kassian A. Kovalcheck, Jr.'s speech: Joe, President Powell, ladies and gentlemen. I face a number of exceedingly difficult, if not mutu-

[1]Delivered to The Brigance Forum at 8 P.M., April 7, 1988, in the Lovell Lecture Hall of Wabash College, Crawfordsville, Indiana.

[2]For biographical note, see Appendix.

ally exclusive, tasks, this evening. The first is to determine the treatment to accord Professor O'Rourke's introduction. Were I to ignore his statements completely you might believe that I simply take the kind of remarks as my due and, by my silence, you might think I acquiesce or agree with his misstatements and hyperbole. For example he said that I wrote home as a freshman and said he wouldn't let me debate with the varsity, "I guess he doesn't want to win." That was untrue. I was already on the varsity, O'Rourke wouldn't let me debate with the novices as well, though I was eligible, and this prompted my embarrassingly humble statement that "I guess he doesn't want to win." To acknowledge his remarks, however, would require me to be as inventive and as kind to Professor O'Rourke as he has been to me. Rather than indulge that bland unctuousness and reverse our 27 years of argument, permit me to relate a true story that happened a few weeks ago. A student of mine was in the law library, working on an assignment. Her name is Tara McCreery and in the course of being in the library a few law students started talking to her. It turned out they were from Wabash College (how unusual for Wabash men to want to speak to young women) and in the course of the conversation she mentioned that she had a professor who had gone to Wabash. She mentioned my name and the Wabash men indicated they had heard it before and even said that they had taken courses from Joe O'Rourke, a man who had taught me. At which point Tara blurted out, no doubt involuntarily: "My God, you mean he's still alive." That could sum up my reactions to O'Rourke.

The second task, though easier, is to acknowledge the honor of presenting the William Norwood Brigance Forum. Since I was among the first of the students to come to Wabash after Brigance's death, there is a special way that I feel myself to be a part of the legacy and tradition he provided. That is a tradition that was and is embodied in the Speech program at Wabash College and I feel a deep sense of gratitude at having been permitted to be a part of that program, particularly through the teaching of Joseph O'Rourke and Victor Powell, and am also grateful for having the opportunity, through tonight's lecture, of joining that tradition again.

But if the honor is great, so is the burden, for to have a lecture worthy of the tradition of W. Norwood Brigance, in spite of what O'Rourke said about my sense of humility and ego, may exceed my capacity. When I was first asked about the lecture, I was told that it should relate to the issues of the American public platform. At least one of the issues of the public platform that I thought Brigance found compelling was the opportunity for participation, and it is the question of the freedom of the public platform that forms the focus for this evening's lecture.

The current issues of *Frets*, "the magazine for acoustic string musicians," and therefore not read by those who like children's music and/or rock and roll, highlights an artistic travesty that is about to strike America. After August of 1986 the United States Immigration and Naturalization Service began tightening controls on the issuance of H-1 Visas—temporary work permits necessary for foreign musicians or performers who seek to tour the United States. It is now necessary for performers to prove "preeminence" in order to obtain an H-1 Visa. The potential for abuse is ominous. The possibility of the INS being influenced by the husband of Tipper Gore, should he achieve greater status, is striking, let alone the idea of what Jimmy Carter used to call "bloated bureaucrats" deciding what music and art is preeminent enough for us to hear and see. The first notable challenge by the Immigration and Naturalization service has fallen on English guitarist John Renbourn when the INS last December asked for additional information concerning his qualifications. Mitch Greenhill, Renbourn's U.S. manager, noted the following difficulties:

> Renbourn seems a singularly unlikely target. Not only is his preeminence as a guitarist well established—through his work with Pentangle, his 1982 Grammy nomination, and appearances at Carnegie Hall, the Wolf Trap Foundation, and other major venues—but John has already been granted H-1 visas several times, most recently in the *summer* of 1987. Had the INS' astute music mavens, a la star-stripping restaurant critics detected a recent slump in his playing? A few botched arpeggios, perhaps, a hammer-on that pulled off? Hard to say. And hard to determine—since their letter while dealing with specific points in the application was unsigned. This might be the work of that rarest and most ominous of music critics, one who needs no byline.

Greenhill then noted the major problem with having the INS make such determinations:

> Thus, if Renbourn is denied permission to perform in America, American audiences are denied access to his musical sensibility, to his "services of an exceptional nature." Culturally, this makes us poorer. And the political implications—for a society which counts freedom of speech among its strengths—are chilling.

Now, I have not come here this evening to discuss the plight of this English guitarist. It is possible that the Republic will not be shattered nor the First Amendment in tatters if we miss out on hearing medieval madrigals or one more example of poacher-gamekeeper ballads. It is also possible that this is the type of issue that will attract the attention of young people. Perhaps we will have a new protest movement in defense of English guitarists or Irish Rock Bands, for if we are to believe Allen Bloom's *Closing of the American Mind* we can do anything to the current crop of college students but interfere with their music. The problem I'm here to discuss is more serious, for if it is distasteful to have federal bureaucrats determining the nature of artistic preeminence and quality, what Americans will be able to hear and watch, it is more than distasteful, it is outright dangerous and a threat to the basis of democracy to have federal bureaucrats determining what ideas Americans can be exposed to and what people will be able to present ideas to Americans. It is the ability of our State Department to control freedom of speech by visa denial that I wish to discuss this evening, and by the conclusion of my lecture I hope to establish that even with recent Congressional efforts to improve the situation the freedom of the public platform and the marketplace of ideas is threatened by the abuses of the State Department, past and present, Republican and Democrat, liberal, conservative, moderate.

At the moment the United States Department of State has the power to deny a visa to foreigners who are invited to the United States for the purpose of engaging in public discourse. The most recent example occurred a month ago. On March 5, *The Washington Post* announced that the State Department denied a visa to Gerry Adams, a member of the British Parliament representing West Belfast and president of Provisional Sinn Fein, a legal political party in Northern Ireland. State Department spokeswoman Donna Sherman stated that Adams was "ineligible under [the section] of the Immigration and Nationality Act which excludes from admission to the U.S. people who are personally involved with terrorist activities." When asked to specify the activities, Ms. Sherman stated: "Our information is that as president of the Provisional Sinn Fein, Mr. Adams is personally and publicly committed to and abets the armed struggle in Northern Ireland, and it's on that basis he was denied a visa."

Before I explain the pernicious nature of such bureaucratic power, permit me to explain a few assumptions I make about the First Amendment and the nature of freedom of speech.

Assumption #1: While freedom of speech may have a beneficial psychological impact in permitting us to "sound off," the most beneficial aspect of the First Amendment is a guarantee that ideas will not be stifled and that the public will have the opportunity to discover information and political truth. Frederick Schauer, in *Free Speech: A Philosophical Inquiry*, noted that: "Under many formulations of the argument from democracy, freedom of speech is valuable because it allows *listeners* to receive all information material to the exercise of voting rights by members of a sovereign electorate. Indeed, the emphasis on the rights of the listener rather than on the rights of the speaker is one of the most important contributions of the argument from democracy." In short, if we accept the idea of democracy, then we must accept the idea of an informed electorate, and the electorate can only be informed if the government does not interfere with the ability to acquire information.

Assumption #2: Almost any individual, group, or governmental body will seek to control the flow of information to its own advantage. It is true that a great deal of argument and evidence suggests that such control is usually counter-productive, particularly in a free society that protects the rights of rebuttal, and that what is suppressed will emerge eventually. But that does not deny the impulse to control information to the advantage of the individual group, or governmental body that has the opportunity or power to control the information.

Assumption #3: Suppression can work. Any number of people argue that suppression is ineffective and return to Aristotle's dictum on truth emerging if we have two equal advocates. Yet Aristotle never claimed truth would emerge if we failed to have two equal advocates or if one of the advocates was not permitted to speak at all. Even in that remarkable work that I first explored under the relentless grilling of Professors Powell and Charles, John Stuart Mill's *On Liberty*, the declaration exists that suppression works. Mill stated that we should never conclude that suppression fails because it is clear that truth can be hidden for a long period of time. Mill said that "the dictum that truth always triumphs over falsehood is one of those pleasant falsehoods which men repeat after one another till they pass into commonplaces, but which all experience refutes. History teems with instances of truth put down by persecution. If not suppressed for ever, it may be thrown back for centuries. . . . It is a piece of idle sentimentality that truth, merely as truth, has any inherent power denied to error of prevailing against the dungeon and the stake. Men are not more zealous for truth than they often are for error, and a sufficient application of legal or even of social penalties will generally succeed in stopping the propagation of either. Schauer even suggests that there are times "when opinions are suppressed precisely because they are (or are perceived to be) true. More commonly, opinions are suppressed because their expression will or is thought to cause certain undesirable consequences unrelated to the truth or falsity of the suppressed opinion. The reason individuals, groups, or governments seek to suppress information is that they know such suppression can prevent, or at the least, delay the acceptance of ideas hostile to their interests.

With my assumptions out in the open, allow me to return to my main theme: the Department of State has, and has had, the power to control the marketplace of ideas by denying entry visas to potential foreign speakers. A partial list of those denied entry includes several members of the British Parliament, notably those interested in Irish questions, such as Gerry Adams, Owen Curran, Bernadette Devlin, and Ian Paisley; writers such as Gabriel Garcia Marquez, Carlos Fuentes, Pablo Neruda, Jorge Luis Borges and Julio Cortazar, and even Nino Pasti, retired NATO General that our State Department thought might provide "propaganda and disinformation" relative to the initial deployment of Pershing and Cruise missiles in Europe. How did the State Department acquire such power? The answer to that requires the tortuous tracing of our history back to that unhappy McCarthyite period of the early 1950s.

During the early 1950s the United States was mired in its own fears over Communism, particularly the fear that we were being subverted from within. It appeared as a deeply held belief that governmental employees were at work who had not admiration or respect for democratic principles and who sought to turn our government away from the desires of the democratic voice and the rule of law. (Of course we had to wait until the arrival of the current administration to discover how well founded such a fear could be.) It was also feared that the Communist message was so powerful that we had to prevent our people, particularly our children, from hearing the message, much as we wish to avoid drug dealers or CIA recruiters on college campuses today. In the face of those fears a number of pieces of legislation became law. One of the worst examples was the Immigration and Nationality Act, Public Law No. 414 (1952), otherwise known as the McCarran-Walter Act. The McCarran-Walter Act was written and passed without public hearings. President Truman vetoed the bill, calling some of its provisions worse than the infamous Alien Act of 1798. The Senate and House in June, 1952 overrode the veto.

Two sections of this bill have particular impact on freedom of speech. Section 212(a)(28) denies an entry visa to any foreigner who believes in communism or anarchism, writes about those doctrines, or belongs to an organization that promotes those doctrines. This section of the bill can still be employed. For example, at the very moment we were engaged in that famous non-trading with the Soviets to get the release of Nicholas Daniloff, an American newsman charged with spying in Moscow, our Immigration and Naturalization Service had detained a correspondent for a Socialist newspaper in Belgian "after immigration officials found Communist documents in his baggage when he arrived at Newark on a flight from Brussels." The journalist, Mr. Tom Ronse, was disturbed that a federal law permitting his detention existed but the Immigration and Naturalization Service eventually decided not to send him back to Belgium. Prior to 1977 the Attorney General could waive this excludability when it was judged necessary, but the so-called McGovern Amendment altered that discretion and required instead that the "Secretary of State 'should' recommend to the Attorney General that a waiver be granted except in national security cases, which must be certified to both houses of Congress. Steven R. Shapiro, a staff attorney for the New York Civil Liberties Union and a professor at Brooklyn Law School, has pointed out that we need a lot of waivers, for this law, read literally, would exclude almost everyone from Eastern Europe. During 1985, for example, 47,853 visitors were deemed excludable but 47,038 waivers were issued. Thus, as Shapiro notes, "815 foreign visitors were excluded from the United States under Section 212(a)(28) because of their political beliefs or associations. This is an incredible power to give a government agency.

If Section 212(a)(28) encroaches on the concept of freedom of speech, Section 212(a)(27) tramples it into dust. This section says foreigners can be banned if they come in "solely, principally, or incidentally to engage in activities which would be prejudicial to the public interest, or endanger the welfare, safety, or security of the United States." Additionally, terrorists are excluded under a 1982 amendment to Section 212(a)(29) that bars aliens likely to engage in espionage or sabotage. Section 212(a)(29) also refers to "other activity subversive to the national security." This is the kind of language that non-well-meaning government officials could use to seriously curtail freedom of expression. And of course that is exactly what government officials have done.

Just look at some of the past examples of the State Department decision making. James J. Kilpatrick (he has to be good because his column appears in the *Indianapolis Star*) provides one of my favorite examples. Farley Mowet, a Canadian writer and author of, among other things, *Never Cry Wolf*, a best-seller turned movie that often appears on the Disney channel, has been prevented from entering the country. Government sources said Mowet was once quoted as saying he shot a .22-cal. rifle at U.S. Strategic Air Command planes. Mowet denied firing any shots and said the story went "back to a time when another writer and myself discovered there was a cache of atomic bombs at a SAC base in Stephenville, Newfoundland. We announced formation of the Newfoundland Revolutionary Society and said we were goint to steal one A-bomb. . . . I said if the American Air Force interfered, we would stand them off with our trusty Siwiling gun. That's a 19th-century muzzleloader. It has a range of 40 yards. Kilpatrick explained that this was intended as satire in the tradition of "The Mouse That Roared," but that our officials had no sense of humor.

Some of the examples of State Department decision making have been taken to court. The Supreme Court on October 19, 1987 ruled that the State Department could not deny visas to foreigners merely because they were affiliated with communist organizations. The case of Reagan v. Abourezk hinged on four people denied visas: Nicaraguan Interior Minister Tomas Borge; two members of the Cuban Communist Party, Olga Finaly and Leonor Rodriguez; and Nino Pasti, the already mentioned retired NATO General. The groups that had invited these individuals to speak challenged the State Department decision, and the U.S. Court of Appeals for the District of Columbia on a 2-1 decision (with Judge Robert Bork in dissent) said the State Department needed to certify to Congress that these speakers represented a threat to the national security, rather than simply a problem for general foreign policy concerns. This is almost a classic case of how a government agency will overstep even broadly based powers.

In the face of all these examples Congress attempted to end what almost everyone believed was a national disgrace. Rep. Barney Frank and Sen. Daniel P. Moynihan introduced HR 1119 and S. 28 "to limit the grounds and improve the process for excluding aliens from the United States." Frank and Moynihan sought improvement for deleting Section 212(a)(28) that excluded solely on the basis of affiliation with communism or anarchism (there was some thought that the anarchists would not attempt to re-assassinate President McKinley) and by redesigning the rest of the document so that the Attorney General in consultation with the Secretary of State would have to provide a factual basis for "reasonable grounds" for belief that issuing a visa or permitting admission to the United States would violate paragraphs 27 or 28: that is, that they are coming in "solely, principally, or incidentally to engage in activities which would be prejudicial to the public interest, or endanger the welfare, safety, or security of the United States," or are likely to engage in "other activity subversive to the national security."

When Congress passed these bills into law civil libertarians were pleased and *The Washington Post* declared that "Congress lifts political beliefs bar to aliens under The McCarran-Walter Act." The civil libertarians and the *Post* should have waited a bit before making these pronouncements, for it isn't clear that freedom of speech is any better off after these amendments as before. It is possible that the Belgian journalist may be unharassed, but everyone else could still be in trouble.

Permit me to explain my pessimism. The language left to the law is sufficiently vague that government officials who wished to thwart freedom of expression might still be able to do so. Clearly we have government officials who would like to thwart freedom of expression. Two examples should establish this truth. In 1984 the State Department proposed legislation to control terrorism that was introduced in the Senate by Strom Thurmond—S.2626, 98th Congress, 2nd. session. This bill said that anyone providing training, support (presumably money) or recruitment for any "foreign government, faction, or international terrorist group" designated by the State Department as a terrorist group could be fined up to $100,000 and/or imprisoned up to 10 years. The State Department was to declare all such groups in the Federal Register and the legislation had an interesting clause:

(e) For the purpose of this section, any finding of fact made in any determination or renewal issued pursuant to subsection (d) shall be conclusive. No question concerning the validity of the issuance of such determination or renewal may be raised by a defendant as a defense in or as an objection to any trial or hearing if such determination or renewal was issued and published in the Federal Register in accordance with subsection (d).

In other words, once the Secretary of State determined that something was terrorist that was to be that, and you could not use as a defense the question of whether the designation was or was not accurate. Of course it is unlikely that the courts would have accepted such a clause and even the United States Senate allowed this bill to die in committee. But it does indicate something about the thought processes of the State Department.

In other words, once the Secretary of State determined that something was terrorist that was to be that, and you could not use as a defense the question of whether the designation was or was not accurate. Of course it is unlikely that the courts would have accepted such a clause and even the United States Senate allowed this bill to die in committee. But it does indicate something about the thought processes of the State Department.

The second example is even more recent and I take [it] even more personally. *The Washington Post* of March 27, that's right, only 11 days ago, reported the University of Maryland librarian Hebert N. Foerstel had discovered that an FBI agent was attempting to get librarians to provide information about the reading habits of individuals with "East European or Russian sounding names." The new FBI director, Mr. William S. Sessions, apparently told Rep. Don Edwards (D. California), who inquired about this process, that he would examine the policy but that Americans must understand that libraries are "where people are being recruited for foreign and hostile intelligence sources." I'm personally not thrilled with the FBI checking on the reading, or any other habits, of people with Eastern European sounding names.

This goes right back to the second assumption I made at the beginning of the lecture. Any individual, group, or government would be willing to exclude ideas if they find some advantage in the exclusion. What we have to be careful to understand, however, is that my first assumption is the critical sssumption. Even our highest courts have been willing to abide by exclusion decisions on the grounds that foreigners have no claim on the First Amendment until they are admitted to the country, and all willing to grant great discretion to the State Department on the grounds of Exclusion. But my first assumption is that what is essential about freedom of speech is the American audience's freedom to hear rather than the foreign speaker's freedom to speak. If we are to have people making decisions, even indirectly, about legislation, then we have to have information, and that information can only be provided when vested parties do not have the right and power to exclude some of the information. When any body has such a power we need "continued vigilance" if we are not to surrender some of our ability to function in a democratic society.

Permit me to use the example of Gerry Adams to make the case. This may turn out to be the first case determined under the new legislation of Frank and Moynihan, and a coalition of Irish-American groups have joined together to initiate a lawsuit challenging his exclusion. Gerry Adams is president of Provisional Sinn Fein, a party that is dedicated to the policy of a united Ireland and a party that does not renounce force as an option for the creation of such a united Ireland. The British government views Provisional Sinn Fein as the political wing of the Irish Republican Army and views Gerry Adams, as leader of Sinn Fein, as the virtual head of the Irish Republican Army. Nonetheless, while the IRA is an outlawed organization in Britain with membership alone being sufficient grounds for a lengthy jail term, Sinn Fein is a legal political party and Gerry Adams is the member of Parliament for West Belfast. He is not charged with terrorism, he is not charged with being a member of the IRA, he is not, at the moment (for this could change quickly given the curiosities of the British legal system in Northern Ireland), charged with anything. For the past few years he has been invited, usually during the month of March for March is the big Irish-awareness month in the United States, by Irish-American organizations to speak about issues of Northern Ireland. One such organization that has extended an invitation is the Ancient Order of Hibernians, an organization that has as members such people as Emmett O'Connell, Managing Director, Eglinton Oil and Gas; Dennis P. Long, President, Anheuser-Busch, Inc.; James A. Delaney, President, Rand Development Corporation; and Michael B. Brosnan, Vice-President, Merrill-Lynch. (This sounds more like a list of potential members of the Republican Club of Wabash College than a bunch of potential anarchists and communists, doesn't it.) Repeatedly, our State Department has denied Adams a visa to speak to such people.

In point of fact, Gerry Adams would not say anything that American citizens haven't said. No doubt he might be more academic and therefore boring than the current spokesman for Northern Irish Aid, Mr. Martin Galvin. Why, then, does the State Department wish to exclude him? Two possible reasons come to mind. The first is that although Mr. Adams would not introduce new arguments or ideas, his very presence would attract an audience. If an Irish-American such as Martin Galvin appears before the Ancient Order of Hibernians and says that the British refuse to obey the rule of law in Northern Ireland, television and the newspapers won't pay much attention. If a member of the British Parliament who is suspiciously linked to violence makes the same claim, the television cameras and the newspaper reporters will be there. This will prove, at the least, embarrassing to our British friends and, at worst, could actually change opinion in the United States and create the call for a different policy. To claim that the ability to create an audience is pivotal to the entire conception of freedom of speech misses the point. The State Department is not in the business of guaranteeing the public platform.

Secondly, the State Department views visa denial as a means of sending a message to foreign governments, both hostile and friendly governments. As Steven Shapiro notes: "Under this theory, the executive's ability to grant or deny visas for ideological reasons is a way of signaling other countries about America's position on certain political issues. For instance, the refusal to permit representatives of the Irish Republican Army into the United States helps to reassure the British that we do not condone the activities of the IRA. This is a tool the State Department has and one that it is reluctant to surrender.

The fact remains that whatever the reason for the exclusion, the public platform remains the poorer. As citizens we have less chance to hear and know, or even to become interested in the questions that concern us. Censorship by visa denial can meet my third assumption. It works and the ideas might not get out. And the Adams case provides the worst of examples. The hope of the new legislation was that we would not be excluding those who would simply be stating the ideas that American citizens can freely state. Adams is exactly the type of instance that the new legislation sought to avoid, and the fact that the State Department was willing to exclude in this instance indicated how strongly they intend to hang on to their prerogatives.

The frightening part of all this is not, of course, in the names and examples I've mentioned. Farley Mowet simply makes us look ridiculous to Canadians and to anyone who has read his books. Patricia Lara, a Columbian journalist, was able to use her visa denial and detention to compare the United States to the Soviet Union. This might make us look bad, but doesn't represent the real danger. Certainly the case of Gerry Adams presents little genuine difficulty for the public forum. There is absolutely nothing Gerry Adams would have said that has not and will not continue to be said, legally, by hundreds if not thousands of Americans. We are not prevented from adequate information on the Irish question, and it is even possible to ask, though O'Rourke might hate me for saying it, why we spend so much time on this fly-speck in the North Sea. If the Irish hadn't produced so many writers, reporters, television commentators, and college professors we could probably forget about them. What is frightening, then, is not in the stories that are reported and make it to the newspapers and television, but in the stories that we fail to hear about. What is frightening is not the stories that have plenty of advocates in the United States but in those stories that the State Department keeps from us.

And make no mistake the State Department is not in the business of encouraging public discourse. Steven Shapiro has noted that the ideological exclusions are not a partisan issue; both Republicans and Democrats have made use of the powers of the McCarran-Walter Act: "The Kennedy Administration excluded Carlos Fuentes, a noted Mexican writer and diplomat, from the United States in 1961 after he had been invited by NBC to participate in a debate on the Alliance for Progress. The Carter Administration denied a visa to Italian satirist and playwright Dario Fo. The State Department said of Fo "It's just that Fo's record of performance with regard to the United States is not good. . . . Dario Fo has never had a good word to say about this country. And you have already been exposed to the litany of people excluded by the Reagan Administration. George Shultz seems like a nice man, almost professorial. You can almost picture George Shultz in class talking about American Diplomatic History or a course in Foreign Relations. But he may not be as one with all of us on the issue of the public platform. Secretary of State George Shultz has had a variety of opinions about the public platform. For example, in January of 1986 he assured an international writers conference in New York that the Reagan administration would "never deny physical access to anyone because of the beliefs he or she may espouse." Earlier, Shultz had said, "As a general proposition I think we have to favor freedom of speech, but it can get abused by people who do not wish us well, and I think we have to take some reasonable precautions about that. Well, part of those precautions appear to me to fly in the face of the changes Congress made in the law on exclusions. Gerry Adams, after all, was denied a visa.

There are some problems with worrying about this legislation. It does trouble me, for instance, that we seem to worry more about the exclusion on the left than on the right, though it is possible that we have excluded more on the left than the right. John Corry, writing in the *New York Times*, noted that there "wasn't much public outrage when the Carter Administration used McCarran-Walter to exclude Ian D. Smith, the Prime Minister of Rhodesia. . . . When the Reagan Administration excluded Robert d'Aubuisson, the leader of the far right in El Salvador, only Senator Jesse Helms seemed upset." Mr. Corry might have added that his own newspaper, the *New York Times*, had no objection to the exclusion of Owen Carron, a Sinn Fein member of the British Parliament and only published an editorial on the virtues of free expression when the State Department, under the pressure of Irish-American groups, also excluded the Rev. Ian Paisley. But in spite of the universal inconsistency and the ability of groups only to be concerned about exclusion when it affects them, I believe it is critical for us to remain dedicated to a free public platform. I'll concluded by agreeing with *The Washington Post*, for a change, when it said:

> Two hundred years ago the men who wrote the Bill of Rights took a chance on the intelligence and good judgment of their fellow citizens. They gambled that if Americans were free to hear every viewpoint, challenge any theory and debate the merits of any controversial idea, they would choose the right course. It is this freedom of speech, so cherished by citizen and protected by courts, that should not be penalized when invoked by foreigners.

When we consider the history of exclusion, when we list the names of those excluded, when we ponder the possibility of issues we never heard about because of exclusion, it should be clear that we still need eternal vigilance. As long as any part of government seeks to limit debate, as long as any agency has the power to control ideas we still need eternal vigilance. I don't know about you, but I suspect that Sam Adams and the Sons of Liberty would not make it past our State Department.

THE INTIMIDATED PRESS[1]

ANTHONY LEWIS[2]

The election of a new President was one of the key events of 1988. Yet after the votes were counted, only 50.16 per cent of eligible Americans had voted—the poorest U.S. turnout in 64 years and the lowest of any major industrialized country in the world. (Richard L. Berke, *New York Times*, December 18, 1988, p. 18)

What accounts for low voter turnout? According to one poll, 63 per cent of Americans considered the 1988 presidential campaign to be "abysmally negative." Former New York major John V. Lindsay observed,

> As one who has been involved in seven presidential campaigns for over thirty-six years, run eight times for political office, including once for President, this campaign was the worst in my memory. Voters were repelled by the poisonous mudslinging: the low vote reflected voters' disaffection. (*Congressional Record*, February 28, 1989, p. E537)

New York Times editorial columnist Anthony Lewis said,

> The 1988 campaign left some reporters who covered it, and their editors and producers, feeling uncomfortable. One said she thought she had been complicit in a fraud on democracy. Another said: "I feel dirty."

Lewis made these remarks in his Frank E. Gannett lecture in Washington, D.C. on Monday, November 28, 1988. The speech was made possible by a grant to the Washington Journalism Center from the Gannett Foundation for "an annual lecture . . . on a journalistic subject of importance and interest to thoughtful laymen as well as to media leaders." The Washington Journalism Center is an independent, nonprofit, tax-exempt educational institution supported entirely by funds from the media, foun-

[1]Delivered as the Frank E. Gannett lecture in the Presidential Ballroom of the Capitol Hilton Hotel in Washington, D.C., at 8 P.M. on November 28, 1988.

[2]For biographical note, see Appendix.

dations, and other private sources. Founded in 1965, the center aims to foster a broader understanding of national issues through strengthening the coverage of public affairs in all of the news media.

Lewis delivered the eleventh annual Gannett lecture. Previous lecturers included such distinguished journalists, editors, and publishers as Walter Cronkite, Ben Bradlee, Carl Rowan, Julian Goodman, and Austin H. Kiplinger. Lewis spoke to an audience of some 400 journalists and government officials at 8 P.M., November 28, 1988, in the Presidential Ballroom of the Capitol Hilton Hotel.

The *Christian Science Monitor* quoted from Lewis's address in an article on press coverage of the 1988 campaign (December 9, 1988, p. 3) and *The New York Review of Books* published a revised version of the lecture. (January 19, 1989, pp. 26–28)

Anthony Lewis's speech: Seventeen years ago *The New York Times* and then *The Washington Post* published the Pentagon Papers, and fought off the Nixon Administration's attempt to stop further publication. Examining that episode afterward, a law review article by Professors Harold Edgar and Benno Schmidt, Jr. of the Columbia Law School said it marked "the passing of an era" for the American press. It was an era, they said, in which there was a "symbiotic relationship between politicians and the press." But now, by printing the secret history of the Vietnam War over strenuous official objections, establishment newspapers had "demonstrated that much of the press was no longer willing to be merely an occasionally critical associate [of the government], devoted to common aims, but intended to become an adversary. . . ."

A year after the Pentagon Papers, *The Washington Post* began looking into Watergate. What it published, in defiance of administration pressures, set in motion a process of law and politics that ended in the resignation of the President. That surely seemed to confirm what Professors Edgar and Schmidt had said. The symbiotic relationship was over. We now had an independently critical press.

I thought about Professors Edgar and Schmidt this past September when I read an editorial in *The Washington Post*. It was about the statement by the Speaker of the House, Jim Wright, that the C.I.A. had admitted, in secret testimony, helping to arouse anti-government protests in Nicaragua in order to provoke repression that would harm the image of the Sandinistas. The editorial was critical—of Speaker Wright, not the C.I.A.

The Speaker's statement was harmful to the Nicaraguan opposition, the *Post* said. It noted Mr. Wright's claim that what he said had already appeared in other news reports. But that explanation, it said sternly, failed to consider "the crucial authority that a Congressional figure can add by his confirmation." Finally, the editorial came to the question whether the C.I.A. had in fact sparked the Nicaraguan protests. That would have been "incredibly stupid," it said, and public testimony in Congress had absolved the C.I.A. of the charge.

The C.I.A. has in fact done some "incredibly stupid" things, in Nicaragua among other places. I think a genuinely critical press would have taken a hard look at the facts before chastising a Congressional leader for improper leaking or abuse of authority in this case.

But what struck me about the editorial, and the reason I mention it now, was not so much its factual assumptions as its reverential tone. Its premise was that legitimacy rests in the executive branch of the United States government, not the legislative. Congress, along with the rest of us, owes respect to the secrecy that the executive, with its special knowledge and expertise, deems necessary in the interest of national security.

Ladies and gentlemen, those were the very attitudes that the *Times* and the *Post* and other newspapers rejected when they published the Pentagon Papers. As a result of the Vietnam War they had come to realize that executive officials did not always have superior knowledge and expertise, and did not always tell the truth. They were not entitled to reverence, from the press or Congress. The country would be better off—more wisely led—if policies were subject to unstinting scrutiny, including a good many policies covered up by secrecy.

Of course my point does not lie in the particular editorial, and I know that there were reasons to question Speaker Wright's wisdom in speaking out when he did. But I think the tone of the editorial reflected a general trend. The established press in this country has to a large extent reverted to the symbiotic relationship with the executive branch. We are an adversary only on the margins, not on the fundamentals that challenge power. We have forgotten the lessons of Vietnam and Watergate.

Think about press treatment of the presidency in the 1970s and, by comparison, in the last eight years. In Ben Bradlee's phrase, there has been "a return to deference." We are all uneasily aware that something like that has happened. We are not sure why it came about. But we can place the change in the Reagan years.

When President Reagan took office in 1981, the press at first reported with gusto on the gaps in his knowledge and interest, the confusion of fact and fancy. The evening television news noted his mistakes at press conferences, and newspapers detailed them the next day. But it turned out that the public did not care about Mr. Reagan's flubs. James David Barber, the scholar of the presidency, said the public treated his contempt for facts "as a charming idiosyncrasy." So the press's gusto for recording Mr. Reagan's wanderings from reality waned. More important, the press did not give the public real insight into the working of the Reagan White House—into the confusion and vacuity that have been described so convincingly now in books by former insiders.

After Mr. Reagan had been President for about a year, I wrote a column puzzling over why the press seemed to hold back from giving us an unvarnished picture. The reporting was gingerly, sometimes almost protective. Why? I ventured a few guesses on the possible reasons.

One was Mr. Reagan's political standing. He had won in a landslide in 1980, and rolled over Congress in the tax and budget battle of 1981. He had the most convincing validation a democracy can give, and the public was not interested in carping at the details. Who was the press to challenge that? To put it another way, I thought some in the press were subconsciously asking themselves what our critics like to ask: Who elected us?

Second, some in the press may have felt uneasy because they were liberals. If they did tough stories, they might be accused of treating Mr. Reagan unfairly for that reason—accused, that is, of being insufficiently "objective."

Third, I guessed that some reporters and editors who watched Mr. Reagan were reluctant as citizens to speak out about what they saw. They saw the most powerful of offices occupied by a man with an anecdotal view of the world, giving simplistic answers to complicated questions, or tuning out. They found it upsetting to acknowledge, to the public or to themselves, that American leadership was in such hands.

My friends in Washington did not think much of my speculations; they denied that they were holding back for any such reasons. But looking back now, I still think that my concern had a basis. I believe there were unacknowledged constraints on the vigor of the press in covering the Reagan White House, including the three I mentioned. To them I would now add a weightier fourth reason: in a word, fear.

For nearly 20 years now the political right in this country has been working to intimidate the press and arouse public feeling against it. Spiro Agnew may be taken as the starting point, with his denunciations of the liberal elitist press and the nattering nabobs of negativism. We treat him as a joke figure now, with his notion that someone should start a good newspaper; and, after all, he did turn out to be a particularly cheap crook. But the resentments he touched and aroused were not a joke, and they have not gone away. There are a good many Americans who use the phrase "elitist press." I get letters from them, and I imagine many of you do.

Watergate fed the resentment, the anger. Nixon had his supporters to the end, and they were enraged at the part played in his fall by an unelected press. A certain amount of press hubris about its role made the feelings worse. After the President resigned, even some citizens and politicians who knew he had to go resented what they considered the display of the power of the press. So there was a Watergate backlash against the press. We felt it, we worried about it, and we tried to compensate for it.

Most important of all, in these historical causes, there was Vietnam. Millions of Americans, including some in high office, are convinced that we lost that war because the press showed us the horrors of it in graphic detail, and somehow favored the other side. What the press actually did, in its noblest tradition, was to show the reality that it was an unwinnable war. But the anger remains.

Today intimidation of the press is a standard item on the agenda of the organized political right. There are self-appointed monitors who circulate denunciations of articles and television programs that depart from their ideology. There are groups that support libel suits. And there is Jesse Helms, threatening to buy up a network that is not far enough to the right for his taste.

People in our business tend to have more than the usual amount of courage. But we kid ourselves if we think that pressure from the right has no effect on us, or on the companies that own media institutions. All things being equal, most of us prefer to avoid trouble in life. And editors and publishers know that tough journalism, journalism that may embarrass conservative interests, means trouble.

There was an important example of the effectiveness of intimidation in the election campaign. When Vice President Bush appeared on the CBS Evening News, Dan Rather tried to question him about his role in the Iran-Contra affair. Mr. Bush ducked, weaved, barracked, picked a fight. It was a beautifully staged performance, well prepared by Mr. Bush and his handlers. The purpose was to make it seem that Rather was leaning on the Vice President improperly, and to frighten others away from asking him questions about Iran. And it worked. After that evening nobody in the press went after Mr. Bush about his role in a sustained way, though there is every reason to believe that he was more deeply involved in the affair than he said.

Lately one of the right-wing extremists who goads the press has again denounced Mr. Rather over that episode. It showed, he said, what an unfair liberal Mr. Rather was that he pressed such questions on the Vice President of the United States. *Lèse majesté!* That is where we are: The price of pressing a question of fundamental importance on a political candidate who will not answer is to be denounced as "liberal." And I repeat: it works.

There was another example of the effectiveness of intimidation in the 1988 campaign. That was the handling of the press in the Dan Quayle affair.

I hardly need to remind you what happened. When George Bush chose Senator Quayle as his running-mate, reporters at the Republican Convention soon discovered that Quayle had avoided military service in Vietnam by getting himself public relations duty in the National Guard. How did he get it? By all indications, through family influence. Then came the counterattack. Republicans compared the reporters to sharks in a "feeding frenzy." Senator Quayle staged a press conference in the middle of a political rally in his home town, Huntington, Indiana. When reporters tried to ask questions about the Guard, people in the audience booed. When Ellen Hume of *The Wall Street Journal* stood her ground, the crowd shouted against "the redhead."

On television, that made a wonderful piece of "press harassment," all planned, I repeat, by the Quayle handlers. And then there was another perfect television clip. A few days later Quayle was shown taking the garbage out of his home, and reporters surrounded him and shouted questions. An outrageous invasion of privacy, right? Wrong. What television did not say in showing that episode was that the Bush-Quayle campaign had listed the trash dumping on its schedule as that day's only press availability for Quayle.

There were a lot of questions about Senator Quayle that never got answered in the campaign. How did he graduate from college without meeting the requirements that all other political science majors had to meet? Why was he given a second general examination when he failed the regular one, and what was the nature of the second exam? How did he get into law school when his grades were below the levels expected of other applicants? His academic records would have told us the answers, but Senator Quayle refused to let anyone see the records. I know some reporters were interested, but somehow the questions were not pressed hard enough or often enough to make the refusal to answer an issue, which it properly was.

I wonder what part the intimidating effects of the attacks on the press had in the way the Quayle story trailed off into nothingness. I wonder whether the press would have let such a story about a Democratic candidate trail off. Nowadays, at least, Democrats are not much good at bullying the press. And bullying has its effect.

The 1988 campaign left some reporters who covered it, and their editors and producers, feeling uncomfortable. One said she thought she had been complicit in a fraud on democracy. Another said: "I feel dirty." I think we can identify a number of reasons for those feelings: a number of press failures in the campaign.

One was the failure to make clear how Vice President Bush was insulated from the press, kept away from unprogrammed questions. It was the same kind of insulation practiced in the Reagan campaigns, but this time without the excuse of Mr. Reagan's personal aura to disarm the press. Yet the press essentially accepted the role assigned to it by the Bush campaign, grumbling but in the end largely passive. There was hardly any effort to describe what was going on.

After the election I had a letter from a reader saying that, yes, this had been a frustrating campaign for voters, one in which the candidates had not grappled with the real issues facing the country; but that was not just the fault of the candidates or their handlers. They can only be "handled," the reader said, if the press cooperates. Why didn't reporters traveling on the candidates' planes at least have the backbone to demand weekly press conferences? That would work, he said, "because no candidate can afford to risk the concerted antagonism of his mouthpieces."

I doubt that that remedy would work so easily. It is difficult to get reporters to work in concert, and it should be. The media men have ways to get around us, at least for a considerable time. But surely we in the press ought to be putting up a fight against the insulated campaign, describing it, focusing on it in a sustained way, instead of shrugging our shoulders. The problem was particularly acute this time for television. While George Bush was refusing to meet the press, Michael Dukakis at first held daily press conferences. He was rewarded by having embarrassing bits shown on the nightly news up against sound bites staged by the Bush campaign. Paul Friedman, executive producer of the ABC World News Tonight, said he was aware of the problem but did not know how to deal with it. He and the rest of us had better start trying to figure out how.

A second problem in this year's coverage was fascination with the process of the modern campaign, and with its manipulators: process, not substance. And not values. We celebrated Roger Ailes for his craft as a maker of television ads that created a picture of Michael Dukakis as a friend of murderers and rapists. There were lots of stories about the superiority of the technicians on that side: value-free stories. One newspaper political analyst even wrote a piece arguing that the inferior quality of Governor Dukakis's television ads had "disturbing implications about Dukakis's leadership."

I wonder how Thomas Jefferson, an introspective man, would rate as a political leader by that standard. Perhaps our democracy has been so corrupted by technology that a sensitive person, a Jefferson, can no longer hope to lead it. That may be. But I do not think the press should be cheering the corrupters for their efficiency. I say all that not out of concern for Michael Dukakis, who should have replied to the smears long before he did. My concern is for our business. There were times in this campaign when we looked like theater critics—critics interested only in the artfulness of the scenery, not in the message of the play.

Third, the press in this campaign actually participated in the degradation of the democratic process. It did so by taking up, as if they were real, the non-issues invented to distract voters from the hard economic and other problems ahead. The two so-called presidential debates provided embarrassing examples. I say so-called because of course they were not debates, not head-to-head confrontations like the Lincoln-Douglas debates. They were games, in which members of the press played stage roles. I think CBS News people were right when they decided not to participate in the second.

In that second debate Governor Dukakis was told by one of the journalists that the public didn't seem to like him; he was asked whether a President should be likable. That was one of the questions in the supposed focal point of our great democratic process. Then there was the opening question, put by the moderator, Bernard Shaw of CNN: Would Governor Dukakis favor the death penalty if his wife Kitty were raped and murdered? I leave it to Roger Ailes to comment on that. In an interview in the *Gannett Center Journal*, just published, he says: "It was an outrageous . . . question."

A fourth disturbing feature of the 1988 campaign was the press's inability to deal with lies. For example, the Bush campaign had a highly effective ad blaming Dukakis for the polluted state of Boston Harbor. It showed a sludgy pool of water with a sign saying: "DANGER/RADIATION HAZARD/NO SWIMMING." The picture was in fact not of Boston Harbor, and it had nothing to do with Dukakis. It was taken at an abandoned nuclear submarine repair yard.

What is the responsibility of the press when it is paid to carry such flagrant distortions? As a general rule it is sensible not to try to edit political advertising for truth. *The New York Times* used to print, once a year, full-page ads containing the thoughts of Kim Il Sung, the dictator of North Korea. I think we were right to take the money and let him say whatever he wanted. But it is another thing to refrain from comment on advertising that directly affects the American political process and that is deliberately false. Run the ad, yes, but say something.

That leads to a fifth problem. It is the press's desire to look "objective," which I think has become a dangerous obsession of American journalism.

Go back to Boston Harbor. George Bush took a cruise around it one day during the campaign, and said its condition proved that he was a better environmentalist than Dukakis. Most television networks and stations used the nice visual and a Bush sound bite, without any critical analysis. The simplest check would have shown that Dukakis had a fairly good record on environmental issues, while Bush as Vice President had a negative record and indeed had often pointed with pride to his activity in pushing development over environmental interests. But to report that would not have been "objective."

Some of us remember when we had a hard lesson on the limits of "He said, She said" journalism, when we learned that just repeating what a politician said was not "objective" in the true sense. Senator Joe McCarthy taught us the lesson. When he denounced 57 or 22 people as Communists, the wire services would flash what he said. For a long time they maintained that it would not be right to add any perspective: to tell the readers what had happened to his last charges, and the ones before that. But eventually the services understood that their obligation went beyond carrying the propaganda of a demagogue; they had an obligation to truth.

Serious reporting has to provide perspective on events. That obligation is not to be left to comment on the editorial and op ed pages. In a complicated world the reporter must try to make sense of things for the viewer or reader.

Reporters today are equipped to analyze events. They have had a liberal education, and many have had special training in their fields. In political reporting, certainly, there are men and women with wide knowledge and acquaintance. We need their perspective. But I had the feeling in this campaign that we were not getting enough writing by political reporters following their instincts for the deeper springs of politics. It was only very late in the campaign, for instance, when attention began to be paid to what is surely one of the determining factors in national voting patterns: race.

Instead of old-fashioned political reporting we had more of what could be called market research. The press has generally been using marketing surveys to find out what people want to read and watch. The surveyors, I am told, attach little flashlights to the heads of newspaper readers and note how long the light shines on different parts of the paper. Then the marketeers advise the paper to give readers more of what they like.

Political campaigns have used market research methods since 1968, when the Nixon campaign did so well with them. You know the technique: survey the voters, find out what they want in a candidate, then reshape the image of your man to fit that desire. Now the press seems to have become entranced by market research for campaign coverage. We had "focus groups" of our own, collections of voters whose impressions we reported. We all had polls, and devoted enormous space and time to reporting the results of our own and others'. It all left the impression that the press's main interest was in what tactics were working, who was winning and who was losing, not in the substantive choices facing the country, and not in truth.

We have less individual flavor in our political reporting today: less of the writer with a distinctive style and background and point of view. Those qualities are suspect, I think, because they are not "objective." It is safer to write about polls and focus groups, which are "objective."

The craving for objectivity was carried to great lengths in this campaign. One television report did try to deal with the low road of the Bush campaign. It showed the falsehoods in a Bush ad stating that "Michael Dukakis had opposed virtually every defense system we have developed." But the report went on to show a Dukakis ad that slightly exaggerated Bush positions. The story had to be "balanced." Even editorial pages balanced their criticism of the Bush smears with comments on this or that in the Dukakis campaign, as if its faults remotely approached the impugning of Dukakis's patriotism.

The notion that journalism should be "balanced" goes against the grain of American history and the Constitution. When the Constitution and the First Amendment were written, there was no such thing as a "balanced" newspaper. There were highly partisan, opinionated sheets. That was "the press" that Jefferson and Madison knew and wanted to protect. They didn't love it. After he had been President for a few years, Jefferson wrote a friend: "The man who never looks into a newspaper is better informed than he who reads them, inasmuch as he who knows nothing is nearer the truth than he whose mind is filled with falsehoods and errors." They just thought the press was necessary, to keep the government honest and the republic free. The First Amendment did not guarantee the freedom of the press as a mere common carrier, printing whatever politicians said "objectively." It guaranteed the freedom of independent, opinionated, quarrelsome, irritating newspapers.

For those reasons I find the current fetish of "objectivity" troublesome. Press institutions are much larger now than in Jefferson's day, and they have reasons to carry different points of view. But it does not follow that they should find two sided to every question or regard it as a triumph to be bland.

There are two other points that should concern us as journalists. They go beyond the campaign. They are cultural trends of which the press is a part, and of which the press should be wary.

The first is the growth of a political class in Washington, D.C. That has happened in my lifetime. Before Franklin Roosevelt this city did not amount to much in our national life. It was a sleepy Southern town—a segregated one—that housed a small government with little impact on the daily life of most Americans. Now it is the headquarters of a powerful government that affects us all in myriad ways: our health, our housing, our jobs and so on. It is the center of a vast military-industrial complex. And it has a permanent society of men and women concerned with government, and with the names and numbers of the players. The popular phrase for the phenomenon, awkward but perhaps unavoidable, is the Inside the Beltway Mentality.

Journalists are part of that Washington society: a leading part. And just as the word "Washington" casts a certain spell on the American public now, so the press corps here has a larger influence than ever before on the way the country's newspapers and magazines and broadcasters see things. My concern is that the press is becoming too Washington-centered in its thinking. I say that as an outsider, but not only for that reason.

There is always a danger of seeing the world in too small a circle of acquaintance and thought. I think that is a particular danger now in Washington: a city where access to the great is easy, where quotes can be picked from every tree, where members of the press have almost the dignity of office. Joan Didion did a remarkable piece on the campaign in *The New York Review of Books*. One of her striking insights was how much the press has become part of a new class, a managerial elite. She heard people at the conventions speak of "the process," and she realized what they meant: not the democratic process but the reverse. "The process," she said, was this:

> A mechanism seen as so specialized that access to it is correctly limited to its own professionals, to those who manage policy and those who quote them, to those who ask and those who answer the questions on the Sunday shows, to the media consultants, to the columnists, to the issues advisers, to those who give the off-the-record breakfasts and those who attend them; to that handful of insiders who invent, year in and year out, the narrative of public life.

To be an insider is wonderful fun. But it carries with it the danger of talking to yourself.

My final subject of concern follows from the one just mentioned. It is the worship of the Presidency. Here again the press is in danger of following a cultural trend. Worship may seem too strong a word. I do not think it is.

Since 1933, gradually but inexorably, Americans have come to invest their hopes and fears in the President. He will solve our problems. He alone represents us all: a national view as compared to the narrow parochialism of members of Congress. Along with this mythic popular image has gone a strange ideological strand in contemporary conservatism, arguing that the President should have total power over everything that touches foreign affairs or national security, with Congress as an illegitimate outsider.

All this would astound the makers of our Constitution if they could see it. They did not think of the President as a tribune of the people, not at all. It was Congress, in particular the House of Representatives, that was to represent the popular will. The President was to be a manager, carrying out the policies established by the legislative branch. What a wonderful irony it is that conservatives who want the Supreme Court to be bound by Original Intent in interpreting the Constitution are also devoted to exalting presidential power, which is a mockery of the Framers' intention.

The trouble with myths is that you may come to believe them. When the press looks to the President to solve all problems, when it assumes the legitimacy of his power in all situations, it creates a mystique about the presidency that may be difficult to penetrate. I think that has happened. I think the press finds it very hard to challenge the President of the United States on things that matter.

But there was Watergate, you will say. Yes. But the man in the White House then was a peculiarly vulnerable President, elected but not loved, given to self-destruction. It certainly required courage to challenge, and the courage was there. But the example does not convince me that the press is bold enough to challenge a secure, popular President.

Consider this question: What was the boldest action by the press in the politics of these last few years? I think it was the investigation of Gary Hart's sexual behavior. There again the target was a loner of a politician, without strong personal links to his colleagues in the Senate or to state politicians. And he was not a friend of the press.

What is needed is not confrontation for confrontation's sake. It is the will to press unwelcome questions into the center of presidential policy. It is the persistence to demand answers from Vice President Bush about his role in the trading of arms for hostages, not the brashness to ask Senator Hart: "Have you ever committed adultery?"

We were at fault in not smelling the arms for hostages deal and the transfer of funds to the *contras* before the story leaked in the Middle East. Something had been known about Colonel North's character and activities: enough to arouse the curiosity of skeptical journalists, I would have thought. And that is what we are meant to be: skeptical.

The press cannot do its job if it is bemused by the presidential mystique: That is the argument I make to you most forcefully. If we must learn again what we learned in Vietnam and put into practice in the Pentagon Papers, let us do so. Officials may act in what they sincerely believe is the interest of national security but be wrong—dangerously wrong. The greatest danger, Justice Brandeis said, lies in "men of zeal, well-meaning but without understanding." Some degree of secrecy is necessary in national security matters, but officials will always try to expand secrecy beyond the necessary because it is so comfortable—because it relieves them of the duty to justify their policies. But it is exactly that duty of justification that is at the heart of our system of government. Our premise is that policy will be wiser if those who make it are forced to consider conflicting views and account for their choice.

Executive officials like to argue that those are old-fashioned ideas, that in a world of nuclear weapons a President needs secrecy. But those officials often see it differently when they leave office. David Gergen spoke in this forum two years ago, and he said he thought we had too little reporting on national security matters, not too much. He spoke of the value of accountability and said "the quest for secrecy has led more than one Administration astray." . . .

The press has a critical function to play in our scheme of government. Madison, the author of the First Amendment, defined that function. It was to give information to the sovereigns of this country, its citizens, so they could freely examine "public characters and measures."

The public relies on the press more today than ever. People feel remote from national politics and governance. They feel it has become not a participatory but a spectator sport. They count on us to penetrate the shams and speak the truth to power. They are often angry at us, but they need us. We should not let them down.

Shortly after Watergate, Justice Potter Stewart of the Supreme Court made a speech at Yale about the press. Its performance in the Pentagon Papers affair and Watergate, he said, had brought on the press charges that it was arrogant and exercised illegitimate power. He disagreed. In the last few years, he said, the American press had "performed precisely the function it was intended to perform by those who wrote the First Amendment."

Justice Stewart said it was a great mistake—a constitutional mistake—to see the press "as a *neutral* conduit of information between the people and their elected leaders." Those who framed the Constitution did not intend the press to be "a neutral vehicle" for "balanced discussion." To them "the free press meant organized, expert scrutiny of government. The press was a conspiracy of the intellect, with the courage of numbers."

That is a rather grand description of our business. But we should try to live up to it.

WE ARE ALL ON THIS PLANET TOGETHER

CAN THE WORLD BE SAVED?[1]

Gus Speth[2]

> Today, . . . pollution is occurring on a vast and unprecedented scale around the world. . . . The dramatic changes in pollution in this century are best described in four long-term trends. . . . These interrelated atmospheric issues probably constitute the most serious pollution threat in history.

Thus Gus Speth elucidated the problem he discussed in the speech he delivered to the United States Environmental Protection Agency seminar on June 21, 1988.

Speth has served as President of the World Resources Institute, an independent, non-profit organization, since it was founded in 1982. The institute carries out interdisciplinary policy studies of issues related to natural resources, develops policy choices, and works with government and the private sector in both industrial and developing countries. Earlier, Speth had served as a member and, later, as chairman of President Jimmy Carter's Council on Environmental Quality.

Speth's address was part of a series of biweekly seminars sponsored by the EPA, which invites a distinguished expert to address its staff, other government officials, and agency guests. John Kenneth Galbraith, Ralph Nader, Jacques Cousteau, Barry Commoner, and Paul Ehrlich are among the thinkers, activists, and scholars who have spoken at these seminars.

A capacity audience of about 140 attended Speth's lecture in the EPA Education Center Auditorium in Washington, D.C. Introduced by an EPA staff member, Speth began his speech at 1:00 P.M. A question-and-answer period of about a half hour followed the address. The speech was preserved on videotape, and excerpts from it were reprinted in numerous publications, including the *EPA Journal*, the *Bulletin of the Atomic Scientists*, the *Mining Journal*, the *Washington Post*, and the *Christian Science Monitor*.

Speth organized his speech in a problem-solution pattern: sketching first details of the unprecedented release in this century of pollutants into the atmosphere and the attendant threat to mankind, and then proposing solutions that he considers necessary if the world is to be saved.

Gus Speth's speech: In an amusing scene in a recent popular movie, the intrepid Captain Kirk awakes from the sleep of time travel

[1]Delivered to the United States Environmental Protection Agency seminar in the EPA Education Center Auditorium in Washington, D.C., at 1:00 P.M. on June 21, 1988.

[2]For biographical note, see Appendix.

and, gazing out, sees that his starship is, as hoped, orbiting Earth. "Earth!" he says, "but when?" To which the genetically unflappable Spock, checking his instrument panel, replies, "Judging from the pollution content of the atmosphere, I believe we have arrived at the latter half of the twentieth century." And indeed they had. And so have we. And there is plenty of pollution here to measure.

Today, in the latter years of the twentieth century, pollution is occurring on a vast and unprecedented scale around the globe. Trends since World War II have been in two directions: first, toward large releases of certain chemicals, principally from using fossil fuels, that are now significantly altering natural systems on a global scale and, second, toward steady increases in the release of innumerable biocidal products and toxic substances. These shifts from the "sewage and soot" concerns of the pre-war period to vastly more serious concerns pose formidable challenges for societies—challenges that today's pollution control laws just begin to address.

The dramatic changes in pollution in this century are best described in terms of four long-term trends.

First is the trend from modest quantities to huge quantities. The twentieth century has witnessed unprecedented growth in human population and economic activity. World population has increased more than threefold; gross world product by perhaps twentyfold; and fossil fuel use by more than tenfold.

With these huge increases in economic activity and fossil fuel use have come huge changes in the quantities of pollutants released. Between 1900 and 1985, annual sulfur dioxide emissions increased sixfold globally, while nitrogen oxide emissions increased about tenfold, perhaps more. Another gas formed when fossil fuels are burned is carbon dioxide, one of the greenhouse gases implicated in global warming and climate change. Annual global emissions of CO_2 have increased tenfold in this century, and a dramatic 25 percent increase in the CO_2 content of Earth's atmosphere has occurred.

Second is the trend from gross insults to microtoxicity, from natural products to synthetic ones. Paralleling the dramatic growth in the volume of older pollutants, such as sulfur dioxide, has been the introduction in the post-World War II period of new synthetic chemicals and radioactive substances, many of which are highly toxic in even minute quantities and some of which persist and accumulate in biological systems or in the atmosphere.

One major product of the modern chemicals industry, pesticides, are released to the environment precisely because they are toxic. Projected global pesticide sales for 1990 are $50 billion, a tenfold increase since 1975. Ironically, another major product of the chemicals industry, the chlorofluorocarbons, found wide use in part because they are not toxic. Such are the pathways of our ignorance.

Third is the trend from First World to Third World. A myth easily exploded by a visit to many developing countries is that pollution is predominately a problem of the highly industrialized countries. While it is true that the industrial countries account for the bulk of the pollutants produced today, pollution is a grave problem in developing countries, and many of the most alarming examples of its consequences can be found there.

Cities in Eastern Europe and the Third World are consistently more polluted with SO_2 and particulates than most of the cities in OECD countries. The rivers most severely contaminated by bacteria and other pathogens are in developing countries.

Third World populations now rank high in their exposure to toxic chemicals. In a sample of ten industrial and developing countries, three of the four countries with the highest blood lead levels of their populations were Mexico, India, and Peru; for the same ten countries, DDT contamination of human milk was highest in China, India, and Mexico. And what may be the worst industrial accident in history occurred not in New Jersey or West Virginia, but in India.

These first three trends combine, with others, to produce the fourth, the trend from local effects to global effects. When the volumes of pollution were much smaller and the pollutants similar to natural substances, impacts tended to be confined to limited geographic areas near sources. Today, the scale and intensity of pollution make its consequences truly global. For the first time, human impacts have grown to approximate and to affect the natural processes that control the global life-support system.

Nothing better illustrates this broadening of the concern about pollution from a local affair to a global one than air pollution. Local air pollution is improving in some cities in industrial countries, but it is worsening in others, principally in developing countries, and is hardly solved anywhere. Meanwhile, global use of fossil fuels, and emissions of traditional pollutants such as sulfur and nitrogen oxides that result from it, continue to climb. Acid rain, ozone, and other consequences of these pollutants are affecting plant and animal life—killing forests and fish, damaging crops, changing the species composition of ecosystems—over vast areas of the globe. Depletion of the stratosphere's ozone layer is a matter of such concern that an international treaty has been negotiated to reduce emissions of chlorofluorocarbons, but the latest measurements indicate the current protocol is already inadequate. And, probably most serious of all, the buildup of infra-red trapping "greenhouse" gases in the atmosphere continues. This buildup is largely a consequence of the use of fossil fuels and CFCs, deforestation, and various agricultural activities, and it now threatens societies with far-reaching climate change.

While the regional impacts of a global warming are uncertain and difficult to predict, rainfall and monsoon patterns could shift, upsetting agricultural activities worldwide. Sea level could rise, flooding coastal areas. Ocean currents could shift, altering the climate of many areas and disrupting fisheries. The ranges of plant and animal species could change regionally, endangering protected areas and many species whose habitats are now few and confined. Record heatwaves and other weather anomalies could harm susceptible people, crops, and forests.

These interrelated atmospheric issues probably constitute the most serious pollution threat in history. I say "interrelated" because these atmospheric issues are linked in ways that scientists are still discovering, and the scientists are far ahead of our policymakers. First, they are linked in time. The view is still common today that, initially, we should address local air pollution, then we should turn attention to regional issues like acid rain, and then, at some point in the future, we should address the global issue of greenhouse gases. But the failures of our clean air efforts make urban air quality an issue for today, forcing a 1970s issue from the past into the present. Simultaneously, the realizations that greenhouse gases other than CO_2 double the urgency of the problem, and that societies may have *already* committed the planet to a 1° to 2.5° C global average warming—these realizations are forcing what was thought to be a "21st Century issue" into the present.

These atmospheric issues are also linked in the vast chemical reactor that is the atmosphere, where pollutants react with each other, other substances, and solar energy in a fiendishly complex set of circular interactions. Touch one problem, you may touch them all.

Third, they are linked in their effects on people and on the biota. What are the consequences of multiple stresses—a variety of pollutants, heat waves and climate changes, increased ultraviolet radiation—when realized together? Who knows? We are all still learning.

And these atmospheric issues are linked through the sources of the pollutants involved. CFCs, for example, contribute both to greenhouse warming and ozone layer destruction, but the dominant source of these problems is the use of fossil fuels.

In short, the time to address all these atmosphere problems—local, regional, global—is now. The way to address all these problems is together. And, in the long run, the key to these problems is energy.

What can we say about the U.S. role in causing these atmospheric problems? We should take pride in what has been accomplished to date under the Clean Air Act and various U.S. energy laws. But let's not overdo it. The United States still produces about 15% of the world's sulfur dioxide emissions, about 25% of NO_x, 25% of the CO_2, and we manufacture about 30% of the CFCs. While emissions of criteria air pollutants other than NO_x have fallen over the last fifteen years, a period during which real GNP grew about 50 percent, emissions today still exceed two-thirds of 1970 amounts, particulates excepted. In other words, the bulk of the pollution that gave rise to the Clean Air Act in 1970 continues. Similarly, real strides have been made in increasing U.S. energy efficiency: between 1973 and 1985 per capita energy use in the U.S. fell 12 percent while per capita gross domestic product rose 17 percent. Still, the United States today remains a gas guzzler of a nation, consuming a fourth of the world's energy annually and producing only half the GNP per unit of energy input as countries such as West Germany, Brazil, France, Japan, and Sweden.

Beyond these atmospheric issues are other pollution concerns, and beyond them the challenge of the planet's biological degradation—deforestation, desertification, the loss of biodiversity—in short, the steady process of biological impoverishment. When we take all these challenges together, we see that we are witnessing nothing less than the emergence of a new environmental agenda. This new agenda encompasses the great life-support systems of the planet's biosphere. It is global in scope and international in implication. It is rapidly forcing itself on the attention of policymakers and the public at large.

Almost twenty years ago, U.S. leaders responded vigorously to the environmental concerns emerging then. Today, the new agenda faces us with challenges that are more disturbing and more difficult. It is not enough to say that we must hope that our leaders respond as they did before. We must ensure that they do.

Now, into this troubled present comes a message from the future. Not, this time, from Captain Kirk, but more reliably, from the World Commission on Environment and Development. Consider closely the following passage from the report of the commission, *Our Common Future*:

> The planet is passing through a period of dramatic growth and fundamental change. Our human world of 5 billion must make room in a finite environment for another human world. The population could stabilize at between 8 billion and 14 billion some time next century, according to UN projections. . . . Economic activity has multiplied to create a $13 trillion world economy, and this could grow five- or tenfold in the coming half-century.

Imagine, just as a simple thought experiment, what would happen if greenhouse gases, industrial pollution, and other assaults on the environment rose proportionately with the vast economic growth to which the commission refers. I am not suggesting that this will happen, but thinking this way does highlight the magnitude of the challenge ahead.

In the early 1970s the CBS Evening News with Walter Cronkite ran a series of environmental stories entitled "Can the World Be Saved?." I remember the globe behind this title was firmly grasped by a hand which seemed to come from nowhere. I was never sure whether this hand was crushing our small planet or saving it, but I was sure at least that Cronkite was out to save it. He dramatically presented the much simpler environmental problems of that period to a huge audience, and helped build the powerful environmental consciousness of the day. Today, the question "Can the World Be Saved?" is a much more serious and legitimate question than it was then.

Societies near and far have set two long-term goals for themselves: improving environmental quality, in part by reducing current pollution levels, and achieving a virtual order of magnitude increase in economic activity. Let us not deceive ourselves, or accept blithely the assurances of political leaders who say casually that we can have both. We know from sad experience that we can have economic growth without having environmental protection. But the stakes on the environmental side are much higher now, and they will only grow in the future. I predict that reconciling these two goals will be one of the dominant challenges facing political leaders on all continents in the 1990s and beyond. It will require constant attention at the highest levels of government. It will require strong, effective, smart government.

Enviromentalism began on the outside, on the periphery of the economy, saving a bit of landscape here, bottling up some pollution there. It will inevitably spread as creed and code to permeate to the core of the economies of the world. We will all be environmentalists soon.

If these are the challenges before us, what should be done? Let's rephrase Cronkite's question into a somewhat more answerable one: how can the world be saved? Certainly, we must strengthen the efforts already begun. The regulatory programs of the industrial countries have yielded definite results over the last two decades, and continuing challenges will require that these programs be enhanced. Monitoring and enforcement capabilities must be strengthened; new types and sources of pollution must be tackled; inter-media effects must be attended to; regional and global approaches to pollution control must become increasingly common; and the overall regulatory process must become more cost-effective, efficient, and streamlined. And much, much more attention needs to be paid to the pollution problems of the developing countries. They can learn from our successes and failures, and pioneer new development paths rather than repeat old ones.

Yet, something more fundamental will be needed. From its origins in the early 1970s, U.S. air and water pollution legislation has recognized that tighter standards could be applied to "new sources" of pollution, in contrast to existing plants, because new sources present the opportunity to go beyond "end of pipe" removal of waste products and to build in "process changes" that reduce or eliminate the wastes that must otherwise be removed. This concept—source reduction through changing the basic technologies of production and consumption—*writ large*, is fundamental to solving world pollution problems. "Pollution control" is not enough. Societies must work "upstream" to change the products, processes, policies and pressures that give rise to pollution.

I urged you a moment ago to consider what would happen if pollution increased proportionately with the five- to ten-fold expansion in world economic activity projected for the middle of the next century. That would indeed happen if this growth merely replicates over and over today's prevailing technologies, broadly conceived. Seen in this light, reconciling the economic and environmental goals societies have set for themselves will only occur if there is a thoroughgoing technological transformation—a transformation to technologies, high and low, soft and hard, that are solution-oriented because they facilitate economic growth while sharply reducing the pressures on the natural environment. We speak positively of "environmentally sustainable" development. What this means in the context of pollution is technology transformation.

In this limited sense at least, one might say that only technology can save us. This is a hard thing for a congenital Luddite like myself to say, but, in a small victory of nurture over nature, I do now believe it. I do not diminish the importance of lifestyle changes—some go hand-in-hand with technological change—and I await the spread of more voluntary simplicity in our rich society. But growth has its imperatives; for much of the world it is the imperative of meeting basic human needs. And, we must not forget it is sustainable economic development—growth that takes the pressure of mass poverty off an eroding resource base—that is an essential component of environmental progress worldwide.

For these reasons, we must think explicitly about society's need to accomplish a technological transformation of unprecedented scope and pace. And we must think as well about the interventions that will be needed to bring it about. Although many emerging technologies offer exciting opportunities, and some are moving us in the right direction, no "hidden hand" is operating to guide technology to reconcile environmental and economic challenges.

The two fundamental processes of this transformation are the process of discovery and the process of application. The first is the realm of science and technology, of research and development. Science and technology must have the financial support and the incentives to provide us with an accurate understanding of the Earth's systems and cycles and what our pollution is doing to them; it must deliver to us a new agriculture, one redesigned to be sustainable both economically and ecologically, which stresses low inputs of commercial fertilizers, pesticides and energy; and it must show us how industry and transportation can be transformed from an era of materials-intensive, high-throughput processes to an era that relies on inputs with low environmental costs, uses materials with great efficiency, generates little or no waste, recycles residuals, and is, hence, more "closed."

To guide and speed the application of solution-oriented technologies will require policy action in the form of both economic incentives and direct regulation. It will require institutional innovation at the national and international levels, particularly to speed the process of international agreement and concerted action. Today, the problems are coming faster than the solutions. We will need a new international law of the environment, environmental diplomats, and the integration of environmental concerns into our trade and other international economic relations.

I have become a believer in the ingenuity of individuals and companies to find efficient solutions and to meet challenging goals, if the incentives are there. We need performance standards and economic rewards and penalties that are powerful, that provide the needed incentives, but that do not micromanage the process of technological innovation. This agency is no stranger to technology-forcing. We need more of it. And we should consider economic rewards for those who exceed baseline requirements.

We need to make the market mechanism work for us, not against us. Today, natural resource depletion and pollution are being subsidized on a grand scale around the globe. We have got to get the prices right; to begin by removing subsidies and then to make private companies and governments "internalize the externalities" so that prices reflect the true costs to society, including the costs of pollution. We need an environmentally honest economy.

Let me illustrate these points further by referring to one area where the need for technology transformation is most pressing—the energy sector—and one area where the need for concerted international action is most pressing—the greenhouse effect.

Our energy problems are forgotten but not gone. Energy will return to our political landscape again in the 1990s, driven by a

U.S. oil import bill that was $46 billion in 1987 and could reach $80 billion in 1995, and by the grave atmospheric pollution—local, regional, and global—that our use of fossil fuels causes. I talked earlier about the ways that urban air pollution, acid rain, and the greenhouse effect are all linked together, and linked to our energy use patterns. Addressing our nation's economic, security, and environmental objectives will require a careful process of long-term, integrated energy planning. Put simply, we can no longer safely make air pollution policy and energy policy independently, directed by separate executive agencies with little communication, under laws written and overseen by different congressional committees.

If we and other countries are to meet our economic and environmental challenges, what energy paths should we take? The coming energy transformation, I would argue, must have rapid energy efficiency improvements as its dominant feature, supplemented by increased reliance on renewable energy sources. The potential for energy efficiency gains through technological change is simply enormous. If the efficiency in energy use current in Japan today could be matched in the U.S. and around the world, total economic output could be doubled globally, and virtually doubled in the U.S., without increasing energy use.

Auto efficiency provides a good example of what is possible. Miles per gallon achieved by new cars sold in the U.S. doubled from 13 mpg to 25 mpg between 1973 and 1985. Ford, Honda and Suzuki all have cars in production that could double this again to 50 mpg, and Toyota has a prototype family car that could double efficiency again to almost 100 mpg. I am reminded here that there is a huge role for the private sector in the coming technological transformation. Those companies that see the future can profit from it.

One recent global energy analysis, built up from careful studies of energy use in industrial and developing countries, concluded "that the global population could roughly double, that living standards could be improved far beyond satisfying basic needs in developing countries, and that economic growth in industrialized countries could continue, without increasing the level of global energy use in 2020 much above the present level." In this technically and economically feasible future, total energy use goes up only 10 percent between 1980 and 2020 and fossil fuel use grows even less. In such a low-energy, high-efficiency future, the great energy supply debates, such as coal vs. nuclear, which preoccupy us so, lose much of their significance, and pollution problems are knocked down to more manageable proportions.

Large energy efficiency gains, and the consequent reductions in CO_2 emissions, will be essential in addressing what is probably the most serious environmental challenge of all—the global warming, which seems to have already begun. I recognize the uncertainties remaining in characterizing the greenhouse effect, but given the risks, I would advocate consideration now of a series of international conventions responsive to the various aspects of the problem.

First, we need to secure swift international approval for the ozone layer protection protocol signed in Montreal last year. We need this for its own sake and to continue the momentum that can get the nations of the world back to the table so that a complete, swift phase-out of CFCs can be negotiated. The phase-out is fully justified on ozone layer grounds alone, but the fact is that a CFC phase-out is the fastest and cheapest way societies can do something major to contain the greenhouse effect.

Second, we need an overall global climate protection convention, the prime goal of which should be to stabilize atmospheric concentrations of greenhouse gases at safe levels. This convention should focus particularly on steps needed to secure reductions in CO_2 emissions from fossil fuel use. Two facts stand out in this regard: the U.S. and the Soviet Union together account for almost half of global CO_2 emissions today, and the U.S., the USSR and China together account for about 90 percent of the estimated coal reserves.

Third, the time is ripe for an international agreement to protect the world's tropical forests and to reforest the spreading wasteland areas in many developing countries. The industrial nations have a double stake in halting the now-rapid clearing of the tropical forests. Not only are these forests repositories for about half of the wildlife and genetic wealth of the planet, but CO_2 emissions from biotic sources such as deforestation are estimated to be about a fifth of CO_2 emissions from fossil fuels. Our stake in the salvation of these forests is sufficiently large that we should be more than willing to help provide financial incentives—incentives that will be necessary [if the] tropics are to turn their attention to what often appears as a low priority or even a threat to development and sovereignty. I suggest that we go far beyond the debt-for-nature swaps under way today and consider a global bargain as part of this international convention. This bargain would involve the easing and forgiving of international debts in exchange for forest conservation. Of the top 17 most heavily indebted countries, 12 are destroying their tropical forests at extraordinarily rapid rates, contributing to the world's annual loss of 27 million acres.

And fourth, we need international agreement on the protocol now being developed to limit nitrogen oxide emissions. Unless capped, increasing NO_x emissions will lead to increasing ozone concentrations, and ozone is a greenhouse gas as well as a source of urban and rural air pollution. Many good reasons exist to control NO_x emissions at the international level, and I urge the State Department and EPA to signal U.S. support for the proposed protocol by the fast-approaching July 1 deadline.

Some of you may be wondering: is he going to discuss nuclear power, an available non-fossil source of energy? My concern about nuclear power, as things stand today, is that it probably will not, in the end, provide a major part of the answer to global warming. Its public acceptability is too low and its price is too high. If we try to solve the greenhouse problem by cramming nuclear power down the throats of an unwilling public and unwilling investors, we will be setting the stage for prolonged confrontation and stalemate. And what is going to happen to nuclear power if there are one or two more major accidents like Three Mile Island and Chernobyl? Moreover, I believe there are safer and cheaper alternatives for the short run, including the vast potential for efficiency gains in how we generate and use electricity. For the longer run, I would favor research aimed at reinventing nuclear power in a way that could gain public and investor confidence; we may need it one day. My guess, however, is that before such a new nuclear system could be commercialized in the next century, the price of photovoltaic and other solar energy systems will be competitive. But who knows? We are all still learning.

In all these areas, in seeking these treaties and in setting an international example by acting on our own, U.S. leadership and EPA leadership could not be more important. The world is not exactly waiting on us, but neither will it get very far without us. I hope you will join with me in urging our Presidential candidates to give these issues the time and thought they deserve. We need to know, beyond the level of generalities, how each candidate would address the emerging environmental agenda of the 1990s.

Let me conclude with a word about why I am optimistic that the world can indeed be saved. This address, you have doubtless noted, reflects a deep appreciation of the importance of economic and technological forces in the modern world. One reason for optimism is that science and technology are presenting us with answers. We are in the midst of a revolution in earth science and a revolution in industrial and agricultural technology, both with huge potentials in the areas we have been reviewing.

But if solutions are found, they will come from another realm as well, from the hopes and fears of people, from their aspirations for their children and their wonder at the natural world, from their own self-respect and their dogged insistence that some things that seem very wrong are just that. People everywhere are offended by pollution. They sense intuitively that we have pressed beyond limits we should not have exceeded. They want to clean up the world, make it a better place, be good trustees of the Earth for future generations. With Thoreau, they know that heaven is under our feet as well as over our heads. Politicians around the globe are increasingly hearing the demand that things be set right. And that is very good news indeed.

BIOTECHNOLOGY AT A CROSSROADS[1]

JEREMY RIFKIN[2]

The public debate on biotechnology, which began in the late 1970s and grew in intensity in the 1980s, seems likely to continue into the next century. The issue is whether scientists should be permitted to experiment with the manipulation of the genetic codes of plants and animals. The issue raises serious environmental questions as well as questions of ethics, economics, and even patent rights.

One man sparked much of the controversy: Jeremy Rifkin, the president of the Foundation on Emerging Technologies, who has challenged almost every aspect of genetic experimental through lawsuits, demonstrations, lectures, interviews, books, and any other available public forum. (Ronald Bailey, "Ministry of Fear," *Forbes*, June 27, 1988, p. 138)

Rifkin has a history of political activism dating back to his under-

[1]Delivered on July 12, 1988, at 11 A.M. in the Capitol Ballroom of the Marriott Hotel in Washington, D.C., at the United States Agricultural Communicators Congress.

[2]For biographical note, see Appendix.

graduate days in the Sixties at the University of Pennsylvania, where he was also elected class president and earned a reputation as an accomplished speaker. Subsequently, he gained national prominence as an organizer and agitator for various causes. In the late 1970s Rifkin became interested in the implications of scientific research into recombinant DNA and the host of questions raised by the issue of genetic manipulation.

Since then, Rifkin has become the acknowledged spokesman for opponents of experimentation in genetic engineering. He is in widespread demand on the college lecture circuit. In a 16-month period preceding this speech, he participated in more than one hundred conferences and meetings in eight countries. While Rifkin's background includes no formal study of science, Lieve Cavalieri, a molecular biologist at Sloane-Kettering Hospital in New York, says, "Jeremy is extremely intelligent and grasps scientific issues immediately, if you take the trouble to explain them to him." (Edward Tivnau, "Jeremy Rifkin Just Says No," *New York Times Magazine*, October 16, 1988, p. 42)

On July 12, 1988, Rifkin addressed the 1988 U.S. Agriculture Communicators Congress, a four-day conference in Washington, D.C. sponsored by five national agricultural communications organizations. This was only the second agricultural communications conference, and the first since 1984. Rifkin spoke to an audience of some 400 in the Capitol Ballroom of the Marriott Hotel at 11 A.M.

Following an introduction by moderator Claude Gifford of the Department of Agriculture, Rifkin stepped away from the head table and onto the floor. He removed his coat, loosened his tie, unbuttoned his collar, and attached a lavelier microphone. After asking, "Can y'all hear me?" he spoke, without notes or manuscript, while moving about, up and down the aisle.

Jeremy Rifkin's speech: Good morning! I'd like to try and place into context some of the issues that we think are important in dealing with the public policy implications of biotechnology. First of all let me try to place it within a larger anthropological perspective.

The world community is making a long-term transition. We are moving out of fossil fuels, the energy base for industrial technology, and we're now moving into renewable resources, the energy base for biological based technology. This transformation will be as significant, in my opinion, as the transformation from Medieval agriculture to the industrial, urban way of life of the last 200 years.

And, certainly, it's going to raise profound environmental, social, ethical and economic questions for the whole world family to have to grapple and deal with. I think there's two broad philosophical approaches to organizing renewable resources. The first is an ecological approach, a stewardship approach. The idea is to develop a philosophy of science that works with the environment, that is empathetic to the natural resource base rather than a philosophy of science based on exploitation and short-term gains only.

The ecological approach would be based on a technology assumption where we use new tools to develop sustainability with our resources rather than short-term expedient use. And the ecological approach to the age of biology would be based on an economic theory, based on justice for the homo sapien species and equity and justice for all the other creatures that we have to live with in this small planet. So, there's an ecological approach to the age of biology. There's also another approach to the age of biology, very different in philosophy and in application: genetic engineering. Genetic engineering simply means placing engineering principles into the gene pool. That's why we call it genetic engineering. We're learning how to map genes, program genes, turn on and off genes. We're learning how to recombine genetic traits between unrelated species. We're learning how to apply engineering assumptions into the blueprint for microbes, plants, animals, and the human race.

What are those engineering assumptions that we used during the industrial age? Quality control, the ability to reduce phenomena to a quantifiable standard of measurement, predictability of outcome, utilitarianism, and efficiency. Those are the kinds of industrial-based assumptions that we used for the last two hundred years in organizing inanimate materials during the fossil fuel era.

And, now the talk in the scientific community and among corporate policy makers is to take those engineering assumptions and apply them directly into the blueprint—microbes, plants, animals, homo sapiens. Now, many scientists have said to me, "Well, Jeremy, gee, lighten up. I mean we're just, this is just a more sophisticated approach to the kind of domesticating technologies we've been using since neolithic agriculture. We've been breeding and domesticating for a long time—this is just a more precise way of doing the same old thing we've always been doing." I have to take exception to that.

You see, in nature it is possible to do a lot of manipulation, but you are constrained by biological boundary walls. For example, you can cross a donkey and a horse and get a mule. Correct? But, as far as I know, there's no breeder in history that can cross a donkey and a dandelion and get a damned thing. Now, we have a technology called gene-splicing that allows us in both theory and practice to eliminate the idea of a species as an identifiable being with an egos and telos, you Latin scholars, an essential nature. Now we can perceive of a horse as a series of genetic programs, any one of which can be snipped out and recombined and placed into the germ line of a totally unrelated species. As you know, scientists have taken human genes and placed them in the permanent genetic code of mice, pigs, and sheep. There's no breeding technology in history, my friends, that can do that. Scientists have taken carp genes—trout genes—and placed them into the genetic code of carp fish. Scientists have taken the gene that emits light in a firefly, injected that gene into tobacco plants and those leaves glow 24 hours a day. There is no breeding technology in history that allows us to bypass species borders with this kind of abandon. So, it's going to create a whole new set of questions—environmental questions for sure, but also ethical and philosophical questions. Is there any limit to the amount of manipulation that we ought to be able to do in rearranging the genetic programs between species?

Now, I'm 43 years old. I grew up in the United States in the 1950s. We had two great technology revolutions: nuclear power and petrochemical technology. The scientific establishment and the corporations and the policy makers said "Trust us, we have a technology revolution here with many benefits and with minimum risks." Back in the 50s and 60s we as a society did not ask the hard questions up front. We rushed pall mall into these technology revolutions hopeful that we would be able to resolve all of the problems of society by these tools and we didn't ask tough environmental, social, ethical and economic questions. They simply were not raised. The result—to be perfectly honest—we benefited immensely in the short run from nuclear power and petrochemical technology. We'd all admit that. But, I think every person in this room would also acknowledge that we have also created tremendous long-term environmental, economic and social dislocation as a result of rushing in with these technologies without asking the hard questions up front. Genetic engineering—only benefits, no problems? I doubt it. Now, let me go through several issues we're dealing with to give you an idea of the kind of questions that need to be raised.

Deliberate release of genetically engineered organisms into the environment. Whenever you release a genetically engineered organism into the environment for agricultural purposes, you have to realize that the environmental consequences are quite different than if you introduce a petrochemical into an agricultural environment. First of all, genetically engineered organisms are alive. So, they're inherently more unpredictable in terms of what they will do when interacting in the eco-system.

Secondly, genetically engineered organisms—many of them can reproduce and they mutate and they can migrate off site. They have much greater mobility than any chemical product.

And, finally, third, if you don't like what a genetically engineered organism is doing out there in your agricultural field, you can't simply say "My fault" and recall it to the laboratory. Would you like to try and recall a virus, or a bacteria or even a plant back to the laboratory if it does do damage?

Now, please understand the level of risk and we've perceived it, up to now. Whenever you introduce a genetically engineered organism into the agricultural field, be it plant, animal, or microbe, there's only a small chance that it's going to do any damage. I know you were expecting I'd come here and talk to you about "killer tomatoes" moving on Iowa and andromeda strains heading toward Kansas. Now, we've never said that although we've been accused of it. There's only a small chance that any given introduction is going to cause a problem. But, if it does cause a problem, the long-term impact on your agricultural environment can be extreme and potentially catastrophic. The analogy is exotic organisms. You people that have covered the farm beat for a long time know we've brought a lot of exotic organisms over to North America—many of them fit into our eco-system, but some of them, quite frankly, become pests and we can't get rid of them. Kudzu vine in the South—anybody here from the South. Anybody here from the South? That doesn't make you too comfortable. We can't get rid of that. We brought that over from somewhere else. Dutch elm disease—remember those beautiful tree-lined streets through the Midwest? No more. Chestnut blight. Do we have enough starlings? Gypsy moth. You know how that happened? Some schmuck brought the gypsy moth over—did you hear this story?—for the silk industry. One night it was hot and he was up in Massachusetts. He opened up his bedroom window and the eggs blew out. And, we can't get rid of gypsy moth.

And, these exotics cause hundreds of millions of dollars a year in damage. Now, please understand the scale. In the next ten years industry would like to develop scores, perhaps hundreds of products, to release into the agricultural field.

In the 21st century, our children's century, the ambition is to introduce thousands of genetically engineered viruses, bacteria, trangenetic plants, and animals in massive commercial volumes all over the planet earth. They hope it'll be comparable to the introduction of chemicals. We introduced thousands of chemical products into the earth.

Now, my friends, you don't have to be a molecular biologist, merely a statistician. Let's assume most of these introductions are safe. If only a tiny fraction turn out to be pests, because of the scale of introductions, the biological pollution could well exceed chemical pollution because these products are alive, many of them reproduce, they mutate, migrate and you cannot recall them once they're out there. You're stuck for centuries, perhaps, millennium. Now, many other countries have taken a very sophisticated, prudent approach to the release of genetically engineered organisms. I think in this country a lot of the folks in this country just think it's just Jeremy Rifkin and a few folks. Let me tell you about other countries.

In Germany, one of the three biotech powers, de Vuntegstag commission on biotechnology has recommended a five year prohibition—a moratorium—on any release into Germany because the scientific questions are yet to be dealt with seriously.

In Denmark they have voted legislation that prohibits any release into the environment because these questions are still unredressed.

Japan, which we always point to "if we don't do it they will get ahead of us." No, Japan has never released an organism into the environment and they have a moratorium now, ostensibly they're doing a three-year study to assess the scientific impact.

There are a few countries that have rushed ahead—the United States, France and England—without seriously raising the problems of a risk-assessment science. The botton line, my friends in the agricultural community, is this. There is no science of predictive ecology. It doesn't exist. There is no science of risk-assessment with which we can judge these introductions. We've been asking for such a science for years. There is none. So, we're in the very uncomfortable situation of regulating a technology in this country on the one hand and on the other realizing there is no science to adequately do it with. I think we should heed the call of other countries and impose a five-year moratorium worldwide so that we can bring the best environmental sciences together with our molecular biologists to see if we can hammer out a reasonable risk-assessment science. To do less than that would be a disservice to our children's generation. Deliberate release into the environment.

Second issue: let's examine bovine growth hormone for a minute because it is a classic example of why the blessings of biotechnology turn out to be a curse when you look at them with more serious attention.

Bovine growth hormone, as you know, is the first major product being researched to introduce into agriculture. Two chemical companies, Monsanto and Cyanamid, two pharmaceutical companies, Eli Lilly and Upjohn, are spending tens of millions of dollars in research, field trials in fifteen countries, I think, to introduce a product which they claim will be a 500 million dollar to one billion dollar a year product.

Now, as you know, bovine growth hormone increases milk production between what? Ten and forty percent per cow. Normal increase in milk production, as you know, is what? About two percent a year with breeding. Now, we're talking ten to forty percent. If you measure progress narrowly in terms of more output and less time, this is the most progressive product in the history of animal husbandry. But, if you mark, if you define progress by enhancing the well-being of society, this is the silliest product that's ever come down the pike. That's why we have to redefine our concepts of progress.

The last thing we need is more milk. Every industrial nation in the world is awash in milk surpluses and now these companies come along with a product that will massively increase the surpluses. Parenthetically, this product cannot be used in the third world because in the southern hemisphere at high temperatures, the cows overheat. You do not get as good a production out of them.

So, we have a product that has literally no redeeming social values: it hurts the farmers, it will hurt the tax payers, it might hurt the consumers. The farmer—one study done by Cornell which they've later kind of back-tracked on—Culture and Bowman study that they did, I think with Monsanto—they predicted that if, I think, you eliminate price supports, that within three years of the introduction of BGH up to 30 percent of the American dairy farms may be out of business. Any way you look at it, that's the biggest dislocation in a short period of time in U.S. agricultural history.

Let's say they change their study. Let's say it's only half that. Imagine the devastation to certain regions of the country by introducing this hormone: Wisconsin, western New York, Missouri, Washington state, etc.

A study was just released in Wisconsin. The University of Wisconsin, your alma mater, Chuck, was commissioned by the state legislature to do a study on biotechnology and BGH. The study made the following conclusion: within four years of the introduction of BGH into Wisconsin and around the country, that Wisconsin dairy farmers by year four would lose one hundred million dollars. We have a—by the way there are health hazards to the cows—I don't have a lot of time today to go into it but there have been studies that have shown now that the cows are facing sterility, mastitis, a whole range of production stresses and it stands to reason. If you're going to put massive injections of a hormone into an animal beyond what it was biologically designed for it's naive and disingenuous to believe that won't stress that animal. Many of you are farmers. You know just what I'm talking about with stress related production diseases. Will the taxpayers want to pay to buy up all of the surpluses? You want to see how this is going to float in Washington when it gets in front of the dairy, poultry and livestock committee? Last Monday, we have a coalition—the international coalition against BGH—we're determined that this product will never enter the market place. Last week our international coalition in Europe—we have seven countries organized—farmers, environmental groups, consumer groups. We did a lobbying effort at the European parliament last Monday to vote. The European parliament has voted and recommended to ban commercial use of BGH and to recommend that it only be used by veterinarians for therapeutic purposes which is ostensibly a ban. That recommendation is going to the counsel of the European community. Germany, one of the three big biotech powers, is on record opposing the introduction of BGH.

Now let me give you a little sneak preview of something that's going to come next year. The international coalition against BGH is fully prepared to launch a consumer boycott worldwide if BGH is introduced in any market in the world in the next year and we have prepared the first series of TV, radio spots and print ads which will be used all over Europe and the United States—if you want to hit the lights—let me just give you—you'll be the first to see this. This is what we will be prepared to launch in the spring of 1989. Can we get the lights?

[Radio to television spot:]

With so many chemicals and additives in our food, there's still one that's one hundred percent natural—pure milk. But, now chemical companies want to inject cows with a genetically engineered growth hormone that forces them to produce more milk creating a milk surplus and putting thirty percent of America's dairy farmers out of work. It could be a health hazard to cows and the milk you drink will contain that hormone. What are they doing to our milk?

We will have those available to anyone who would like to see them afterward. We have copies of the TV and radio spots. We're going to ask, demand that labelling be placed on all milk products—BGH, non-BGH—so that the consumers worldwide will have a choice.

Let me try to talk about one more issue. What I'm trying to point out here is there's no fait accompli about the technology. Just because it can be done doesn't mean it will be done. Parts of the biotechnology revolution make sense, they should go ahead. There are other parts that probably have very little socially redeeming value and we as a citizenry have a responsibility to pick and choose. There is an issue tomorrow coming to a vote in the House of Representatives that we've been working on for fourteen months. Back in April of 1987, the U.S. Patent Office issued a policy decision. The decision was that you can now patent any genetically-engineered animal on the planet. If you place a human gene into the genetic code of a pig, since that can't be done through natural breeding, that whole pig is now considered a human invention. In one regulatory stroke, a handful of bureaucrats in the patent office reduced the entire animal kingdom to the lowly status of a commercial commodity indistinguishable from microwave ovens or automobiles or tennis balls. Those are all patented inventions.

Now, I for one, I think there are philosophical, environmental, and economic reasons to oppose the patenting of animals. By the way, I should tell you that by this decision, any number of human genes can be placed into the genetic code of animals and they can be patented. The patent office did offer a reprieve. They did say that we cannot patent a homo sapiens because the 13th amendment and the 14th amendment forbids slavery. So, that was nice of them. By this decision, our children would grow up in a world where they would come to think of all animals as patented inventions indistinguishable from inanimate materials, from chemical materials that we have patented over the years.

Now, don't get me wrong. I'm like a lot of people: I'm not a purist. I do believe you have to manipulate nature to survive. I don't want to take us back into the stone age. I do believe we have to go ahead and proceed on into the future and we have to manipulate and tinker and organize nature, and especially agriculture in order to make a better way of life for us and our kids. But, I do believe there's a margin between mutual give and take so we can sustain a healthy, vibrant, economic agricultural system on the one hand and on the other reducing all of life to strict, utilitarian expediency. The farmers don't want patenting animals. The National Farmers Union, the American Agricultural Movement, Save the Family Farm Coalition—they have all joined in our coalition with many of the animal welfare groups like the Humane Society, the ASPCA—that's an interesting coalition isn't it?—animal rights and farm groups. Things are changing. And, other groups have called for a moratorium on patenting animals. The Wildlife Federation of America, the Consumer Federation of America, the 27 religious leaders of every major protestant denomination in the United States and several Jewish. They're all saying, "Let's look at patenting before we rush ahead." And, all of these organizations are in favor of a short moratorium so that the Congress of the United States can take a long, hard, careful look as to whether this is the road we want to pursue. It makes no sense for two of three men at the patent office to dictate the entire future control of the gene pool of this planet. Whoever controls the gene pool will be effectively as powerful as whoever controlled the oil in the way of minerals in the industrial age—you with me?

So, this a decision that we as a people ought to respond to collectively through our elected representatives. Tomorrow morning two bills will be voted for markup in the House Judiciary Committee on Patents and Trademarks. Both bills I expect will pass and we anticipate that to be a major for our coalition against patenting animals—both bills.

The first bill introduced by Congressman Charles Rowles with 64 congressional sponsors calls for a two year moratorium on patenting animals so Congress can look at this question. The second bill introduced by the chairman of the committee, Congressman Kastenmeyer, calls for major exemptions for farmers and for researchers. You see, under existing patent policy, if you buy a patented animal from a chemical company, and that animal gives birth, you have to pay a royalty because every birth is considered a reproduction, now. You see why farmers are not happy with patenting? It'll mean a few chemical, and pharmaceutical and biotech companies in the next twenty years literally taking over animal husbandry as they have poultry. By this exemption, Congressman Kastenmeyer has put on the table and I think because of the effective lobbying of this coalition for 14 months, farmers making under $2 million gross a year will be exempted from paying royalties and researchers will be exempted from paying royalties for pure research reproduction. Again, when this patent policy was announced, everyone assumed it would be a fait accompli. And, what I'm here to say to you today is that today as Chuck I think mentioned earlier, we're entering a new chapter in our relationship to technology, especially in agriculture. Now, we're going to, as a society, debate the pros and cons of each new technology so we can have a more sophisticated analysis of cost benefit. So, that when we proceed into these new areas we do so with a sense that we've taken care.

You know, when you intervene into the environment, you can never anticipate all of the consequences. Right? There's no fail-safe method of knowing the future. So, the rule of thumb ought to be when intervening in nature, always intervene the most gently, the most careful, and the most prudent course. Never take the most radical and the most adventuresome approach because you can never foresee all the consequences.

Gene splicing, engineering and rearranging the code of plants, animals and microbes. Is that prudent, caring, thoughtful? Or, is that radical, adventurous, and extreme?

Finally, you'll notice in those press releases that we handed out that there's mention of the greenhouse effect. In 1980 I wrote a book called *Entropy* and we developed a project called the Entropy project. We predicted that this would happen. And, the reason I'm glad to speak with you this morning is because it points out the problems we faced and the approach to science and technology we have used in the past. In the last two weeks you've all been reading about the greenhouse effect. My friends, that's the bill for the industrial age. I've often been accused of being against progress and being a Luddite. Well, I'm here to tell you this morning that the real obstacle to progress has been the pursuit of an industrial policy and an agricultural policy that has created now a change in climate so severe that we'll be paying for it for thousands of years in the future. You might have noticed on the cover of *Newsweek* and the congressional testimony NASA, the Goddard Space Institute, the Volagia report—they are now saying in the next fifty years, as a result of industrial pollutants on this planet, the temperature change in the next 40 to 75 years, that's the range, will increase by a greater margin than in the last 18,000 years since the end of the ice age. And, all the eco-systems of the planet will be affected in ways we can't begin to measure. It's being called the greatest social, environmental crisis in world history. And, it will force a readjustment across this planet of the entire way we do business—our science, our technology, our public policy—how we develop our infrastructures and finally how we grow our plants and raise our animals. Because the surveys that I've been reading from the National Academy of Science, the CEQ, EPA suggest agriculture is going to be the first to be affected you've seen the drought this year. According to these studies, between the early 21st century and the end of that century our entire agricultural areas of this country will be increasingly unavailable for agriculture. That's a big adjustment to make in less than 75 years.

We are initiating, by the way, and you know the major cause of the greenhouse effect is auto emissions and coal burning plants. You know what the third greatest cause is? Of the greenhouse effect? How many know? Ten percent of the greenhouse effect is caused by you know what? Fertilizers—the green revolution. Ten percent nitrous oxides in all the studies the third major cause of the greatest crises facing humanity is the green revolution of modern agriculture that we have pursued with great benefit for three decades at the expense of the survival of our planet for the next millennium.

We are initiating a global network, a global coalition which we announced this fall of farm organizations working together with environmental groups, food and consumer groups, religious leaders from around the world and we're going to announce this fall a global coalition of groups. We will seek whole new approaches to orient our agriculture in the future so that it's based on sustainability, it's based on diversification and it's based on a working partnership with our environment so that in 500 years from now and 1,000 years from now our children's children's generation will look back and say we made some wise choices for the future because at this point it's not a matter of who's right and who's wrong and pointing blame. We're all going to be part of this problem in the next 50 years. How will we choose the future of agriculture? An extension of green revolution philosophy, genetic engineering of those plants and animals, or new, sophisticated ecological science based on sustainability?

Finally, let me leave you with the words of the Iroquois Indians. Lest we snicker at the thought of the Iroquois remember Thomas Jefferson was quite enamored with the Iroquois. He borrowed quite liberally from their philosophy to pen his own. When the Iroquois Indians made decisions, they asked "How does the decision we make today affect seven generations removed?" "How does the decision we make now affect our children's children's children's children's children's children's children?" The Iroquois didn't live just for the moment, the quick fix, the short run. They heard their ancestors speak from the grave saying, "Honor the past. We have to have continuity between the generations." But, they also heard their unborn children and all other life not yet here saying, "Speak for us. We're not there yet." So, when the Iroquois made decisions, they did so as part of the continuum of history from the beginning to the end time. Now, I've been in Washington 17 years. You know what the attention span here is? The two-year general election. And in New York on Wall Street, the attention span is the three month profit and loss quarterly statement. Who is more sophisticated: us or the Iroquois? In winning in the short run we lose in the long run. So, together we have a tremendous opportunity and challenge and that's why I'm so grateful to even get this tme to speak with you this morning. We have a tremendous opportunity and challenge to learn from the past and to develop a critical analysis of former agricultural practices so that we can move ahead with a new vision of agriculture that can allow us not only to deal with and adjust to the current greenhouse crisis, but could allow to plan a new agricultural policy for the world in coming centuries that will be based on resacrilizing our relationship with life. Because the new politics of the next century are not going to be based on right wing–left wing. Kids don't understand that politics anymore. The new politics is going to be based on resacrilizing our relationship to living things on the one hand or on the other reducing all of life to programs and chemicals and engineered genes that can be manipulated and rearranged for short term expedient purposes. So, I'm hoping that when we look in back 50 to 75 years from now we can look back and say we carved a new course out, a course based on all of us working together to resacrilize our relationship to life and develop an agricultural policy that can allow future generations to not only survive but to prosper. Thank you.

THOUGHTS ON THE 125TH ANNIVERSARY OF THE BATTLE OF GETTYSBURG[1]

CARL SAGAN[2]

Fifty-one thousand individuals were killed or wounded at the Battle of Gettysburg in 1863. At ceremonies marking the anniversary of that Civil War battle, Carl Sagan described it as "the first full-fledged example of an industrialized war, with machine-made arms and railroad transport of men and materiel. This was the first hint of an age yet to come, our age; an intimation of what technology bent to the purposes of war might be capable."

A Pulitzer Prize-winning professor of astronomy and space sciences, director of the Laboratory for Planetary Studies at Cornell University, and narrator of the successful television series *Cosmos*, Sagan delivered the principal address at the anniversary and the rededication ceremonies of the Eternal Light Peace Memorial at Gettysburg National Military Park, Gettysburg, Pennsylvania, on July 3, 1988.

The battle has been celebrated at the national park every 25 years since the 50th anniversary in 1913, when President Woodrow Wilson delivered the principal address. In 1938 200,000 people attended as Franklin D. Roosevelt dedicated the Eternal Peace flame. (*Americana*, June 1988, p. 51) In 1963 the centennial anniversary, Dwight D. Eisenhower delivered the principal address. Sagan was the first nonpresidential speaker to deliver the main address.

A week of ceremonies and Civil War battle reenactments preceded Sagan's speech. As many as 75,000 observers saw recreations of the fight for McPherson's Ridge, the Cavalry Field struggle, wheatfield battles, and Pickett's charge. Commemorative activities include a display of Civil

[1]Delivered at the 125th celebration of the Battle of Gettysburg and the rededication ceremonies of the Eternal Light Peace Memorial, Gettysburg National Military Park, Gettysburg, Pennsylvania, at approximately 6:30 P.M., July 3, 1988.

[2]For biographical note, see Appendix.

War arts and crafts; a symbolic presentation of battle flags in which the governors of Pennsylvania and Virginia, a New York senator, and other government officials took part; band concerts; lectures; and a ceremony opening the National Park Service's Gettysburg Museum of the Civil War. (*Civil War Times Illustrated*, October 1988, pp. 30–31)

The site for Sagan's speech was the Peace Memorial, located in a beautiful, heavily wooded Oak Ridge area overlooking a dramatic vista of the scene of the three-day battle. The monument itself is in the form of a tall square shaft rising from the center of an elevated platform. Surmounting the shaft is a bronze urn containing what was intended to be a perpetually burning light.

Sagan spoke on Sunday, the final day of the week of anniversary ceremonies. During the afternoon, several bands and choirs performed. An ecumenical church service was conducted at the Lutheran Seminary between 5:00 and 5:45 P.M., which was followed by a procession to the Eternal Light Peace Memorial, where an audience of 30,000 had assembled. The theme of the rededication, which lasted from 6:00 to 7:30 P.M., was "A World United in the Search for Peace." The program began with music by the Morgan State University Choir. After welcoming the audience, Judge Oscar F. Spicer, president of the Gettysburg Peace Celebration, and several others, including the governor of Pennsylvania, Robert P. Casey, spoke briefly. Judge Spicer introduced Dr. Sagan as "a noted author, scientist, and teacher whose awards and honors are almost beyond either counting or recitation." Sagan began to speak at approximately 6:30 P.M., with the setting sun beaming directly over the unveiling and relighting of the memorial.

Sagan's speech is interesting for several reasons. One, in particular, is the way the astronomer skillfully used what was a ceremonial, commemorative occasion to discuss a controversial issue. After calling the battle the first "full-fledged example of industrialized war," he traced the development of modern weaponry and military tactics up to the present and then addressed his main topic: the threat of nuclear war. Sagan argued that throughout history warriors have made mistakes and killed their own. That risk is one humanity can no longer afford, and Sagan devoted more than half of his speech to that danger.

The speech was the joint product of Professor Sagan and his wife, Ann Druyan, who work closely together on most of the speeches, articles, and publications that appear under his name.

Carl Sagan's speech: Thank you Judge Spicer. I'm moved and honored to join you in the commemoration of this doleful and instructive milestone in world history.

Fifty-one thousand human beings were killed or wounded here, ancestors of some of us, brothers of us all. This was the first full-fledged example of an industrialized war, with machine-made arms and railroad transport of men and materiel. This was the first hint of an age yet to come, our age; an intimation of what technology bent to the purposes of war might be capable. The new Spencer repeating rifle was used here. In May 1863, a reconnaissance balloon of the Army of the Potomac detected movement of Confederate troops across the Rappahannock River, the beginning of the campaign that led to the Battle of Gettysburg. That balloon was a precursor of air forces and strategic bombing and reconnaissance satellites.

A few hundred artillery pieces were deployed in the three-day battle of Gettysburg. What could they do? What was war like then? Here is an eyewitness account by Frank Haskel of Wisconsin, who fought on this battlefield for the Union Armies. It is from a letter to his brother:

> We could not often see the shell before it burst, but sometimes, as we faced towards the enemy and looked above our heads, the approach would be heralded by a prolonged hiss, which always seemed to me to be a line of something tangible terminating in a black globe distinct to the eye as the sound had been to the ear. The shell would seem to stop and hang suspended in the air an instant and then vanish in fire and smoke and noise. . . . Not ten yards away from us a shell burst among some bushes where sat three or four orderlies holding horses. Two of the men and one horse were killed.

It was a typical event from the Battle of Gettysburg. Something like it was repeated thousands of times. Those ballistic projectiles, launched from the cannons that you can see all over this Gettysburg Memorial, had a range, at best, of a few miles. The amount of explosive in the most formidable of them was some twenty pounds, roughly one-hundredth of a ton of TNT. It was enough to kill a few people.

But the most powerful chemical explosives used 80 years later, in World War II, were the blockbusters, so-called because they could destroy a city block. Dropped from aircraft, after a journey of hundreds of miles, each carried about ten tons of TNT, a thousand times more than the most powerful weapon at the Battle of Gettysburg. A blockbuster could kill a few dozen people.

At the very end of World War II, the United States used the first atomic bombs to annihilate two Japanese cities. Each of those weapons had the equivalent power of about ten thousand tons of TNT, enough to kill a few hundred thousand people. One bomb.

A few years later the United States and the Soviet Union developed the first thermonuclear weapons, the first hydrogen bombs. Some of them had an explosive yield equivalent to ten million tons of TNT; enough to kill a few million people. One bomb. Strategic nuclear weapons can now be launched to any place on the planet. Everywhere on Earth is a potential battlefield now.

Each of these technological triumphs advanced the art of mass murder by a factor of a thousand. From Gettysburg to the blockbuster, a thousand times more explosive energy; from the blockbuster to the atomic bomb, a thousand times more; and from the atomic bomb to the hydrogen bomb a thousand times still more. A thousand times a thousand, times a thousand is a billion; in less than one century, our most fearful weapon has become a billion times more deadly. But we have not become a billion times wiser in the generations that stretch from Gettysburg to us.

The souls that perished here would find the carnage of which we are now capable unspeakable. Today, the United States and the Soviet Union have booby-trapped our planet with almost 60,000 nuclear weapons. Sixty thousand nuclear weapons! Even a small fraction of the strategic arsenals could without question annihilate the two contending superpowers, probably destroy the global civilization, and possibly render the human species extinct. No nation, no man should have such power. We distribute these instruments of apocalypse all over our fragile world, and justify it on the grounds that it has made us safe. We have made a fool's bargain.

The 51,000 casualties here at Gettysburg represented one-third of the Confederate army, and one-quarter of the Union army. All those who died, with one or two exceptions, were soldiers. The best-known exception was a civilian in her own house who thought to bake a loaf of bread and, through two closed doors, was shot to death; her name was Jennie Wade. But in a global thermonuclear war, almost all the casualties will be civilians, men, women and children, including vast numbers of citizens of nations that had no part in the quarrel that led to the war, nations far removed from the northern mid-latitude "target zone." There will be billions of Jennie Wades. Everyone on Earth is now at risk.

In Washington there is a memorial to the Americans who died in the most recent major U.S. war, the one in Southeast Asia. Some 58,000 Americans perished, not a very different number from the casualties here at Gettysburg. (I ignore, as we too often do, the one or two million Vietnamese, Laotians, and Kampucheans who also died in that war.) Think of that dark, somber, beautiful, moving, touching memorial. Think of how long it is; actually, not much longer than a suburban street: 58,000 names.

Imagine now that we are so foolish or inattentive as to permit a nuclear war to occur, and that, somehow, a similar memorial wall is built. How long would it have to be to contain the names of all those who will die in a major nuclear war? About a thousand miles long. It would stretch from here in Pennsylvania to Missouri. But of course, there would be no one to build it, and very few to read the roster of the fallen.

In 1945, at the close of World War II, the United States and the Soviet Union were virtually invulnerable. The United States, bounded east and west by vast and impassable oceans, north and south by weak and friendly neighbors, had the most effective armed forces, and the most powerful economy on the planet. We had nothing to fear. So we built nuclear weapons and their delivery systems. We initiated and vigorously pumped up an arms race with the Soviet Union. When we were done, everyone in the United States had handed their lives over to the leaders of the Soviet Union. Today, if Moscow decides we should die, twenty minutes later we're dead. In nearly perfect symmetry, the Soviet Union had the largest standing army in the world in 1945, and no significant military threats to worry about. It joined the United States in the nuclear arms race so that today everyone in the Soviet Union has handed their lives over to the leaders of the United States. If Washington decides they should die, twenty minutes later they're dead. The lives of every American and every Soviet citizen are now in the hands of a foreign power. I say we have made a fool's bargain. We—we Americans, we Soviets—have spent 43 years and vast national treasure in making ourselves exquisitely vulnerable to instant annihilation. We have done it in the name of patriotism and "national security," so no one is supposed to question it.

Two months before Gettysburg, on May 3, 1863, there was a Confederate triumph, the battle of Chancellorsville. On the moonlit evening following the victory, General Stonewall Jackson and his staff, returning to the Confederate lines, were mistaken for Union cavalry. Jackson was shot twice in error by his own men. He died of his wounds.

We make mistakes. We kill our own.

There are some who claim that since we have not yet had an accidental nuclear war, the precautions being taken to prevent one must be adequate. But not three years ago we witnessed the disasters of the Challenger space shuttle and the Chernobyl nuclear power plant, high technology systems, one American, one Soviet, into which enormous quantities of national prestige had been invested. There were compelling reasons to prevent these disasters. In the preceding year, confident assertions were made by officials of both nations that no accidents of that sort could happen. We were not to worry. The experts would not permit an accident to happen. We have since learned that such assurances do not amount to much.

We make mistakes. We kill our own.

This is the century of Hitler and Stalin, evidence—if any were needed—that madmen can seize the reins of power of modern industrial states. If we are content in a world with nearly 60,000 nuclear weapons, we are betting our lives on the proposition that no present or future leaders, military or civilian—of the United States, the Soviet Union, Britain, France, China, Israel, India, Pakistan, South Africa, and whatever other nuclear powers there will be—will ever stray from the strictest standards of prudence. We are gambling on their sanity and sobriety even in times of great personal and national crisis, all of them, for all times to come. I say this is asking too much of us. Because we make mistakes. We kill our own.

The nuclear arms race and the attendant Cold War cost something. They don't come free. Apart from the immense diversion of fiscal and intellectual resources away from the civilian economy, apart from the psychic cost of living out our lives under the Damoclean sword, what has been the price of the Cold War?

The American cost we can readily tabulate. (The Soviet cost is, very likely, about the same.) By the time the Reagan Administration leaves office in January, 1989, how much will the United States have spent on the Cold War? The answer, in current dollars, is about $10 trillion. That's the one with the big "T"; ten *t*rillion dollars. Of this sum, more than a third has been spent by the Reagan Administration, which has added more to the national debt than all previous administrations combined, back to the presidency of George Washington.

How much could you buy for $10 trillion? The answer is: everything. You could buy everything in the United States, except the land. Everything. All the houses, airplanes, factories, skyscrapers, highways, railroads, stores, homes, food, clothing, medicine, furniture, toys, games, baby's diapers. . . . Everything in the United States but the land could be bought for what we have spent on the Cold War. A business that spent its capital so recklessly and with so little effect would have been bankrupt long ago. Executives who could not recognize so clear a failure of corporate policy would long before now have been dismissed by the stockholders.

What else could the United States have done with that money (not all of it, because prudent defense is, of course, necessary, but with some fraction of it; a third or a quarter, something like that)? We could have made major progress toward eliminating hunger, homelessness, infectious disease, illiteracy, ignorance, poverty, not just in the United States, but worldwide. We could have helped make the planet agriculturally self-sufficient and removed many of the causes of violence and war, and this could have been done with enormous benefit to the American economy. Think what prodigies of human inventiveness in art, architecture, medicine, science, and technology could have been supported for decades with the tiniest fraction of that money, and how they could have enriched our lives.

We have made a fool's bargain. We have been locked in a deadly embrace with the Soviet Union, each side always propelled by the abundant malefactions of the other; almost always looking to the short term—to the next congressional or presidential election, to the next Party Congress—and almost never seeing the big picture.

Dwight Eisenhower, who was closely associated with this Gettysburg community, said "The problem in defense spending is to figure out how far you should go without destroying from within what you are trying to defend from without." I say we have gone too far.

How do we get out of this mess? A Comprehensive Test Ban Treaty would stop all future nuclear weapons tests; they are the chief technological driver that propels, on both sides, the nuclear arms race. We need to abandon the ruinously expensive notion of Star Wars, which cannot protect the civilian population from nuclear war and subtracts from, not adds to, the national security of the United States. If we want to enhance deterrence, there are far better ways to do it. We need to make safe, massive, bilateral, intrusively inspected reductions in the strategic and tactical nuclear arsenals of the United States, the Soviet Union, and all other nations. (The INF Treaty represents a tiny step, but in the right direction.) That's what we should be doing.

Because nuclear weapons are comparatively cheap, the big ticket item has always been, and remains, conventional military forces. An extraordinary opportunity is now before us. Something no one had anticipated, something approaching a miracle has happened in the Soviet Union. There is somebody in charge there, somebody not just more reasonable than any Soviet leader in recent memory, somebody not just smart, but somebody with a long-term vision, with concern for precisely the same problems in his nation that we should be concerned for in ours. There is a clear commonality of purpose. Mr. Gorbachev has proposed massive conventional force reductions in Europe; he's willing, he says, to do it asymmetrically, in which the Soviets reduce their forces more than the Americans do. I say such conventional force reduction is in the interest of peace, and in the interest of a sane and healthy American economy. We ought to meet him halfway.

The world today spends $1 trillion a year on military preparations, most of it on conventional arms. The United States and the Soviet Union are the leading arms merchants. Much of that money is spent only because the nations of the world are unable to take the unbearable step of reconciliation with their adversaries. That trillion dollars a year takes food from the mouths of poor people. It cripples potentially effective economies. It is a scandalous waste, and we should not countenance it.

It is time to learn from those who fell here. And it is time to act.

In part the American Civil War was about freedom; about extending the benefits of the American Revolution to all Americans, to make valid for everyone that tragically unfulfilled promise of "liberty and justice for all." I'm concerned about a lack of historical pattern recognition. Today the fighters for freedom do not wear three-cornered hats and play the fife and drum. They come in other costumes. They make speak other languages. They may adhere to other religions. The color of their skin may be different. But the creed of liberty means nothing if it is only our own liberty that excites us. People elsewhere are crying, "No taxation without representation," and in Southern Africa, or the West Bank of the Jordan River, or Eastern Europe, or Central America they are shouting in increasing numbers, "Give me liberty or give me death." Why are we unable to hear most of them? We Americans have powerful nonviolent means of persuasion available to us. Why are we not using these means?

The Civil War was mainly about union; union in the face of differences. A million years ago, there were no nations on the planet. There were no tribes. The humans who were here were divided into small family groups of a few dozen people each. They wandered. That was the horizon of our identification, an itinerant family group. Since then, the horizons have expanded. From a handful of hunter-gatherers, to a tribe, to a horde, to a small city-state, to a nation, and today to immense nation-states. The average person on the Earth today owes his or her primary allegiance to a group of something like 100 million people. It seems very clear that if we do not destroy ourselves first, the unit of primary identification of most human beings will before long be the planet Earth and the human species. To my mind, this raises the key question: whether the fundamental unit of identification will expand to embrace the planet and the species, or whether we will destroy ourselves first. I'm afraid it's going to be very close.

The identification horizons were broadened in this place 125 years ago, and at great cost to North and South, to blacks and whites. But we recognize that expansion of identification horizons as just. Today there is an urgent, practical necessity to work together on arms control, on the world economy, on the global environment. It is clear that the nations of the world now can only rise and fall together. It is not a question of one nation winning at the expense of another. We must all help one another or all perish together.

On occasions like this it is customary to quote homilies; phrases by great men and women that we've all heard before. We hear, but we tend not to focus. Let me mention one, a phrase that was uttered not far from this spot by Abraham Lincoln: "With malice toward none, with charity for all . . . " *Think* of what that means. This is what is expected of us, not merely because our ethics command it, or because our religions preach it, but because it is necessary for human survival.

Here's another: "A house divided against itself cannot stand." Let me vary it a little: A species divided against itself cannot stand. A planet divided against itself cannot stand. And [to be] inscribed on this Eternal Light Peace Memorial, which is about to be rekindled and rededicated, is a stirring phrase: "A World United in the Search for Peace."

The real triumph of Gettysburg was not, I think, in 1863 but in 1913, when the surviving veterans, the remnants of the adversary forces, the Blue and the Gray, met in celebration and solemn memorial. It had been the war that set brother against brother, and when the time came to remember, on the fiftieth anniversary of the battle, the survivors fell, sobbing, into one another's arms. They could not help themselves.

It is time now for us to emulate them, NATO and the Warsaw Pact, Israelis and Palestinians, whites and blacks, Americans and Iranians, the developed and the underdeveloped worlds.

We need more than anniversary sentimentalism and holiday piety and patriotism. Where necessary, we must confront and challenge the conventional wisdom. It is time to learn from those who fell here. Our challenge is to reconcile, not *after* the carnage and the mass murder, but *instead* of the carnage and the mass murder.

It is time to act.

DETERMINING OUR PRIORITIES AND COMMITMENTS IN EDUCATION

WHOSE CHILDREN ARE THESE?[1]

JEFFREY R. HOLLAND[2]

Publication in the early 1980s of scholarly studies deploring the condition of American education prompted a continuing debate. Sparked by a commission's report that there is a "rising tide of mediocrity" in our schools and in the academic performance of students, the public became alarmed and the mass media's attention turned the issue into a controversy. Since then, the quality of American education had been widely discussed in speeches, articles, studies, and conferences. In the ensuing debate, student scores on various academic achievement tests were stressed, with examination results being used to compare today's school children to those of ten or 20 years ago, and American students to students of other countries. Questions regarding teacher qualifications and pay, discipline in the home and in the schools, funding for education, and racial and ethnic discrimination have become critical issues in the heated debate over the state of American education.

Asked to address the 1988 Conference of the Association for Childhood Education International (ACEI) in Salt Lake City on April 23, 1988, Jeffrey R. Holland emphasized a different approach: the personal relationship of the teacher to the student. The ACEI is an organization of 13,000 members, including teachers, parents, and others "interested in promoting good educational practices for children from infancy through early adolescence." It seeks to promote the rights, education, and well-being of children in the community as well as at home and school; to raise the standards of preparation for teachers and others involved in the care and development of children; and to inform the public about children's needs.

More than 530 persons, including educators, day care workers, and ACEI members, and representatives of 40 states and five foreign countries—including a delegation of 30 from Taiwan—attended the three-day conference. Dr. Holland, the president of Brigham Young University, was the keynote speaker at the second general session of the conference, whose theme was "The Child and the Family." He has degrees in English, religious education, philosophy, and American studies from Brigham Young and Yale universities. Approximately 500 conference members heard Holland's keynote address, delivered at 10:30 A.M.

[1]Delivered as the keynote address to the 1988 Conference of the Association for Childhood Education International at 10:30 A.M., April 23, 1988, in the Grand Ballroom of the Marriott Hotel in Salt Lake City, Utah.

[2]For biographical note, see Appendix.

in the Grand Ballroom of the Marriott Hotel in Salt Lake City.

Following the conference, in the organization's newsletter, the deputy executive director of the ACEI reported favorably on the attendance, sense of revitalization and new enthusiasm, and effectiveness of the keynote speeches. (Jerry Odland, *ACEI Exchange*, July 1988, v. 56, no. 6, p. 2) President Holland's address was reprinted in *Vital Speeches of the Day*.

Jeffrey R. Holland's speech: Urie Bronfenbrenner once noted that every child, every boy and girl, deserves at least one adult who is absolutely crazy about them. He has also described the heart of family life as an irrational commitment of family members to each other. But there is much in a child's world—our world—which wars against such affection.

Bronfenbrenner noted in a recent speech in Washington, D.C., that "the [apocalyptic] horsemen of modern times are poverty, chaos, isolation and abandonment of our responsibility to love our neighbors."

I am going to assume today that professionals who work with children have, from their own experience, discovered that poverty is ever with us and that chaos, when it comes, is like riding a tornado *without* the magic solution given Dorothy and Toto in *The Wizard of Oz*. My guess is you have already discovered that your professional work cannot relieve all of the family poverty *or* the chaos which can swirl just outside the boundaries of your classroom and then all too often sweep right on through the middle of it. However, I am going to assume that Bronfenbrenner's latter two horsemen, "isolation and abandonment of our responsibility to love our neighbors," can be addressed and can be alleviated, in part, by how you operate with children. You can do something to overcome a child's sense of isolation or lack of love, and you can do it in a way that the effects last beyond your own immediate limits of time and space, beyond the child's direct experience with you.

In making this claim regarding your potential influence with children I must admit that I have not done an exhaustive review of your professional literature. But I have an instinctive hunch, some personal experience, and a few case studies which suggest that my view of your indelible influence is right.

Let me give you two quotes from children who have known trouble. James Michener is quoted as having said:

> I was born to a woman I never knew, and raised by another who took in orphans. I do not know my background, my lineage, my biological or cultural heritage. But when I meet someone new, I treat them with respect. For after all, they could be my people.

Second, a teenage girl who confided to her teacher:

> Mrs. Wilson, my older brothers and sisters have hit the streets. I don't know where they sleep at night and I don't know what they might be "getting into." My mama's had a lot of different boyfriends, but lately she's been sick and they don't come around any more. My brothers and sisters say, "Why don't you leave, why don't you get out of there." Mrs. Wilson, I don't want the kind of life for myself that my mama has had, but I don't want to move out. I feel she needs me. How can I help her?"

I have begun with these two unusual, but not unlikely, cases, because I wish to have my remarks today apply broadly—broadly to all early childhood educators, and broadly to all children from all types of families. I am not interested in distinguishing between one kind of teacher and another, or one kind of family and another, or one kind of child and another. Your responsibility in those early childhood years is basically the same. Neither you nor I have the right to disparage our own effectiveness regardless of how difficult and frustrating some days are. Nor worse yet do we have the right to disqualify some children because of the backgrounds from which they come.

So I will be direct in sketching professional action which I feel will benefit the children you serve.

The danger, or presumption, in doing this is that I do not speak from the ranks of your profession. You may wish to discount my observations because of that (you probably already have), but I, too, am a teacher and I am a parent. And, what I have to say about your professional role is of importance and interest to parents.

The first question, then, for those who would work with children is to ask themselves the Bronfenbrenner question: "How crazy am I about working with children?" Or, better yet, "How crazy am I about the child I am working with?" (All of this assumes you have already answered the question for yourself as to whether or not you are just simply crazy.) In asking this question, I am assuming the principle that one cannot give what one does not have, any more than you can come back from where you have not been. Children do not know what training you have. They have never seen a resume and would probably not show any interest in one if they did. But they are interested in you. What they see of you in the classroom is what they get. So what *do* you have which qualifies you for work with children *in their eyes*? It is not your professional training. That comes next. What you have is what has made your professional study worthwhile. It is what has made you willing to meet challenges and to stay in the profession, in spite of any host of difficulties you may have encountered. It is, of course, love. Bruno Bettelheim may have been right when he used "Love is not enough," as the title for his book on what children need, but whatever the other factors are, first place in those qualities essential for child development still belongs to love, especially love of the individual child. It is a prerequisite, a must, a given, for anyone who would teach those in their early childhood. It is the *sine qua non* of your profession. It is the "absolutely indispensable, essential thing." It is the foundation for every other quality you must have.

This need is exemplified by how one pre-schooler responded to his teacher on his first day at our BYU early childhood education laboratory. He was more than hesitant. The teacher extended a hand. The boy retreated. She asked a question. He shook his head. She did not move forward. The boy retreated until his back was to the classroom wall. She knelt. She asked him more questions. More head-shaking followed. Then she picked up a book, showed a picture and asked a question. No head-shaking. She asked another question. Now a nod. She explained something and the boy took a slow step forward. No questions now, but explanations. The teacher was pointing to the blocks, to the individual coat racks and to the outdoor playground. Two more steps forward. Another nod of the head. The teacher extended a hand. Once he took her hand, the teacher paused to explain they were going to walk over to the clay table. With the goal in sight, he led the way, but gripped the hand of a teacher, newly trusted.

What made such a transformation possible in such a brief exchange? What invited this boy to give up his hesitation, his fear? I know that the formal answer could be a technical one. I know that those trained in observation could note that the teacher followed correct procedures. That is, she knelt down at eye level. She did not move forward, which could have been seen a silent sign of pressure on a child who already had found, quickly enough, his back against the wall. I recognize also that the teacher's use of questions and illustrations may have been derived from her rehearsals of such things in her practicum the previous semester.

But ultimately, it was her love and interest in that child which spoke to the child. Whatever guileless children may not see about adults in this sophisticated world, one thing they do seem to see is when love is feigned, when interest is artificial. Especially in times of their own fear would they be sensitive to the difference between someone acting out a role of kindness and love, as opposed to someone truly giving kindness, truly offering love. That young boy didn't want to know *anything* about building blocks, and coat racks and clay tables *until* he knew what he had to know about *her*—this woman, this stranger, this teacher. "Does she love me?" He was asking—even if he didn't know he was asking. "Does she love me? Let's get that settled and then we can talk about clay tables." So it is the quality of love, or your spirit of compassion, or your interest in the well-being of children *which you bring* to your training, to your classrooms and daily tasks, which most qualifies you for the work you have undertaken.

We have all heard that people do better on the job or in a profession when they love what they do. Surely that must be true in early childhood education. But it cannot be just a love of organization, or a love of administration, or a love of teaching per se. It must be founded above all on a love for the children themselves.

Of course, some children may not respond easily or immediately. Some children can be a little harder to love than others, at least at first. I am not asking that you and I be supermen or superwomen, that we somehow insist that we can succeed with anyone and everyone all the time and everywhere. But I am asking that we be free of the prejudice we sometimes carry with us, and which, frankly, often seems justifiable because of our experience. It is in this regard I would recall the example of Michener's youth. In the absence of a "real" family, Michener adopted as his family the family of mankind. Someone showed him how to love, perhaps a teacher helped do that. His books, in fact, reflect a remarkable love affair with peoples and cultures around the world. His stories almost always follow a family across generations. He seems not to discriminate because of his past experience without a family; he has retained this love of humanity of which I speak. Someone helped him do that. It may have been someone just like you.

In your world, what if, for example, you have found that children from certain backgrounds are more difficult to reach? You may begin to make the mistake of deciding in advance which children you will be successful with and which ones it will be fruitless to encourage. Whatever our experiences with children, we cannot afford to make such decisions in advance. We will not be naive about what the outcomes of our efforts might be, yet we will allow our best efforts in behalf of children to be given without reservation, no matter what our past experiences might hint.

I have set the stage for my first point: Success as an early childhood educator depends more on what you are than on what the children are. The love you have for children may not be enough, but if you do *not* have it, not much else, including your training, will be worth much.

My second point is a broader version of the first, and it is illustrated in the experience of a teacher who faced what she thought was "burn-out." She was no stranger to the demands of professional life. The hallmark of her service was her nurturing attitude toward all children, especially those who would be seen by most as disadvantaged. She had begun to despair over some of the children who seemed so lost, so limited, and in some cases, so neglected at home. What the textbooks said about how to reach such children, about how to encourage them, began to seem hollow to her. She bounced around so much in her feelings toward them that she began to wonder if she were suffering from some form of chemical depression. Whatever the cause, she vacillated between feeling that there was something wrong with her, or there was something wrong with "this current crop of pre-schoolers. They just don't respond like they used to." Then her mother died.

To go to the funeral, this woman broke away from her duties at the pre-school for a week. After the funeral she attended to some of her mother's affairs and then, deliberately, traveled home by train in order to have time to think. She had been very close emotionally to her mother, in spite of the separation geographically, and now she wanted to reflect on the meaning of being without her.

The frustrations in her professional life seemed an added burden. The idea of going back to those "children" brought, in her words, "an intensely disheartening feeling." The closer the train got to home, the less she understood her feelings.

After a weekend of shopping aimlessly, gardening without energy and sitting in front of television programs she did not remember, the day of return to action dawned. She felt as if she were preparing for battle instead of for pre-school, as if she were a soldier rather than an educator.

The first day back was all that she had expected (or should we say, dreaded). Her impatience was followed by resentment which became an expression of despair. Yet, by the end of the day, she felt she had done a good job of hiding all these feelings. She greeted and smiled at children and teachers alike, was efficient as ever at the snack break, told the stories she knew well, and yet inside she felt miserable. Moreover, the children seemed more distant or unresponsive than in previous weeks.

The last straw that day actually turned out to be the beginning of a transformation in her feelings. She had come around the corner to discover Rachel plucking the last chrysanthemum from the pot in the hall. Rachel's five-year-old hand could barely grasp a fresh, and by now quite complete, bouquet. (Rachel, by the way, was the child who seemed most distant, most inattentive, and most disruptive of the school activities, especially that day.) In a voice trembling and stern, this teacher demanded, "What *are* you doing?"

The girl's reply was, "Mrs. Terrell, you used to be like a mother; would these flowers help you to be like a mother again?" (Mrs. Terrell felt she had been slapped in the face—hard. *You used to be like a mother*. What did that child mean?) But Rachel went on: "I know you are fussed in your mind. Wouldn't you like some flowers?"

Mrs. Terrel thought, "Fussed in my mind." You mean it shows? To a five-year old? She spoke:

"Rachel, what is a mother like?"
"A mother is like you used to be. A mother likes being with children."
"But Rachel, I like being with children. I've just . . . well, I've been . . . well, Rachel, my mother . . . passed away, and . . . "
"You mean she died?"
"Yes, Rachel, that's what I mean."
"Did she live until she died?"

Mrs. Terrell thought, what kind of question is that? "Well, honey, of course. All people live until they die; they . . . "

"Oh, no they don't, Mrs. Terrell. Some people seem to die while they are still walking around. They stop being what they used to be. Mrs. Terrell, don't die just because your mother did. Be alive while you are alive."

Did this child understand what she was saying? Could she be that profound? Or was she just delivering typical five-year-old nonsense—the stuff children talk about when they still haven't put everything together—as the textbooks would say, "when a child's efforts at assimilation and accommodation have not yet produced logical or mature ways of understanding." Rachel may have said something she did not understand, but it was Mrs. Terrell who seemed to be dying "just because her mother did."

That night Mrs. Terrell put it all together. Reading in her journal she reviewed thoughts written twenty years earlier, after her first experience as a pre-school teacher out on her own. What were her words at the end of that first day? Boldly written in her journal—in fact, the only block-printed letters on a page of cursive comments—were the words, "I've never felt more alive."

Now to the moment of truth. What had changed within her? Was it that children, who once had been a source of life for her, were now a burden? What had happened that would prompt a five-year-old girl to ask her if she could "be like a mother again," and why would the phrase "be alive while you are alive" not leave her mind?

The answer took several more weeks to understand, but once Mrs. Terrell saw it, she became again what she used to be. Rachel wasn't around to see it, for the school term was over. And, although Mrs. Terrell had never heard of Urie Bronfenbrenner's modern apocalyptic horsemen of "isolation and abandonment of the responsibility to love our neighbors," she discovered that her own felt isolation, her own despair in the midst of life, was rooted, not in what children had become (they had not changed), but in what she had become. She had become one who refused to love the children. She had become one of the horsemen by her own choice. She was withholding what she heretofore had given freely. She stopped feeling sorry for herself; she decided that life was not a burden, life looked again like it always had. She decided not to die while still walking around. She would be as alive as she knew how to be, and she would be "like a mother again."

The point of Mrs. Terrell's experience is this. However good we are with children, our abilities, talents, commitments and love originate from within and are not determined by what is without.

And, our refusal to be true to the best in us may be what tarnishes our view of the Rachels all around us. Even our professional training benefits us only when we live by our beliefs and commitments. If those beliefs include a love of children, and a desire to promote their well-being, then all our professional experience will work for our good. Challenges can be met; we can be alive until the end of our lives.

Your best professional motivation, of course, the one which is life-giving to both you and to children, is an expression of your commitment to act in the children's best interests. While you cannot dictate the quality of life in the homes of the children you serve, you can determine the quality of their early childhood education experience. That experience is best when it approximates, in structure and quality, what parents at their best give their children. You act in children's best interest when you do what the best parents would do.

What you do in your classrooms will never replace parents, but what you provide can be supportive of parents who, overall, are wanting to do the right things. And, on those occasions when children come to you from families who do not seem to be acting in behalf of their children, you can be supportive of what those parents *could* be. The atmosphere you provide is what children from both backgrounds need. Both groups of children can benefit from what you offer, and your responsibility is to offer that which is mutually beneficial.

Your task is to nurture and invite and love and care so that at least two of Bronfenbrenner's ugly riders are forced to dismount in your presence. How realistic is such a task? Are you being asked to give more than you can? Is such a task really more tied to the land of Oz than to reality? I have suggested that the answer to that question depends less on who the children are than on who you are. And, who you are depends less on your professional training than on your professional beliefs.

What stands *do* you take regarding isolation and the responsibility to love your neighbors? If, for example, some parents simply are not the neighborly type, what are you to do? If you discover some parents are the antithesis of neighborliness, that is, they physically abuse their children, what are you to do? An act of love would be to notify authorities. And most states, including Utah, have laws which require the notification of authorities when evidence of abuse is discovered.

But what about children who seem neglected or emotionally battered? You want your pre-school to be more than a haven for a few hours for children who go home to horror. You wish to invite parents to see, to change, to be true to the best in them, just as you are giving your best. One of your goals may well be to make bad parents good and good parents better. You want their involvement. You cannot afford to be content to do what you do *in spite* of parents. Your responsibility is to reach out to them, even when they refuse to respond. Such parents may, themselves, be companions of Bronfenbrenner's riders of isolation and refusal to love. So you remember you are committed to act in the children's best interests and you do whatever you can.

The vast majority of parents of pre-schoolers are interested in learning more, in giving their best. That includes learning from you what you know about child development, about stages of growth, about the importance of nurturance and sociality. It includes showing parents the difference between putting pressure on children and inviting them to discover and learn; the difference between affirming a child's worth and making constant negative comparisons. It is legitimate also to demonstrate to parents the difference between work and play, as well as the need for parents to be involved with their children in both.

You are offering more than technical expertise or professional advice when you meet with parents. You are demonstrating that you are an ally in their task of rearing the next generation. In all that you do, and I am emphasizing this again deliberately, however good you work, and whatever the quality of life parents provide, there is no comparable substitute for families. Your best opportunity to act in children's best interest is to strengthen parents, rather than think you can or will replace them.

Now I realize that many of you have long experience in your field. You have seen the strengths and weaknesses of parents at close range. You may think I am overestimating parents' strengths or underestimating their weaknesses. But I would like to believe that *most* parents, including single parents, will respond to your invitation, example and interest in their child precisely because they are interested and involved over the child's lifetime. Your influence, however powerful, is but for a season. Parental involvement is for a lifetime. Take full advantage of your opportunity to introduce new, strengthening dimensions to the relationship of parents and children. When you do these things, you are, in Rachel's words, "like a mother" or, more importantly, helping a mother "be like a mother."

What I am saying about your profession and about your responsibility is even more needed when you discover those few families who have gone awry. When you realize that some families threaten, rather than promote, a child's well-being, you may be one of the first ones to have an opportunity to affect both parents and children. That is important because in most instances where families have been destructive of one another, the first attempt at help is to invite them to rebuild their relationships on a proper foundation. In cases of abuse of children by parents, it is hoped that they will change. Thus, your parent education programs can play a role in the necessary building. But even when such efforts fail, what do help agencies, communities and governments working in behalf of such children do? They do find them another family. An imperfect family is a better haven for mistreated children than any other agency or institution, however well-managed. So, in a sense, the extent to which you can help any family in a way is a way of helping every family. And overall, you help children most when you help link them to their parents over issues of development, learning and love.

Obviously, I feel that every child who participates in early childhood education should have more than just parents who are absolutely crazy about them. I am asking that early childhood educators be as irrational in their commitment to children as good parents are. I am asking early childhood educators to being an irrational, selfless love of children to their professional work. I am asking those who educate children in the primary grades to consider this: if we stripped away salary, status, facilities, recognition and all other material rewards of the profession (however great or small they may be), we would still be able to find an attitude of commitment, a love of children and an interest in their positive growth and development. Money, training, recognition—nothing can give to professionals the kind of commitment of which I speak. Actually, what I am asking of you I would ask of all educators; yet, young children seem so vulnerable and so full of possibilities that when we do not give them our best when they are young, the impact seems greater and more lasting than when they are confronted by other kinds of neglect later. You have the potential of being an early, intense influence for good on the children entrusted to your schools.

I know that you try to structure a learning environment, a supportive atmosphere, for children. But the most important feature of any environment is the human component. The quality of school environments begins not with colored carpets or beautiful bulletin boards, but with the quality of attitude in the teacher in you.

If educators and parents can share the common attitudes and commitments I have been describing, then perhaps I can propose my final point: Early childhood educators at their best, will love the children as parents do, will have personal commitments which are more fundamental than what training or salary can buy, *and* will seek to turn children and parents to each other in quality relationships.

An essential part of your profession is to be interested in promoting the family connection. By so doing, you set in place an influence which extends beyond the classroom, and beyond the here and now.

For all our social problems—and there are many—we have come a long way in our world. You do not work with children enslaved by the color of their skin or a pledge to a sweat shop. Neither are our children granted status automatically because of family connections. And yet the isolation and the lack of love that too many of our children feel are perhaps even more significant obstacles in their progress.

A past leader of the church that sponsors BYU had this to say about caring for children:

> If you will keep your [children] close to your heart, within the clasp of your arms; if you will make them . . . feel that you love them . . . , they will not commit any great sin. But it is when you turn them out of . . . your affection . . . that [they will be driven] from you. . . . If you wish your children . . . to love the truth and understand it . . . prove that you do love them by your every word and act to[ward] them.

In your efforts, remember, as Rachel taught Mrs. Terrell, that children will likely measure all that you do against all that you are. For if Rachel can invite an outstanding teacher to return to being her best, surely we can encourage each other never to be guilty of letting our commitment to the children die while we are still living among them.

IN SEARCH OF EDUCATIONAL ALCHEMISTS[1]

DONALD M. STEWART[2]

During the first week of February, 1989, more than 400 black students from Ivy League and Boston area colleges participated in a three-day conference at Harvard University titled, "Why We Can't Wait: The Future of Black America." The conference, conceived and organized by two Harvard students, David Adams and Michael Gaouette, and sponsored by the Harvard-Radcliffe Black Students Association, considered problems facing blacks and heard calls for a renewed sense of commitment toward the black community.

David Adams said he did not see enough commitment on the part of black students to working with blacks less fortunate than themselves. "Often black students feel they have arrived because they made it into a prestigious institution," he observed. "There is definitely a level and inactivity and lack of cohesiveness, and we wanted to address some of those problems." (*Chronicle of Higher Education*, February 15, 1989, A31)

In addition to a variety of workshops on topics ranging from black entrepreneurship to the paucity of black professors, students attending the conference heard speeches by Representative William H. Gray of Pennsylvania; former Gary, Indiana, Mayor Richard G. Hatcher; Harvard Law Professor Derrick A. Bell, Jr.; and Dr. Donald M. Stewart, President of the College Board. The conferees also tried to establish a coalition of black students to improve conditions at colleges and universities.

Donald M. Stewart's impressive qualifications as a speaker include his experience as a university administrator; his involvement in community leadership; his continuing research in the field of education; his service as president of Spelman College for ten years; and, perhaps most important, his position as head of the College Board. The College Board—an organization of public and private institutions, systems, and associations of higher education, including public and private secondary schools as well as school systems and associations serving secondary education—provides direction, coordination, services, and research in helping students make the transition from high school to college. The board sponsors a variety of guidance, admissions, and placement examinations, including the Scholastic Aptitude Test (SAT), which is widely used by college administrators to determine student achievement. Stewart addressed the conference at an hour-and-a-half session on the afternoon of February 4, 1989.

Donald M. Stewart's speech: Good afternoon, ladies and gentlemen. For so many reasons, it is a pleasure to be with you today. Harvard is a special place for me. In the late Middle Ages, I was a

[1]Delivered at the conference on "Why We Can't Wait: The Future of Black America" sponsored by the Harvard-Radcliffe Black Students Association at Harvard University, Cambridge, Massachusetts, on February 4, 1989.

[2]For biographical note, see Appendix.

graduate student here and at the Kennedy School. And as some of you know, my son, Jay, is a junior and is with us this afternoon. I have many friends and colleagues from Harvard including one of the Trustees of the College Board, Dean Whitla, and Professor Nate Huggins, who serves on our Minority Affairs Committee, whose insights have helped me formulate my ideas for this afternoon.

I see that we have an hour and a quarter for our encounter today and my goal is that most of that can be spent in a dialogue. Fortunately, there has been some hard research on audience response to speakers. The first ten minutes, there is pretty good attention and understanding, the second ten minutes their minds begin to wander. After twenty minutes, they start to have sexual fantasies. So, I hope that you are going to enjoy at least the last part of what I have to say.

The question you have asked me to address today, "Savior or Curse—Is the Public Education System Meeting the Needs of Black America?," is a most provocative one. And without wishing to be too academic, I should observe that it raises other questions by the very way it is posed. The first is, should we assume that American public education today, in a cause and effect fashion, can answer the "needs" of any group in the population? In my opinion, we should be careful in thinking about social problems and solutions from a simple perspective of cause and effect. Rather, as you will see, I would propose that it is more like the Cartesian calculus, in which a number of different variables interact and through interaction create an environment in which desirable or undesirable consequences can occur. If one wanted a social scientific model, it would be closer to that great German economist and sociologist Max Weber, whom I'm sure you have studied. In his book "The Protestant Ethic and the Spirit of Capitalism," he portrays a situation in which the independently evolved spiritual and economic forces of protestantism and capitalism developed an amazingly powerful resonance with each other in 18th century England and 19th century America, one which has transformed the world. For better as well as worse, no doubt, but transformed it nevertheless.

The second question I would like to ask is: can we accurately say, today, in 1989, that there is such a thing as "Black America," that is, a nation within a nation? As much as I want to believe in it and, in fact, do believe in it, I must recognize that we are undergoing a demographic earthquake in which American society is becoming "multi-cultural" and in which, like parts of the atom, each seemingly unitary sub-group is emerging as diverse and difficult to define accurately—notwithstanding our new nomenclature, African-American. Fourth generation children of Japanese-Americans, and newly arrived Laotian immigrants are both "Asian," and yet as different as can be. There is, similarly, a significant socio-economic and sociocultural difference between most of you in this room, and young people of your age still tragically trapped in inner-city ghettos, yet we are still one people and with all of our differences, we ought not forget it. However, conditions are often so different that, in terms of public education's ability to "meet the needs" of the entire spectrum, we would have to make some major distinctions, even if we are made to feel personally guilty in the process.

When we speak of "blacks *in* America," I can answer generally the question you have put to me rather easily. No, public education is not serving the needs of blacks in America. By the same token, a case can be made that for the vast majority of students, public education is not serving the needs of *anybody* in America.

As various recent studies have shown, for example, the United States lags well behind, even dangerously behind, other industrialized nations in mathematics learning. According to the report on the Second International Mathematics Study, entitled *The Underachieving Curriculum*: "Five areas of mathematics were tested at the eighth grade level. For three of the topics, the United States scored at or near the international average. On the remaining two topics, the U.S. scores were among the lowest one quarter of the countries." It is somewhat daunting, I should add, to look at the category of "measurement" and see the United States 18 out of a field of 20, only ahead of Swaziland and Nigeria.

As American students progress through high school, "The U.S. results were even more disappointing than for the eighth grade. The U.S. never achieved as well as the international average." While, to be sure, there are special problems related to the study of mathematics, there have been similar ones in the teaching of science. Just this week, a five nation study including Korea, Canada, the U.S., Spain and Ireland, showed that, here too, the U.S. is at the bottom.

In his essay "It Ain't No Consolation," from the anthology, *Educating Black Children: America's Challenge*, Harvard Professor and Dean Alvin Pouissant noted: "If it's any consolation, it appears that American education is short-changing just about everybody—rich and poor, urban and suburban, advantaged and disadvantaged, black and every other color." In this regard you may be aware that Albert Shanker, who for years has been the out-spoken, activist president of the American Federation of Teachers, believes that our schools are serving only 20 percent of the students at best. As he puts it, placing the blame on the system not the students, "We are turning out 80% lemons."

According to Shanker: "The percentage of 17-year-old youngsters still in school who can take six fractions and put them in places according to size is about 12%. There's a shocking result on the ability to figure out a bus schedule or a time-table. . . . The number of 17-year-old kids who can figure out which train to catch in Philadelphia in order to get to Washington at a particular time is 4.9%. Recent results in science and math indicate that about 5% of the kids leaving high schools can really begin college science or mathematics."

The essential problems in public education today are not just those resulting from years of discrimination by race, although we all know this is the legacy we must bear as black people. But the reality is that blacks are behind a student population that is, itself, far back of where it should be. Overall, we have a dysfunctional system that is (a) swamped by other social problems; (b) oriented toward creating a society for the 19th rather than the 21st century; (c) trapped in its own bureaucratic structure; and (d) given the other social afflictions, unable by itself, no matter how configured, to answer the "needs" of any group in society. As Mary Futrell, President of the National Education Association (NEA), commented: "We've so overregulated the schools, they're almost teacher-proof."

A group of concerned business men, the Committee for Economic Development, has decided that, by the time youngsters get to kindergarten, it is already *too late* effectively to address the problems that will keep them from doing well in school, not to mention going on to higher education. As a result, business people are directing a tremendous amount of focus and energy on developing resources to help young people from pre-natal to three years old. Tragically, a black baby born in Washington D.C.

has less of a chance of living through its first year of life than a child born in Jamaica. We are also at the bottom infant mortality rates.

We must realize, therefore, that the public school systems cannot cope with problems unremedied from the first six years of life. If a child is born with low birth weight and therefore brain weight, as is too often the case when children have children, that child can never make it up. At this point in time, just fixing the schools won't serve the needs of blacks in America which begin long before children go to school.

However, to answer your question in another way, public education is, in and of itself, neither savior nor curse. It is only one piece in the puzzle.

Is it an important piece? Unquestionably, and in our society, where minorities are disproportionately among the poor, and the poor are disproportionately dependent on public education, it is a very important piece.

A basic problem with public education in the United States is that it has changed little since it was designed to turn out a labor force ready to accept the discipline of the factory with strong backs and minimal competence in basic skills. But, even if a young person "dropped out," until fairly recently there were plenty of jobs. The crisis which has brought into focus this fatal flaw in public education is that most new jobs require education through and beyond high school. The 27 million people in this country who are functionally illiterate, the 700,000 who are dropping out each year, and the 700,000 more who drift through the system and graduate with functional illiteracy, face a future in which they will be, to use the sociologists' term, functionally disinherited by America. In a tremendously competitive international economy, in which America's fast-fading edge of high technology is our one competitive hope, higher order thinking skills, verbal and computer literacy, and math literacy with some acquaintance with the calculus, is what the work force is going to need as we struggle to stay even with the Japanese and Europeans, and as you personally change careers five or six times in the course of your professional lives. As Donna Shalala, president of the University of Wisconsin, likes to put it, "the purpose of the liberal arts is to prepare you for your third job, not just your first."

Once again, in this kind of demanding new environment, those groups of people with the least resources are going to be most severely hurt. According to the report of the Commission of Minority Participation in American life, in 1986, 31% of blacks and 27% of Hispanics had incomes below the poverty level—nearly three times the rate for whites. Median black family income was only 57% of that of whites, $17,604 as opposed to $30,809. If I had to say, globally speaking, what is the most serious problem facing humanity, apart from the vulnerability of the geophysical environment (if you don't have a field, no games can be played) it is the tension created by a two-tier society: groups of people with education and resources confronted by groups without education and without resources. This is as true in London as it is in Tel Aviv or Boston or Buenos Aires or Jakarta or Los Angeles. Interestingly, however, as this room and this meeting attest to, while race plays an important part in America, what we are really witnessing in the United States and the rest of the world is the emergence of an endemic, universal problem of economic class, an "underclass," if you will, to use the phrase of Professor William Julius Wilson: those who have at least the basic educational and financial resources needed versus those who don't. My friend and longtime mentor, Marian Wright Edelman (who parenthetically helped introduce me to the woman who became my wife and Jay's mom and whose son, Josh, is a student here), President of the Children's Defense Fund, tells us that a growing number of young families of all races and backgrounds are losing any possibility of achieving the American dream.

A significant part of the problem is due to teenage pregnancy, as I mentioned earlier, children having children. Marian has told us: "Our children need help in preventing too early sexual activity. Pregnancy and parenthood. Each year thousands of children get pregnant, two-thirds of whom are not black, not poor, and not in inner cities, and a half-million give birth, a population equivalent to the city of Seattle. Why should you care?" she asks. "Because teen pregnancy is the largest single reason why girls drop out of school, and it also contributes to boys dropping out. One of two children in a female-headed household is poor, but if that household is headed by a mother under twenty-five, three out of four of these children are poor." Youths from poor families—and again, teen pregnancy is both a consequence of and cause of poverty—youths from poor families are four times more likely as non-poor youths to drop out of school and to have poor academic skills. Hopefully, these families are going to be among the first beneficiaries of our "gentler and kinder" nation. We'll wait and see.

I note with pride and pleasure that today the doors of education are open. We have come a long way since the 1950s and early '60s and the great struggle lead by Martin Luther King, Jr. In his extraordinary "Letter from Birmingham Jail" he says: "One day the South will know that when these disinherited children of God sat down at lunch counters, they were in reality standing up for the best in the American dream and the most sacred values in our Judeo-Christian heritage, and thus carrying our whole nation back to great wells of democracy which were dug deep by the founding fathers in the formulation of the Constitution and the Declaration of Independence."

I believe the South and the nation now know that. Yet there is much more to do, and the voices of reaction are still with us. Far too many students are either not entering high school or are entering unprepared. Many that do enter find that educational opportunity received does not guarantee educational success. Too many of our minority youth are still being short-changed at lower levels of public education. According to a survey conducted by the National Assessment of Educational Progress, "although both black and Hispanic students demonstrated improvements in mathematics proficiency between 1978 and 1986 . . . black 17 years olds were only marginally more proficient than non-Hispanic white 13 year olds." As reported by the Educational Testing Service's publication *Focus*: "Recent report cards on writing have produced similar results. Even by age nine, the average reading proficiency and writing proficiency of Black and Hispanic nine year olds is considerable lower than that of comparable white students."

What we are also realizing, as research in this report affirms, is that middle school years are crucial "because it is here that students begin to be directed toward academic, general or vocational tracks. 'If we don't get kids on to academic tracks . . . the probability that they will get into college is remote.'" We know from our programs at the College Board that successful intervention "must be sustained through high school and must provide a mix of services, including counseling, developmental courses, role models and test preparation."

This same problem exists, in a different way, in higher education. As Michael T. Nettles has commented in his book *Toward*

Black Undergraduate Student Equality in American Higher Education, "Over the past two decades, Black Americans have gained access to the full range of America's colleges and universities. However, they continue to be underrepresented at most predominantly white universities, particularly at the most selective and most prestigious institutions." Conversely, they are over-represented in two-year and community colleges. The same, to be sure, holds true for Hispanic students and other minority groups. And not only is this unfair to them, it is proving to be a disaster for the nation. Again, as Martin Luther King, Jr. said in his Birmingham "Letter": "Injustice anywhere is a threat to justice everywhere." Educational deprivation is *real* injustice that none of us can tolerate.

By the year 2000, one third of the nation's school-aged children will be minorities, and two decades later, that percentage will have risen to 40%. In California, as of this year, there is no single majority group in the population, which means that California now has a "minority majority." Your generation reaches maturity in the full bloom of a demographic revolution in this country.

And in terms of black kids, there is good news. The decline in college attendance has bottomed out. Between 1977 and 1987 average SAT scores for black students increased by 21 points on the verbal portion and 20 points in math. In contrast, scores for white students rose just one point on the verbal and remained the same for math. Of course, there is still a gap that is far too wide, but this gap points to the unfinished agenda of achieving true social and economic equality here in this country. We are also witnessing extraordinary success of blacks and other minorities with the College Board's Advance Placement program. The growth in scores of three or higher by minority students [is] far outpacing the overall growth of this successful program itself. In 1988, the AP program grew 13 percent. And the number of minority students nationwide with a score of three or better has grown 37 percent.

Sadly, both in higher education and in society, the one group most at risk are black males, who suffer to a greater degree from debilitating health problems, a higher death rate, a lower life expectancy, and a greater incidence of serious disease. A recent report by the National Coalition of Advocates for Students has found that "Black public school students suffer more than twice the corporal punishment and school suspensions as their white counterparts." Needless to say, black male students suffer the most from this. In his book, *Black Men*, Lawrence Gary found that "male black students account for 29% of suspensions, 27% of expulsions, and 29% of corporal punishment."

That is outrageous. But it appears to be part of larger pattern in the schools.

In light of abilities to achieve which have been demonstrated over and over again, it is disheartening, to read a recent report from the American Council on Education, to discover that "a consistent and disquieting finding is the extent to which aspects of the American school experience can inhibit the satisfactory academic achievement of blacks (particularly black males), e.g., . . . teachers consistently give less attention, less praise and more criticism . . . their chances of attainment are thereby diminished. Moreover, teacher expectations of black male achievement are lower, and become self-fulfilling conditions in the consistent award of lower grades." Speaking for this black male, in the prophetic words of Langston Hughes: "They'll see how beautiful I am/And be ashamed—I, too, am America."

Clearly, public education is failing in its role of insuring equitable life chances for minorities. David Kearns, CEO of Xerox who is tremendously concerned about minority achievement, reported at our National Forum in Washington a few months ago that fewer than two-thirds of black 18 or 19 year-olds complete high school. For Hispanics, the figures are even worse—barely half hold high school diplomas. A dozen years ago, one out of every three black high school graduates went to college; today, it's down to one out of every four. In making this assertion about public education, we must remember two things. First of all, a school that is doing a bad job with youngsters on one end of the spectrum, is in all likelihood doing the same bad job at the other end of the spectrum. You rarely find schools that teach one group well and another poorly. Secondly, there is considerable variation in the quality of public education as one moves from cities to suburbs around the nation. A minority student in a public high school in Greenwich, Connecticut, for example, is going to have a much better education on the average than one in New York City. In some cases, there is not even a warm body, not to mention a well-trained teacher, standing in front of the class in New York.

By the same token, there is no lack of bureaucrats. John Chubb, a senior fellow at the Brookings Institution, writing in *The New York Times*, noted that "New York City has 6622 fulltime employees in its public school headquarters. That's one external administrator for every 150 students."

"By comparison," he continues, "the Roman Catholic Archdiocese of New York has only . . . 30 central administrators; no more than one for every 4000 students." And, can you guess which school system is performing more effectively for its students? Of course, the results of poor public education are reflected in the performance of those trying to enter the workforce. For example, in 1988, 23,000 people took an exam for entry-level jobs at New York telephone, which required simply an eighth grade level of reading. Fully 84% of the applicants failed.

The most tragic example of big city public schooling in America, however, is probably in Chicago. This is a system with 596 schools, serving 420,000 students of whom 60% are black, 24% Hispanic, 13% white, and 3% Asian. Close to 10% of these have limited proficiency in English. Almost 70% live below the poverty level. 45% drop out. 40% of the students are failing two courses a year. In one fourth grade class, every one of the 22 students had to attend summer school because the teacher was incapable of preparing them for fifth grade. Dismaying though it is, I would like to quote from a *Newsweek* article about some more of the specific problems.

"On any given day, 45,000 Chicago public school students—one in nine—are absent. But many are just following their teacher's lead. In May, some 1,250—5 percent of the total—called in sick each day. The Board of Education does not have enough substitutes, so as many as 11,160 students were teacherless."

As you might imagine, the results of this kind of situation are disastrous. According to *Newsweek*, "roughly half of Chicago's public school students drop out before graduation. When American College Test scores were averaged, half the city's high schools ranked in the lowest 1 percent nationally."

By the same token, cities like New York have extraordinary honors public high schools, such as Hunter College or Stuyvesant High Schools which are fully as competitive as Harvard—and full of minorities. Not surprisingly, the educational outcome is exceptional. Unfortunately, just the reverse can be said about schools with few resources serving young people from difficult educational and personal circumstances who lack family and other kinds of support. The educational output of these schools is abysmal. Therefore, as the title of my talk goes, we are "In search of educational alchemists," namely people and institutions who are able to take poor and educationally underserved youngsters of all backgrounds and successfully transform them and their lives through quality education.

One hopeful sign in 1989 is that the problems in public education have now become "front burner" problems, especially with the renaissance in concern for education among governors. Fortunately, political and business leaders have become more sensitive in their approach. As Mary Futrell wisely pointed out: "Don't come to us and say, 'This is the plan.' If you do, the education community will resist. But if you come and say 'We will work with you to help determine what the plan should be,' you will have 100% cooperation." And there are some very imaginative programs. Here in Massachusetts, for example, Governor Dukakis unveiled a teacher training program in which experienced school teachers will share in the responsibility of training the next generation of the state's teachers.

On a conceptual level educational leaders like Al Shanker and Mary Futrell are talking about the need for a new metaphor by which to understand the essence of schools and schooling. For too long, we have considered schools as factories in which the students are inert raw material on whom the workers, namely the teachers, "attach" educational elements. This has led to such nonsensical comment by teachers as, "I taught him, but he didn't learn." Instead of a "factory" model, we need a corporate, "outcomes" model, in which student abilities are the product. Students are viewed as the "employees," and teachers as the "managers" who must be given the freedom and flexibility to figure out the best way to make their "workers" productive.

Now, what I am about to say will come as no surprise to you who are still deeply involved in the process of learning, but one of the discoveries currently being made as to how to teach and motivate young people most "at risk" of dropping out, is simply to *pay attention to them*.

A few weeks ago, the ABC evening news reported on two programs in New York City which were having tremendous success in dealing with at-risk students. The first program is a small, caring high school for at-risk students from various parts of the city.

In addition to their academic classes, students participate in a regular encounter group to make up for the lack of family and community support, in which any subject of concern can be talked about. And some 90% of these students, who otherwise would have mostly dropped out, are completing their studies in a safe and happy environment, as opposed to the dangerous and divisive situation often found in large schools.

On the theoretical level, this is an appropriate point to observe that part of what has happened in our public schools systems is a function of the inherent problems with large bureaucracies. Max Weber, in his sociological studies, not to mention Franz Kafka in his logical nightmares, or Milan Kundera in his sexual tragi-comedies, have each analyzed the problems that such organizations have in maintaining their legitimacy in the eyes of those served by them. Some of you might feel this way about aspects of Harvard. Forgive me if I don't share all your views, but one day you will see how one's memories as alumni are alchemists, too.

The second project is creation of a high school *within* a community college, mixing college and high school faculty, so that high school students rub shoulders every day with slightly older students, just like themselves, who are now involved in postsecondary studies.

Well, you have been most patient with these comments. And no matter how much fun you may now be having, I also have in mind Mark Twain's remark that "To be talked to death is a horrible death."

By way of conclusion therefore, I would like to summarize these narrative thoughts in a conceptually more rigorous way.

In view of the enormous social and demographic changes of the last several decades, and those which await us, the system of public education is only one of the forces acting upon individuals. Unfortunately, those with the least resources are the most likely to receive the least assistance from the public system, whether in academics or guidance services.

For reasons of political and economic competition, the nation can no longer afford the loss of 1.4 million illiterate young people every year. In addition, there are the moral and democratic imperatives of providing every one with a high quality education. As social analyst and pollster Lou Harris observes:

The hard truth is that there have been few substantial changes in education in the U.S., but almost the entire world around us has changed radically. . . . We now have terrible and even radical challenges and changes to make to survive. In short, we have to become a nation that *thinks* for a living. The key for education [he concludes] lies in the *standards* that must be adopted and then strongly enforced.

It seems to me that there are at least half a dozen imperatives or standards which, generally speaking, need to be followed in order to assure that traditionally underserved groups receive the high quality education which they deserve and which the nation and not to mention the black community desperately needs them to have.

The first imperative is that we must change the metaphor by which we understand teaching and students. As suggested by Al Shanker, students should be looked on, not as "products," but as "workers." The "product" of schooling should be their ability effectively to learn and to master higher-order thinking skills. The teachers are not "workers," but "managers," who, as in any successful business, do well only insofar as their workers are inspired to work well.

The second standard we must maintain is that education must be empowering. In the process of learning, in the atmosphere of the school environment, kids must feel, in Jesse Jackson's colorful words, that "I want to be a tree shaker, not a jelly maker." Of course, one does have to be a little careful. As comedian Lily Tomlin noted, "I always wanted to be somebody. Now I realize I should have been a bit more specific."

The third standard is that we must have meaningful and rigorous measurement of knowledge and skill levels.

Access to real knowledge for all students is the fourth standard. In a publication entitled "Access to Knowledge: Removing School Barriers to Learning," which the College Board has published with the Educational Commission of the States, we make the following self-evident, but often disregarded, point: "children assigned to low-ability classes are taught different, less socially-valued knowledge and skills. . . . Regardless of ability or motivation, the academic mobility of these students is constrained . . . by contrast, teachers in high ability classes more often encourage critical thinking and independent questioning. They are more enthusiastic, better organized and make lessons clearer."

The next standard I would like to propose is that curricula in middle and high schools should prepare *all* students for the possibility of successful participation in higher education.

The sixth imperative is that we must reverse the plunge in the number of minorities who are going into teaching. Currently it stands at 12%. By the 1990s, it may drop to 5%, precisely at a time when the number of minority school children, not just in the inner cities but everywhere, is mushrooming. We cannot afford to have a system in which a multi-cultural student body is taught predominantly by representatives of a single ethnic group.

The final standard that I would like to propose today is that all students should have the opportunity to do honors and advanced-level work.

In some profound way, I believe that what we have been talking about is captured in a remark by Marian Wright Edelman: "the moral litmus test of a society is how it treats its children." Looking around this room, it is clear that part of our society, at least, would score very high on any such test.

Notwithstanding all the challenges we still face, and all the problems which the past has created and left for us to deal with, I believe that the nation is finally returning to its sense, and recognizing the deep need for conscientiously understanding, loving, and caring for all its children, how they grow, and how they learn. The poet Carl Sandburg observed: "Always the path of American destiny has been into the unknown. Always, there arose enough reserves of strength, balances of sanity, portions of wisdom to carry us to a fresh start with ever renewing vitality."

I salute you for the wisdom you show in seeking to discuss this subject in all candor and openness. My guess is that there are several educational alchemists of the future sitting in this room today full of strength, sanity, and that ever renewing vitality. And I want to thank you for the invitation to take part in your work.

EDUCATION IS WHAT IT IS ALL ABOUT[1]

CHARLES B. REED[2]

At a time when college sports are more popular than ever, academic institutions are confronted with scandalous revelations of unethical behavior, rules-breaking, and lawlessness on the part of student-athletes, coaches, administrators, and boosters. In addition to preferential treatment of athletes in the classroom, which included altered grade transcripts, false course credits, and forgery, there was the usual widespread assortment of recruitment violations, illicit payments to athletes, disregard for studies, the use of steroids, drug abuse, and the filing of assault and rape charges against numerous ballplayers. Moreover, in 1988 the crimes of mail fraud and racketeering were added to the list of abuses spawned by the pervasive "winning-is-the-only-thing" attitude in college sports.

In an editorial, *Insight* magazine observed:

> Each fresh revelation of contamination within the "jockocracy" of intercollegiate athletics poses the question with repetitive insistence: How deep is the rot? The answer is evident, at least to anyone capable of tying his own shoes. The rot is wide, deep, and nasty.
>
> To admit, however, that we know why so many "student athletes" fail to earn even a devalued college degree and often leave campuses in worse shape for the future than when they were recruited—to admit full knowledge of the reasons and yet avert our eyes as we do would be an intolerable hypocrisy for most of us. Thus, from college presidents genuflecting to the mystique of competitive sports to you and me in front of the television set, there is an unwillingness to acknowledge what a corrupt and corrupting stew we're helping to stir.
>
> We rationalize that there are benefits that overarch abuses in intercollegiate athletics: the opportunity for young men and women, particularly members of minority groups, to aspire to higher education by means of their athletic capacity and the economic usefulness of revenue-producing sports in underwriting athletic facilities for the general run of students. . . . [However], testimony in a Chicago trial of two sports agents in April 1989 undermines these cozy rationalizations. In dramatic testimony one of the attorneys indicated that the athletes' transcripts included *credit* courses in "billiards, karate, tennis, ancient athletics, recreational leisure, jogging, speed-reading, advanced bowling, and advanced slow-pitch softball—so much for the myth of higher learning in jockocracy." (Woody West, April 24, 1989, p. 64)

[1]Delivered at the 83rd annual convention of the National Collegiate Athletic Association at approximately 4:00 P.M., on January 9, 1989, in the Continental Ballroom of the San Francisco Hilton Hotel, San Francisco, California.

[2]For biographical note, see Appendix.

In an effort to remedy abuses prevalent in college sports, the National Collegiate Athletic Association Presidents' Commission prepared a report on the proper role of athletics in higher education. A highlight of the 83d annual convention of the NCAA was a day-long session on January 9, 1989, featuring a discussion of the initial findings in the research regarding student athletes.

In two morning sessions, panelists discussed the study methods and results and reviewed the findings from a national perspective. After an honors luncheon, with television newscaster Kathleen Sullivan as master of ceremonies, the Forum examined the study from the standpoint of implementation of the report's recommendations. Panelists at this third session included college and university athletic directors, chancellors, and presidents, and one former student-athlete—five men and two women. Charles B. Reed, Chancellor of the State University System of Florida, was one of the seven speakers addressing this session. The meeting was held in the Continental Ballroom of the San Francisco Hilton, the convention headquarters. Approximately 1200 persons heard Chancellor Reed's speech. His listeners included convention delegates, university presidents and administrators, athletic directors, and representatives for both men's and women's college sports programs. Because seven speakers had been scheduled in the two hours set aside for the discussion, the speakers' remarks were brief.

Charles B. Reed's speech: Good afternoon. To begin my comments, I want to borrow a line from Governor Mario Cuomo of New York. He recently told an audience in Washington that, back when he was considering running for president, late one night, the devil came to him and offered him a deal.

Governor Cuomo said, "He offered me the presidency in exchange for my soul. So I said: 'What's the catch?'"

I think we need to think about the report of American Institutes for Research in this light, and ask the question: If we are going to have big-time intercollegiate athletics in an environment of academic excellence, what's the catch?

That catch is, I think, not that we're trying to do two things that are totally incompatible, but that we've lost our sense of proportion and our sense of priority.

We often hear conversations within the NCAA that come to the conclusion that we "must not kill the golden goose," meaning television contracts. Well, I think the golden goose really isn't broadcast revenues, but American higher education itself.

Our sense of proportion should tell us that. Anyone who has trouble deciding whether education or athletics is more important should recognize that we could easily have higher education without athletics.

Ask yourself: What would we do differently if tomorrow there were no such thing as intercollegiate athletics? We'd still teach every course in the college catalogue. That wouldn't change one bit. We'd still conduct research at the same pace. We'd still perform public service.

What we wouldn't be doing in American higher education is bending or breaking the recruiting rules, stealing players and coaches from each other, struggling to keep our more rabid and fanatical boosters under control and trying to prevent the academic reputations of our institutions from being mocked or disgraced by our athletic programs.

Ask yourself another question: Is there another single reason why more university presidents have had to resign, or have been dismissed, than problems with athletics?

And finally, ask yourself this one: What's more important in the life of a student-athlete—winning, or graduating? I say, graduating is more important. And I think the real values of our universities are not merely what we say they are. Our real values are reflected not in words, but in the way we conduct ourselves. No institution is value-free. We either live up to high standards, or we don't.

Sometimes the recognition of our own imperfections prompts us to consider abandoning all pretense of amateurism and declaring the tradition of the scholar-athlete an unattainable myth. Some say we should openly pay our athletes, not require them to make progress toward a degree, and create a semi-professional feeder system for professional sports.

I disagree. I think the way to avoid hypocrisy is not to abandon our ideals, but to make a greater effort to live up to them. And so we return to the issue of setting a priority. I think that priority ought to be graduating, on time, and at the same rate, if not at a higher rate, than students as a whole. Notre Dame, Penn State, and Georgetown show us clearly that this is possible.

I know this can be done because I've seen it happen time after time. And frankly, I would not be here today as Chancellor of the State University System of Florida were it not for the athletic scholarship that made it possible for me to attend George Washington University, where I ultimately earned all three of my degrees.

I think we have to set graduation rates—not the score of the game or the won-loss record—as the priority, for three reasons.

First, it gives the student athlete a chance at life after college.

Second, it sends the right message to younger students.

Third, it preserves the values of our society and of our universities.

Let's look at these points one at a time.

The first point is the future of our student athletes. Our system today throws up the photos of, to name two athletes from my own system, Deion Sanders and Sammy Smith, off to the National Football League without degrees, to make millions of dollars.

Those two students will make enough money that, with some good advice, they'll be set for life even without degrees. But if they'd finished college, they'd be in a better position to evaluate the financial advice they'll get, and also have the basis for a second career after their knees give out. But they are two in a million.

Most of our student athletes never get a shot at professional sports. Most who do don't last long enough to have what could reasonably be called "a career" as a professional athlete. What about those people who, having been exploited, now compete in the job market with former students who earned their diplomas?

Ask yourself this question: Which applicant would you rather hire: someone whose academic focus was on remaining eligible for sports, or on graduating? Someone who barely passed a freshman algebra course, or someone who majored in computer science?

Second, we need to send a message to the younger students in the junior high schools and high schools of the nation that goes beyond the message of Proposition 48. We need to tell them that sports can be a meaningful part of life, but that hardly anybody makes a living in sports. Your odds of becoming a rock star or an astronaut are about the same as starting for the New York Knicks.

So we need to tell the next generation of student athletes that, if they are unprepared academically to do college work they can forget about playing college sports. In my experience, there are few better motivators for athletes than threatening to withhold participation in sports. Make it stick and you'll make it work.

Third, making academic success the true focus of intercollegiate athletics keeps us true to the purpose of our universities. Education is what it's all about, not touchdowns, skyhooks, or home runs.

So let me make the following modest proposal:

1. Abolish spring training for football. This report tells us that athletes spend less time on the books than they do on sports. Let's cut back on some of the athletic distractions.

2. Reduce eligibility from four years to three. Let our freshmen find out where the library is and experience a degree of academic success first.

3. Report annually our graduation rates by institution, by sport, and by gender. We've started doing this in Florida, and we're beginning to see the results. Until now, only the coaching staff has been held accountable, because we don't keep score in the academic area.

Let's start keeping score, and compete with Notre Dame and Penn State and Georgetown not just on the field, but on commencement day.

4. Finally, let's extend the score-keeping to junior high and high schools, by making it clear that we do not recruit and will not accept as athletes students whose grades and test scores predict academic failure.

I realize not everyone is going to agree with everything I say here today. That's fine. But I think one thing we can all agree on is this:

Education is what it's all about. And if we make graduating the priority of every student athlete, we'll be dealing honestly with our student-athletes, we'll set a positive example for younger students coming up, and we'll be true to the values that our institutions are supposed to embody.

Otherwise, when the devil offers us a bowl bid in exchange for our soul, we'll ask: "What's the catch?"

Thank you.

COMMENCEMENT REMARKS: LEARNING TO CARE AND SHARE

A SHARED REALITY[1]

BILL MOYERS[2]

In a commencement address in 1983, U.S. Senator Terry Sanford of North Carolina, a former state governor and university president, observed, "Communicating with college students is always somewhat of a challenge. It is not that I have too much difficulty understanding your changing expressions and attitudes. It is that I forget what you never saw." (*Representative American Speeches, 1983–1984*, p. 46)

Returning 32 years after being graduated to deliver the commencement address at his alma mater, the University of Texas at Austin, Bill Moyers had similar feelings. He wondered,

> . . . at commencement if a stranger from one generation can say much that is helpful to members of another standing on a different doorstep in time. Just as life is a particular life, so a generation lives in its own unique time, and you must make your own map into the unfamiliar country of the future.

Nevertheless, Moyers sought to bridge the generational gap in a thoughtful address that combined reminiscences of his Texas boyhood and his experiences as an undergraduate with reflections on aspects of Texas and American history and a sketch of challenges facing the graduates. Pleasant, congenial, and at times humorous, Moyers skillfully developed a serious theme.

If any of the 2200 graduating students or the 10,000 others in the audience were unfamiliar with who Bill Moyers is, in his introduction Dr. William Cunningham, President of the University of Texas, cited some of the speaker's many accomplishments. Calling him one of the nation's most distinguished broadcasters and writers, Cunningham noted that Moyers had won almost every major award in television, including ten Emmy awards, three Peabody awards, the Ralph Lowell medal for contributions in public television, and the Alfred I. DuPont–Columbia University award. He is also renowned as executive editor of the acclaimed public television series, *Bill Moyers' Journal*; as editor and chief correspondent for *CBS Reports*; and as senior news analyst for the *CBS Evening News*. Cunningham emphasized Moyers's media accomplishments, but many listeners remembered him from the Sixties as a special assistant, press secre-

[1]Delivered at the spring commencement exercises of the University of Texas on the south mall of the Austin campus at 7:30 P.M. on May 21, 1988.

[2]For biographical note, see Appendix.

tary, and speechwriter for President Lyndon B. Johnson and as deputy director of the Peace Corps.

Moyers delivered his address at the spring commencement of the University of Texas on May 21, 1988. The exercises were held on the south mall of the campus with the state capitol visible toward the south. The procession began at 7:30 P.M. following a carillon recital, a concert and processional by the university Longhorn Band, an invocation by a clergyman, and a welcome.

Bill Moyers's speech: I often wonder at commencement if a stranger from one generation can say much that is helpful to members of another standing on a different doorstep in time. Just as a life is a particular life, so a generation lives in its own unique time, and you must make your own map into the unfamiliar country of the future. Life after college is where you get your answers questioned, in your own conversation with the world.

However, I do have some very specific thoughts for one member of your class who is graduating tonight and who shall remain anonymous not because you can trust a journalist to protect his sources but because I actually do not know his name. I will refer to him as UT Socrates, because he is a philosopher of Texas Metaphysics. He wrote an essay two years ago for a class in which he talked about the meaning of life, and a mutual friend here sent me an unsigned copy in a plain brown envelope. I was immediately struck by this opening proposition: "It seems like no matter how you fry it, life adds up to the same old enchilada . . . transitory and always out of reach." UT Socrates went on to raise questions that just about everyone asks within the 30 years after he or she has left this university: "What are we here for and what does it matter? Why risk the disillusionment of truly experiencing your own limitations and boundaries? Is there really a point since we're going to die anyway?" While the questions may be universal, UT Socrates offered a very personal prescription for the predicament of existence; he called it "Texas Metaphysics."

Now philosophy under Dr. Ginascol here some 30-odd years ago was not my long suit, but I think I dig "Texas Metaphysics," as defined by this inquiring native Socrates. It consists, in his words, of "an early rise, a nice long run, or a swim in Barton's. Then coffee, bran muffins, orange juice, and the morning paper, followed around noon by a ride to Lake Travis, plenty of cold beer, and an afternoon with friends skiing and soaking up the sun. And in the evening, a little Larry McMurtry or Dostoevsky, maybe the VCR, some home-cooked fettuccini Alfredo, and red wine." I've left out a few things, but in UT Socrates' words, "that's enough to get started with." He went on to ask: "Who gives a blankety-blank if we are waging war in Nicaragua? Or if there are hungry people right here in Austin, Texas? Sure, I want to save the world," he said, "who doesn't? But I'm not Martin Luther King or Jesus Christ. I wouldn't know where to start and I'm not sure I would want to. I'm scared to be heroic. What if I fail? What the hell would I do then? No, thanks," he said, "I'll stick to Texas Metaphysics."

You may be surprised, UT Socrates, whoever you are, but Texas Metaphysics is bottled in other states, too. You're not alone in longing to embrace life in its most commonplace texture. No less an erudite man than my friend Alistair Cooke has said that no generation should take the world crisis so seriously that it forgets what we may have been designed for in the first place: finding work that's interesting, meeting someone to love who loves you back, sitting under a tree, hitting a ball and bouncing a baby.

Those seem to be the essential ingredients of Texas Metaphysics and occasionally I myself have indulged in the applied philosophy of the field. But UT Socrates asked another question. He asked a question I couldn't have answered 30 years ago, and I'm not sure I can answer it now but I'm going to try. He asked, "Why does life always seem, even in the midst of Texas Metaphysics, just outside your grasp?" I'm going to come back to that.

First, I want to acknowledge to UT Socrates and to all of you that your generation faces circumstances today that Judith and I did not face when we left here in 1956. Frankly, I don't envy you the difference. America then was an exuberant place of seemingly inexhaustible possibilities. The economic boom that followed the second world war was lifting our boats to heights our parents never dreamed of. In my junior year here I went to work for Lyndon Johnson's television station at $100 a week. Not bad considering that tuition was $40 a semester, our apartment at 507-A East 18th was $40 a month, and a complete meal at Scholz Garten—Swiss steak, salad, potatoes, bread, pie and coffee—cost 65 cents. But the point is that with that first job as a junior at The University of Texas I was instantly making more than my father ever made. I was 20, and he was 50. Like millions of his generation he had been struck down by the Depression before he had gotten on his feet. Even when he retired in 1969 he was making no more than I had made in my first job here at the University. So, my generation was being carried by that buoyant economy to a standard of living our parents had worked hard all their adult lives without achieving. By 1959 the average white male—and white males were about all that economically counted or were counted in 1959—could look forward to a 49 percent increase in income over the next decade and to paying only 16 percent of his earnings for a mortgage.

It's a different story today, and I apologize on a solemn and sacred and festive occasion such as this for talking about money, but some of you may move to New York one day. You should know about another Texan who moved to New York. He'd been there for six months. As he was walking home he was stuck up by a mugger who said, "Give me your money or I'll blow your brains out." And the Texan replied, "Go ahead and fire away, buddy. You can live in New York without brains but you can't live without money."

Most of you are going to have to run fast just to stand still, and you'll find it hard to surpass your parents. The average 30-year-old today—male and female—is likely to be making less in real dollars than 10 years ago, and 40 percent of the income—40 percent, not 16 percent—will go for the mortgage.

Already, more and more people are finding a middle-class standard of living hard to achieve and hard to maintain. Those who manage it do so only at great personal sacrifice by sending more family members to work, working longer hours on multiple jobs, marrying later, having fewer children, delaying the purchase of a home, taking on more debts, and spending bigger chunks of income for today's needs instead of saving for the future. This is changing our social fabric, affecting the way children are raised, spouses relate, and communities operate. Where I live in New York, villages and towns that once relied on volunteer firemen can no longer count on young people to enlist; they have to work long hours and commute too far to perform what once was a civic duty.

You know the story well here in Texas, here on the front lines of what economists are calling America's quiet depression. In the decade of your majority we've experienced the worst recession since the 30s, the deterioration of our manufacturing base, a loss of America's economic supremacy, a burst of speculation in stocks and bonds unequalled since 1929, and the biggest stock market collapse in nearly six decades.

This erratic economic behavior has taken a toll: average hourly wages dropping since 1973, disposable household income—what you have after taxes—growing much more slowly, the economy expanding at a slower rate, the distribution of income becoming more unequal. More than one American in seven is poor today, compared to nine 10 years ago. Here in Texas more than one in six women live below the poverty line. A million or so Texas children are poor—one child in five. Meanwhile, the rich have carved out for themselves the largest share of the national wealth since 1947. "Trickle down" has become "soak it up."

Listen in some quarters and you will hear predictions of worse days ahead; that the United States, like empires of the past that lived beyond their means and took no thought of the morrow, has begun an irreversible slide. Because we have not been investing in modern industries, because we have been cutting back on our investment in education and universities like this, because we've not been rebuilding our infrastructure, it's said our problems are going to intensify.

Listen in yet other quarters where I travel and you will hear it said that even if the trend of economic stagnation reverses, even if wages and incomes get better, the slow growth and the greed have done too much damage, the polarization between rich and poor will increase, and the class divisions between us become more aggravated. Even if some of you do better individually, the society you live in runs the risk of being poorer and less just, less equal and less creative.

No, I do not envy you the budget deficit, the trade imbalance, the burden of debt, the decline of savings, the dangerous dependence on foreign capital, and the higher poverty rate. Some graduation present my generation is handing you! Your elders have been on a spree, reveling in "the celebration of individual cunning in the single-minded pursuit of wealth and status." Now, it's no longer morning in America but high noon, and you're expected to handle the reckoning.

Now for the bad news. To cope with this difficult future, we are being told that your generation must come to terms with living in a bitterly competitive world, that you must compete not only with each other, the very people sitting at this moment beside you in those chairs, but with other nations. There is some truth in that—considerable truth in that—but it isn't the whole truth. If we're to build a common future—your generation and mine—we cannot talk about the new economics of competition without talking about a new ethic of cooperation. This means recognizing our capacity to make common cause with others and the necessity of creating a political culture that nurtures and honors obligation and trust.

This is not a new idea, although it is one widely ignored of late. Gilbert McAllister taught it in his anthropology courses here 30-odd years ago. That's where I had my first de-programming. I went to see Dr. McAllister this afternoon. He's 85. We sat and talked for a long time. We talked again about the time he spent among the Apaches as a young graduate student before he came here to teach. I said, "Do you remember telling us all those years ago about what you had learned from the Apaches?" He thought a minute and said, "I'm not sure I can remember the exact words but I think I talked to you about reciprocity." "That's right," I said, "reciprocity." Then he got going. "You know, in the Apache tongue, the word grandfather is the same word for grandson—grandfather, grandson—it's all one word. The Apaches believed in the reciprocity of generations—in both linking and in locking one generation to another." Reciprocity. Mutual help. Reinforcing. Time and time again in this class, he'd look back over the sweep of time to tell us that human beings have advanced more in the past through having learned the value of cooperative caring behavior than through their ability to compete successfully.

Robert Cotner taught right over there in Garrison Hall but he used to hold forth on the same lessons of American history. I still am not sure of the answer to the question he asked in our final exam: "Did Lincoln make his times or did his times make Lincoln?" I think I answered, "Yes." But I haven't forgotten Dr. Cotner's message that the building of this country, like the building of this university, was a social, not a solitary, endeavor. Yes, the cruelty, the exploitation, the racism, the chauvinism deeply stained the record. Dedicated to the proposition that all men are created equal our ancestors violently dispossessed the Indian and nurtured slavery in the cradle of liberty. But there was another strain in American life. For all the chest-thumping about rugged individuals and the self-made man, the ethic of cooperation inspired a social compromise that gave us, in our best moments, the texture of a common endeavor. It was this talent for social cooperation that provided a resilient environment in which American capitalism flourished. Individual initiative succeeded only when it led to strong systems of mutual support. In the words of Edward Ericson, president of the American Ethical Union, we had to move beyond the laissez-faire philosophy of "live and let live" to the active and affirmative notion of "live and HELP live." I couldn't sit in my clearing in the woods while you sweated and strained alone to raise your barn. The neighborly thing was for my neighbors and your neighbors to come together to help you. The barn-raising became a social occasion, a way of expressing solidarity and caring. You helped to deliver one another's babies. When a family was sick, you took turns sitting at the bedside or helping with the meals. And when a neighbor died, you helped dig the grave.

Earlier this week I sat on the porch with my father over in my hometown of Marshall and listened as he reminisced again—as he likes to do—about his days as a boy on the Red River, just south of what then was Indian country. He was born in 1904—Teddy Roosevelt was president. He was 14 when his own father died during the flu epidemic in 1918. Neighbors washed my grandfather's body and neighbors dug his grave and neighbors laid him away in the earth. Even as late as my high school days my father was one of several men in town who would sit up all night beside the corpse of a friend. "Why did you do that," I asked, "especially when you had to work hard all the next day driving that truck?" Without pausing, he said, "Because it was the thing we did." The thing WE did.

Last Sunday after delivering the commencement address at North Texas State University, I drove home from Denton to Marshall along the road I used to hitchhike when I was a freshman going to and from campus. I was so much in a hurry then and looking so much to the horizon that I never looked back. It wasn't until many years later that I realized that the road I was traveling was what once was called the Old County Line Road, down which settlers came 150 years ago from eastern points through Jefferson, south of Clarksville, on to McKinney to settle in that part of the country. It took six hours to make the trip last Sunday, when it normally takes three hours, because I kept getting out to read the historical markers. Not far from where I used to stand and hitchhike at a juncture in the road I found a marker whose few details reinforced the broad outlines that Robert Cotner used to hold forth with right over there in Garrison Hall. The marker records that John McGarrah brought his family to Texas in 1842 and near this spot founded the town of Buckner. Soon thereafter a church grew up; then a school; then a trading post, indicating neighbors had settled nearby. Four years later, on the Fourth of July 1846 he and his neighbors elected their first public officials and opened a post office. Standing there, taking this all in, I was struck by the inevitable progression of civilization from individual initiative to public cooperation through voluntary associations of mutual help: first, the prime family unit; then the wagon train; then the church and the school; then a trading post for the goods of survival and comfort; then a local government for roads and public order; then a communications outpost—the post office—for contact with others; and then a public holiday for mutual celebration and recreation.

This is the story of how you got here tonight; how I got here thirty years ago; how in the year 2020, children not born now, your children, will come and sit where you sit because individual initiative became volunteer association, to build a great public effort that results in The University of Texas. That is civilization. It's a web of cooperation joining people to family, friends, communities, and country, creating in the individual a sense of reliance on the whole, a recognition of the self rooted in companionship with others, through powerful loyalties to the common good: "Habits of the Heart," as a recent book by that name called it.

All history has been a struggle to widen the circle of the heart until the affections that flow from it reach out to include a larger and larger number of neighbors.

It isn't just in these parts that the ethic of cooperation kept people going. My friend and journalistic colleague, Al Levin, and his wife, Hannah, are here tonight from New York. Their daughter, Juliette, received one of the excellence in teaching awards this morning at the Graduate School. Al and Hannah Levin know that back in the East, where we live now, ethnic churches and the synagogue, together with the carpenters' hall and other mutual endeavors, were driving forces behind democracy—agencies that permitted waves of immigrants to coalesce and survive in an unfamiliar land. Mutual help, you see, was a shared reality. A family's savings might buy passage in steerage for an only son. He would toil in the shops or factories to send back to the old country for a brother, then a bride, then for more brothers and more brides. "It was just the thing WE did." They do it now from here to Los

Angeles. Fathers, brothers, aunts and uncles, drawn by El Norte, coming to toil and sweat, living many in a room or house, sending their money back home to help others to live and come, too. "It was just the thing WE do."

I can hear some of you say, "Moyers, you're just being romantic. The frontier is long gone. Let the dead bury the dead. Please move over, we need to compete."

Well, it's true, America is different. Robert Reich tells us just how different in his recent book, *Tales of a New America*. By the 1980s, rather more Americans lived on military bases than lived in what could be called "neighborhoods" in the traditional sense (card games on the front porch, kids running over lawns and fields, corner soda fountains, town meetings, PTAs, etc.); the majority lives in suburban subdivisions that extend helter-skelter in every direction, bordered by highways and punctuated by large shopping malls; or in condominiums, townhouses, cooperative apartments, and retirement communities that provide privacy and safety; or inhabit dilapidated houses and apartments in far less fashionable areas. Many work at some distance from home and socialize with friends selected on some other basis than proximity. We don't have neighborhoods the way we used to have. What's happened is the center has dropped out. It's what our fundamentalist friends have been angrily grieving over for so long now. Gone is the comforting sense of community where everyone was perceived to share enduring values. But all of us are affected. The sense of loss is widespread. It is as if a huge spiritual void has appeared in our collective psyche, making us more nervous, vulnerable, uncertain, and amenable to nonsense, violence, and triviality. So we seek refuge in the comfortable lie rather than face the uncomfortable truth. The lie is that John Wayne never lived. The truth is, his name is Woody Allen. And there's no standing tall in a world of Woody Allens without standing together.

In a society of shards and fragments, tossed and torn by centrifugal forces, together seems an unnatural act. But that's the point. Civilization is not natural. It's an accomplishment of culture. It is not just what happens; it is what we make happen. It's the thing WE do. Furthermore civilization is cost-efficient. John McGarrah up on the Old County Line Road—before he could have a trading post, before he could satisfy what he was going to do with his M.B.A, there had to be a community and there couldn't be a community unless its members agreed on the difference between a horse trader and horse thief. The distinction, you see, is not the weight of money. The distinction is ethical. Without it, society is a war of all against all; a free market for wolves becomes a slaughter for the lambs. A stable system of law, clean and safe streets, secure pensions for everybody who works, and schools where children learn enough to cope with the world whether they live in poor or rich neighborhoods—all of this is part of the bargain we strike with each other and the bargain is civilization.

I brought something to make a point. They tell me people don't remember what they hear at commencement. Maybe you'll remember this—a loaf of bread. In the last 30 years, I've decided that bread is the great reinforcer of the reality principle. Bread equals life. On the frontier they had to produce this themselves. But if you're like me, you have thousands of times repeated the ordinary experience of eating bread without a thought for the process itself. This was brought to me the other day by a friend who said: "I depend for bread on hundreds of people I don't know and will never meet. If they fail me, I starve. If I cannot give them something of value in exchange for this, I fail them. Bread and life are shared realities. No one prays the Lord's Prayer in the first-person singular. It is always, "Give *us* this day *our* daily bread." Our very lives depend on the ethics of strangers, and most of us are always strangers to other people. If you want to see a monument to this, look around. Literally, look around. Think of all the people you will never know and will never meet who raised this university up from just a dream. I assure you it wasn't built by the taxes my parents paid. That wouldn't have dented the cost of being here even in 1954. The $80 Judith and I paid together in tuition each semester was a mere token of the real cost of our experience here. This institution we owe to the vision, the sweat, and the gift of strangers. It is this ethic of obligation—live and help live—which inspires the young to die in battles for their country's sake, the old to plant trees they will never sit under, and men and women to build universities for kids not their own. The ethic of cooperation.

Which brings me back to our friend, UT Socrates. In his essay, he said, "I'll just stick to metaphysics, Texas Metaphysics. However," he went on to say, "in contentment I still feel the need of some eternal bliss." And he asked, "Why does life always feel like it's just outside your grasp?"

Here's my answer: It most seems that way when the circle of human fellowship is broken, and we act for ourselves alone. It most seems that way when we mistake the grasp for something for the embrace of others. Texas Metaphysics is a good philosophy as far as it goes. But it's what I do and not what we do and it won't get *us* in the year 2020. For that, we need a larger idea and a sense of our place in it.

My final word is not original. A journalist is a professional beachcomber on the shores of other people's wisdom. This comes from a young writer named Michael Ventura, who lives now in California:

> The dream we must now seek to realize, the new human project, is not "security," which is impossible to achieve on the planet Earth in the latter half of the 20th century. It is not "happiness," by which we generally mean nothing but giddy forgetfulness about the danger of all our lives together. It is not "self-realization," by which people usually mean a separate peace. There is no separate peace . . . . The real project is to realize that technology has married us all to each other . . . that until we are more courageous about this new marriage—ourselves all intertwined—there will be no peace and the destination of any of us will be unknown. . . . Men and women, black, brown, yellow, white, young and old . . . we must go wherever it is we are going together. There is no such thing as being alone. If you are the only one in the room, it is still a crowded room. But we are all together on this planet, you me, us: inner, outer, together, and we're called to affirm our marriage vows. Our project is to learn how to consummate, how to sustain, how to enjoy this most human marriage—all parts, all of us.

Thank you for inviting me home. Thank you for listening. Good luck to each one of you on the way to 2020.

THESE THINGS WE KNOW[1]

JOHN HOPE FRANKLIN[2]

Traditionally, commencement speakers have praised the graduating students for the achievements, passed to them the torch of leadership, then challenged them to solve the problems of the world. Recently, however, it has become fashionable to invite a distinguished public figure,

[1]Delivered at the 207th commencement exercises of Louisiana State University in the campus Assembly Center in Baton Rouge at 9:30 A.M. on May 18, 1988.
[2]For biographical note, see Appendix.

scholar, or celebrity to address a subject of his choosing, regardless of its relevance to graduation ceremonies.

Occasionally, commencement speakers adroitly combine both objectives: they acknowledge that the graduates and their families are deservedly proud of their achievements, while they also call attention to an issue of overriding concern and challenge their audience to seek its resolution. This was true of the address delivered by the historian John Hope Franklin at the commencement exercises at Louisana State University on May 18, 1988.

Dr. Franklin, James B. Duke Professor of History at Duke University in Durham, North Carolina, considered "one of the world's foremost scholars on slavery and racial equality" (Baton Rouge *Morning Advocate*, May 19, 1988, 11D), was the first black to deliver the commencement address at LSU. The 207th commencement exercises began at 9:30 A.M. in the campus Assembly Center, with Chancellor James H. Wharton presiding. A processional played by the LSU Symphonic Band, the singing of "The Star Spangled Banner," an invocation by a campus clergyman, and remarks by Chancellor Wharton preceded Professor Franklin's address. Franklin's audience included the 1975 graduating students, their parents and friends, and faculty representatives. Immediately following Dr. Franklin's address, Dr. Allen A. Copping, President of the Louisiana State University system, conferred degrees on the graduates, and two honorary degrees were presented.

Franklin began his address with reminiscences about his enjoyable "in and out" association with Louisiana State University that he has sustained for more than four decades. After congratulating the graduating students and their parents, he moved on to discuss what the graduates had learned—what we know—and some things we may not know. He cautioned the graduates, and the country, on being too quick to lecture, and to condemn, other countries, when the example we present to the world might be better. He challenged his listeners to help solve this nation's own glaring social, political, and economic problems.

At the conclusion of his address, Dr. Franklin received a standing ovation. (Baton Rouge *Advocate*, May 19, 1988, p. D11)

John Hope Franklin's speech: Mr. President, Members of the Graduating Classes and their loved ones, Members of the Faculty and Administration, Friends and Alumni, Ladies and Gentlemen:

First of all, permit me to say that it is a great honor and pleasure for me to be here and to participate in the commencement exercises of this great institution. I have been in and out of Louisiana State University for more than forty years. I did research here, for the first time, in 1945; and I have returned to use the rich resources of the library and archives on several occasions. In 1972 I delivered the Walter Lynwood Fleming Lectures here, and the Louisiana State University Press has graciously published my works from time to time. In several divisions and departments of the University, there are personal and professional relationships that I greatly cherish. Indeed, in the city, and at Southern

University, I have friendships and associations that have been sustained for more than fifty years. For many reasons, therefore, I am delighted to be here.

Secondly, permit me to extend to the members of the graduating classes, their parents, loved ones, and friends, my heartiest congratulations for reaching this significant milestone. By your arrival at this juncture, you have indicated a capacity and a willingness to pursue additional studies or to take up the duties and responsibilities of a constructive contributor to some aspect of life here—or elsewhere. I hope that the members of the graduating classes will join me in expressing thanks to the officers and instructional staff of the university and to the parents and others who have made this day possible by their sacrifices, patience, dedication, and contributions in numerous ways. For their help I know that the graduates are truly grateful.

There are those, moreover, whom you have never seen and will never know who have contributed much to the enormous fund of knowledge from which you have drawn and will continue to draw. They are the dreamers, the gifted scientists, the talented humanists, the poets and philosophers, the great men and women who, through the ages, have stimulated our thinking, inspired moments of grandeur for us all, and moved us to work even beyond our own capacities to fulfill the dreams that each of us holds for tomorrow. We are grateful to them for helping us to see and appreciate the distinction between ourselves and lower orders of beings.

On this occasion, if I had the talent, I would not speak at all, but I would do something like Johannes Brahms did when he wrote the "Academic Festival Overture" to mark his attendance at the commencement exercises at the University of Breslau in 1879. Or, perhaps, I would like to have already composed a piece such as Aaron Copeland's "Fanfare for the Common Man," with which Copeland was serenaded as he rose to speak at the commencement exercise at Brooklyn College in 1975. Unfortunately, I can provide you with neither an academic festival overture nor a musical fanfare of any kind. You will, therefore, have to bear with me as I attempt to make some very brief remarks on this important and exciting occasion.

Perhaps this is one of the last times that you will have an opportunity to reflect in any formal way on what you have learned during your sojourn here. At the risk of delaying your celebrations—but only for a short while, I can assure you—I invite you to think about what you have learned and what you now know as you go down from this place. The sheer volume of information that the members of this class have been able to acquire would put to shame the knowledge available to college graduates of a mere half-century ago. For those of us who are separated from this graduating class by a half-century or more, it is difficult not to envy you for the wonderful academic fare on which you have been able to feast. With a curriculum much richer in so many ways than ours was, you who graduate today have been exposed to new sciences such as nuclear energy and space technology and a completely new language of the computer, to say nothing of the availability to you of numerous African, Asian, and exotic languages from the four corners of the earth. These areas have brought within your reach the great civilizations as well as the immortal wisdom of the great sages of China, Japan, India, Russia, and Egypt, to name a very few.

I assure you that I do not envy you for your academic achievements, whatever they may be. I can only congratulate you for what you have done here and hope that you will use what you have learned in a way that will bring great credit to you and the society of which you are a part. Indeed, it is about those things you know that I wish to speak quite briefly.

Since you have mastered the curriculum of this university—or at least have successfully coped with it—you know the fundamentals set forth in the core curriculum. You have learned a foreign language and some of you, hopefully, have become fluent in it. You have become familiar with some of the world's great writers and thinkers, and some of you have arrived at the point where you not only can appreciate them but can also view them critically and constructively. Many of you have mastered the language of the computer and have gained some understanding of the scientific world. All of you have achieved some specialization whether in an undergraduate major or in a graduate or professional area. For your efforts and for your success you have earned the commendation of us all.

There are some other things you know. You have doubtless learned to look at the world in the breadth and depth that it deserves to be viewed. This means, of course, that it is no longer feasible or even becoming to look at the world as an appendage to this country and thus to be judged solely by western or American standards and traditions. You should certainly be beyond the royal sovereign in "The King and I." You will remember he ordered that in his country geography had to be taught so that it showed Siam as the largest land mass not only in Asia but in the western world as well. This appears to be absurd, on the face of it; but you must be certain that you know it is absurd. Your knowledge of this matter has significant implications for the way you view certain current developments. For example, we are in the midst of what some regard as a great debate over the future curriculum of the university. At Stanford University it centers on whether students should be exposed to a larger slice of non-western studies in order to understand what the rest of the world is like. Even before the issues became clear there were those who opposed the very idea of an undergraduate curriculum embracing, say, African, Hispanic, Asian, or Afro-American studies. The United States Secretary of Education severely criticized Stanford and other institutions for yielding to the pressure of what he called "trendy lightweights." Regardless of the outcome of that debate, we need to know much more about the world in which we live. If we can learn more about the Soviet Union, the People's Republic of China, the emerging third world, and the multifaceted aspects of our own ethnic and racial diversity, we can arrive at a more intelligent understanding of how we should frame our own agenda as we react and respond to peoples in other parts of the world.

We also know that we in this country do not have a monopoly on creativity and ingenuity. It should be easy for us to appreciate what others can achieve as we witness the inundation of our markets with foreign automobiles, electronic products, clothing, and other manufactured goods. These are areas in which we formerly claimed a superiority that could not be challenged; but we have surely been overtaken in many of them. That is all right, we say to ourselves, for we have already made the transition from an industrial economy to a service and information economy. But even as we make the declaration, we witness gains being made by other countries in the new areas that we propose to claim as our very own.

If that is not sobering enough, we need only to remember that thirty years ago the capability of producing nuclear weapons was limited to less than a half dozen countries. Today, the number has more than doubled, and some of those are countries that we previously regarded as too backward, too small, or too poor to belong to the nuclear club. Many among us, including our leaders, condemn other countries for doing what we did almost a half century ago. Their priorities are all confused, we insist. Instead of developing a nuclear capability they should use their resources to feed their poor, develop their economy, and build a social and political system that will sustain them in the long run.

Before we sermonize too much, however, about what other countries should do with their resources, it is well to remember that we have our own very serious social problems. Today millions of Americans live below the poverty level, hundreds of thousands of Americans have no home, we have the largest trade imbalance in the history of our country, and our great-grandchildren will do well if they can pay off the federal budget deficit that we have amassed in the past eight years! Perhaps some of *our own* priorities are confused or misplaced. As we go about the world, flexing our muscles by invading Grenada, telling the Angolans what kind of government they can have, insisting that Central Americans model their governments on ours, and proceeding to militarize outer space, we would do well to reexamine our own priorities. Perhaps if we used our great resources in feeding the hungry, housing the poor, and healing the sick around the world, we might go far in dissolving the specter of ideological conflict that seems to haunt us endlessly.

Perhaps the best thing that we can do for an ailing world is to make our way of life work in such a way that it will be a shining example for the rest of the world. This means that we will not be moved to celebrate the anniversary of our invasion of one of the great powers of the world, Grenada, whose location is a bit hazy to many of us. Rather, it means that we should make certain that our economic and social system is working at a level that will inspire the Grenadans to follow our example, and that it works so well that we can assist Grenada and other countries in their quest for a better life. It means that perhaps our best approach to the problems of Angola is not to cheer the rebels, but to seek a policy toward Angola *and* South Africa that will make that part of the world a place of peace as well as a land of plenty. And we should make certain that we know where it is. (A few years ago when I returned from Senegal some solicitous friends said they hoped I was not exposed to the fighting. I assured them that I was not, since the nearest fighting to Senegal was, perhaps, among the gangsters of New York. After I returned from a later trip to Zimbabwe, some solicitous friends expressed relief that I had not been near the area where South Africa had been dropping bombs! One of the places I visited in Harare, the capital, was the headquarters of the African National Congress which South Africa had bombed a few weeks earlier.) I suppose one must excuse the citizens of a great world power if they do not know where the places are that help shape our foreign policy. We are too busy shaping theirs!

The examples we set before the world would be more impressive and attractive if they were marked by consistency as well as logic. We encourage in every way possible the striking workers in Poland, and it is well that we do. But you know, and even the workers in Poland must know, how inconsistent we are in doing so. When the air traffic controllers were in a similar situation in this country in 1981, our government destroyed their union by firing its members because they were striking against the government, which is precisely what the Polish workers have been doing. Why is a strike against one's employers for higher wages and better working conditions in Poland a legitimate pursuit, and a similar undertaking here an illegitimate pursuit?

Because of our long and tumultuous history of human rights and race relations, we know much more about the factors and considerations that are involved in improving them. It is reasonable if other countries look to us for leadership, and we give it willingly, if unevenly. Indeed, we issue a report card annually on which we grade countries on the basis of improvement or retrogression in these areas. We are loud to condemn certain acts of terrorism in the Middle East, but if we act at all about the reign of terror in South Africa, it rarely exceeds a gentle rap on the knuckles. Meanwhile, our own careful and discreet steps toward improved human relations have been challenged if not nullified by an administration and a President who has emasculated the United States Commission on Civil Rights, reluctantly signed the extension of the Voting Rights Act, belittled social programs ranging from school lunches to health insurance for the poor, and just a few weeks ago vetoed the Civil Rights Restoration Bill, only to have it overridden by an aroused Congress. Small wonder that there has been a significant increase in racial incidents on university campuses, largely northern incidentally, an increase in local terrorist groups, and a distressing rise in racial violence in urban centers. One wishes that we had a better record and a better example to present to the world.

You know, even if you did not major in political science, that our adulation of the rights and duties enshrined in our democratic form of government is not reflected in the attention we pay to the political process. We seem to be so busy praising the democratic process and recommending it to others, that we do very little about it ourselves. Thus, we leave elections to a small, highly interested segment of the population. If we get out fifty percent of the eligible voters in an election in this country, it is a rare and remarkable achievement. Two weeks ago, when the primaries were held in the county in which I live in North Carolina, a resounding 21.5 percent of the eligible voters bothered to participate. Compare this with an average of more than 80 percent in the Philippines and in other third world countries with multiple party systems and where voting is not compulsory. We talk about democracy a great deal but we practice it much less than some so-called benighted countries on whom we look with condescension if not loathsomeness.

As you reflect today on what you do know, I suspect that you will conclude that you do not know enough. If you reach that conclusion, you have acquired a distinguishing characteristic of an educated person. You know enough to care; you know enough to want to know more; and you know enough to appreciate the fact that it is in such places as Louisiana State University that the difference will be made between a self-centered, underdeveloped social order and one that is sensitive to the needs of our society and informed about the things that can be done to supply those needs. As you go down from this place today and as you take stock of what these years in this university have meant to you, this is a good time to renew your faith in the process with which you have been concerned here, and by which you have come to know what you do know.

It would be a lavish display of public service if you rallied others, especially the general citizenry, to renew their faith in this major vehicle for the improvement, preservation, and transmission of the very best that our civilization has to offer. It would be an act of courage, moreover, if you insisted that the resources of this country could not be spent better than in the building of an effective, successful educational apparatus for the benefit of our children at every stage of their development. Tell everyone, including our political leaders, that you will bear any burden, pay any price (including taxes), to protect and strengthen the educational institutions of this land.

As you say farewell to this university and to those who have become a part of your lives here, I invite you to join the company of those who believe in and work for the improvement of the human condition through the pervasive power of education and its related enterprises. If you do, you may discover that the company is ever growing and that with your renewed faith the battle for a world in which we can live in peace, prosperity, and wisdom, may, indeed, be won.

GEORGIA—OF 25 YEARS AGO—ON MY MIND[1]

CHARLAYNE HUNTER-GAULT[2]

A significant moment in the recent history of the civil rights movement in America occurred on June 11, 1988, when Charlayne Hunter-Gault, the first black woman to graduate from the University of Georgia, returned after 25 years to deliver the commencement address at her alma mater. That she was the first black speaker to address the university's commencement in 185 years established another milestone.

The significance of the occasion derived from the circumstances of Hunter-Gault's admission to the University of Georgia. Calvin Trillin described the situation:

> By May 17, 1954, when the United States Supreme Court declared racial segregation in public education unconstitutional, most Southern states had already desegregated their state universities, some voluntarily and some under a prophetic series of Supreme Court rulings on the practical inequality of "separate but equal" education. . . . However, in the states of the Deep South where no Negroes attended white universities before 1954 the first assault on segregation came in higher education, and came after the battle lines were drawn.

The enrollment of black students and their freedom to attend classes became the test of the desegregation order, and, according to Trillin,

[1]Delivered at the commencement exercises of the University of Georgia in Sanford Stadium on campus in Athens, Georgia, at approximately 10 A.M. on June 11, 1988.

[2]For biographical note, see Appendix.

> Nowhere was the test more decisive than in Georgia, where Charlayne Hunter and Hamilton Holmes, two Negroes from Atlanta, entered the state university in Athens, in January of 1961. During their first week at the university—which began in relative calm, was climaxed by their both being suspended "for their own safety" after a riot, and ended with their both returning under a new court order—Georgia abandoned its policy of all-out resistance and accepted desegregated education. (*New Yorker*, July 13, 1963, p. 30)

The black students involved in these confrontations became "student celebrities" of a strange new kind, famed for no achievements in athletics or scholarship but merely for going to class and surviving harassment. For many of those students, celebrity status lasted only two or three weeks. However, Charlayne Hunter went on to win several journalism awards as a reporter before achieving national prominence as a correspondent for the *MacNeil-Lehrer Newshour*, a nightly news program on the Public Broadcasting System.

Hunter-Gault addressed the 6200 graduates and their parents, relatives, and friends—total attendance was estimated at 30,000—at the commencement exercises in Sanford Stadium at approximately 10 A.M. It was an emotional occasion. As Anne Hardie reported,

> For some it was a painful trip back in time. Others chose to discard the past and celebrate how far things had come. For the thousands [in attendance] . . . Charlayne Hunter-Gault touched a nerve when she said the school has not fully met its mission to educate all students, both black and white. (*Atlanta Journal and Constitution*, June 12, 1988, p. 2)

And as David Treadwell noted:

> It was an obviously moving moment for Hunter-Gault, who, 27 years ago, had to be shielded from rioting mobs by state troopers when she and Hamilton Holmes became the first black students to enter the university. (*Los Angeles Times*, June 12, 1988, I, p. 4)

Representative Charles Rangel, who inserted Hunter-Gault's speech in the *Congressional Record*, observed:

> Ms. Hunter-Gault expressed feelings and memories that many of us have about the Old South. She spoke not out of bitterness for the misunderstanding and hate she and fellow black student Hamilton Holmes faced in their pioneering roles, but out of warmth for all those faculty and students, many of them white, that pioneered along with them. (*Congressional Record*, June 28, 1988, E2195)

While Hunter-Gault praised the university for its progress, she also noted that of the 6200 students in the graduating class, only 300 were black. According to Ann Hardie,

> Some graduates said the criticism was harsh, calling the speech inappropriate. But afterward Ms. Hunter-Gault was warmly embraced by members of the crowd . . . who accepted the challenge to keep the doors of progress open for blacks at UGA.

National media coverage of the speech was extensive and included an article in the *New York Times* (June 14, 1988, p. 25) adapted from the address.

Charlayne Hunter-Gault's speech: It's good to be back home again, in a place I have always thought of as "our place." I jogged my memory about graduation day here 25 years ago by rereading the address of the late Senator Richard Russell of Georgia, and I knew what I had to talk about today was memory.

It is the memory of many things: Of things taught, like Dr. Charles Kopp's lecture on how "we learn from history that we do not learn from history," and Santayana's admonition that "those who cannot remember the past are condemned to repeat it."

Just the other night, as I listened to the poet Yevgeny Yevtushenko interviewed on the *Newhour*, I remembered that his poetry was one of the passions I pursued at Georgia. Now he spoke passionately about the painful Stalinist period of Russian history, in which, he said, "We destroyed memory, our national memory."

It was the week Robert Kennedy was being honored in our own national memory, and contemplating my return to Georgia, I felt, almost palpably, history coming full circle.

Robert Kennedy came to this campus shortly after I was admitted. While the wound was still wide open, the Attorney General said unflinchingly that the graduation of Hamilton Holmes and Charlayne Hunter would "without question, aid and assist in the fight against Communist political infiltration and guerrilla warfare." I almost fell over; I hadn't thought of it in quite those terms.

Yet, on my graduation day, the words spoken by Senator Russell were wedded to the past rather than a present and future symbolized by our presence in that class.

The senator spoke of the "majesty of local law," a reference to the South's antipathy to the law of the land. The "majesty of local law" meant I could not take a bowling class at the university because the bowling alley was in Athens. The federal law desegregating the campus did not apply in town. Nor did it apply to black citizens from Athens who came to football games on campus. They were forced to sit in what was called "the crow's nest."

Despite those facts of life 25 years ago, a watchfire was lit, celebrating a revelation. Amid misunderstanding and hate, one inquisitive black girl, who dreamed of being Brenda Starr, found the University of Georgia the place to fulfill that dream, as did one gifted young black man who wanted to become a healer.

One thing I want us all to keep alive in memory is that our days as students would have been a sojourn into unrelieved loneliness had not others pioneered with Hamp and me. They were many: faculty and students, all of them white. I must especially remember Salter Stovall, a bona fide white Southerner who boldly sought me out. I confess I was leery when he took a seat next to me during summer school. But when we stopped each other at fall registration, we hugged, and I knew we had stolen each other's heart.

He gave up going to movies because I couldn't get a seat in segregated theaters. He gave up going to the local student hangout because they would not serve me (although he told me it was because the chili dogs tasted funny). We married, despite the uproar he knew it would cause, because we loved each other. While we are now happily married to other people we love—I to Ronald, he to Sue—the reason our marriage didn't work out wasn't because we lacked courage in a time of sea changes.

I have come to understand that in this country only the South has ever been a true melting pot. Through our toil and tumultuous history, we have become a definable people, *sui generis* in the way we talk, our preference for fried food and our humility as we fulfill our hopes and dreams.

No one would pretend that the Old South is dead, that the events of 25 years or even my presence here today have transformed our peculiar world beyond recognition. True, there are more than two black students in this graduating class: 300 out of 6,200. But taken together with the number of black students in the entire school, 1,200 out of 26,000, permit me to say we have failed our responsibility to this institution and this state.

The lessons I learned on this campus provided me with sharp radar for intolerance. Recently that radar has been sounding constant alarms: from campuses, where dissent is now often mean-spirited, and from the White House, where former Education Secretary Terrell Bell recalled he was "shocked to hear racist cliches" and ethnic slurs. Something, I know not exactly what, and probably a combination of things, has changed the consensus we forged.

I was struck the other day by the words of the West African novelist Ayi Kwei Armah: "Our way is not a random path. . . . Our way begins from the coherent understanding." I believe the South's understanding, even when it was wrong, was always more coherent than the rest of the country's and that is one of the few hopeful signs I see.

University of Georgia president Charles Knapp's bold stroke in hiring 15 new black faculty members is part of that equation. When people at the top exercise leadership, even when they don't work miracles, they make things happen. That is true wherever the gap between what should be and what is remains a wide abyss, wherever college administrators, CEO's, news directors and others talk about their philosophical commitment to diversity, but add that they "just couldn't find any qualified" or "willing to come."

The presence of more black faculty members here will not only attract more black students. Together, their presence will move this place—our place—to a new phase in its pioneering history. By the year 2000, one out of three Americans will be a minority. In preparing for the real world, it is our turn.

I first came here, in the words of Stephen Vincent Benet, "A brown girl bearing an idle gift." I stand before you now a woman, who has drunk from the waters and wines of the world: not at peace, but confident of my capacities; praising the Shepherd's and the lawgivers' gifts because we have had our justice after all. If I had it to do all over again, I might have hoped for less of a struggle. But even today, I would welcome the challenge.

REMEMBERING

ROBERT F. KENNEDY REMEMBERED[1]

ARTHUR SCHLESINGER, JR.[2]

Is history the product of impersonal social and economic forces, or can individuals change its course? That question was raised on the 20th anniversary of the death of Robert F. Kennedy. Would he have made a difference had assassination not ended his quest for the Democratic presidential nomination? This question was the subject of intense speculation in the media during the first half of 1988. Several books about Senator Kennedy were published, including an oral history and a collection of his campaign speeches, while *Time*, the conservative *National Review*, the *New York Times*, and other magazines and newspapers devoted special features to Kennedy, whose photo graced the cover of the May 9 issue of *Newsweek* and who was the subject of a special conference, "R.F.K. Remembered," which was held at Loyola Marymount College in Los Angeles on April 23-24, 1988.

"Why, after 20 years, are we recalling the memory of Robert F. Kennedy?" asked Adam Walinsky, a former speechwriter and assistant to Kennedy when he was Attorney General. "In retrospect," he answered, "it's clear that Robert F. Kennedy was the last major leader who allowed us to at least imagine we could realize the ideals of American politics." (*New York Times*, June 6, 1988, p. E31) In *Newsweek* it was noted that:

> The 20 years that have passed since June 6, 1968, have transfigured Bobby Kennedy. In memories, in histories, bull sessions, he has turned into a legend, a man of so many faces, voices, identities that no one can keep track of them all. (May 9, 1988, p. 34)

A 1988 *Rolling Stone* magazine poll of members of the "baby boom" generation showed that Robert Kennedy and Martin Luther King, Jr., were remembered as heroes by 18-to-44 year-olds, and writers for *Time* tried to explain the continuing fascination with RFK in an article titled "The Last Hero":

> It has been 20 years since he died, and still it is to take measure of the man. . . . What echoes today is a memory, almost mythic in proportions. Like all leaders who die young, Bobby is frozen in death as larger than life. As a memory, he evokes an era of political passion that stands in haunting contrast to 1988. As a myth, he is a vessel into which all dreams can be poured. (May 9, 1988, p. 40)

[1]Delivered at a special retrospective conference on the theme "R.F.K. Remembered" in the college auditorium of Loyola Marymount University in Los Angeles, California, at 9:45 A.M. on April 23, 1988.

[2]For biogrphical note, see Appendix.

Organized by the Center for Politics, Ethics, and Public Policy at Loyola Marymount University, the conference memorializing Kennedy attracted some 1500 Democrats and a diverse group of former Kennedy supporters and associates, including Cesar Chavez, president of the United Farm Workers; Ford Foundation president Franklin Thomas; Congressman John Lewis, former head of the Student Non-Violence Coordinating Committee; former California governor Edmund A. Brown, Jr.; writer Jimmy Breslin; athlete Rafer Johnson; and activist Tom Hayden.

The conference included a film, "R.F.K. Remembered," such activities as workshops and panel discussions, and two main speeches, one by the historian and Kennedy biographer Arthur Schlesinger, Jr., the other by RFK's daughter, Kathleen Kennedy Townsend, who told the conference:

> These two days are a time to recall the battles, to tell stories, to laugh, and to be happy that you were part of that joyful time. We want to remember Robert Kennedy because he touched something deep and enduring in each of us. We miss him terribly. . . . It is also an occasion to rededicate ourselves to fulfilling the sense of possibility that he saw in this nation and in each of us. (*Congressional Record*, April 29, 1988, p. E1320)

Arthur Schlesinger, Jr., delivered the conference keynote address in the college auditorium on the campus of Loyola Marymount University at 9:45 A.M. Immediately following his address, Jeff Greenfield, a former Kennedy aide who now is a network news commentator, chaired a panel discussion on "The Legacy of R.F.K."

Arthur Schlesinger, Jr.'s speech: We are gathered here this weekend for a double purpose. This occasion is in part a reunion, the coming together, after long years, of men and women who two decades ago were friends and associates of Robert Kennedy. But it is also, I take it, and more significantly, a reaffirmation—a rededication, twenty years after, to the purposes and ideals for which Robert Kennedy lived, and died.

Those purposes and ideals have lately been out of fashion in the republic. For a moment I would like to carry you back to ancient times. The past, L. P. Hartley once wrote, is another country. From the perspective of the 1980s, the Kennedy years truly seem another country, different in direction, purposes, values, different in the conception of America and in the aspirations for American society. We have been for some years as strangers in a strange land: Reaganland. It requires a leap of the historical imagination to put ourselves back into that remote and exotic time twenty years ago, so near us chronologically; so distant ideologically and emotionally.

However, there is nothing new in such dramatic shifts in the national mood. For there is a discernible rhythm in our politics. American history displays a fairly regular alternation between conservatism and liberalism in our political outlook, an alternation that has taken the form this century of swings back and forth between eras when the national preference is for private interest as the best way of meeting national problems and eras when the national preference turns to public purpose.

In this light, the Reaganite private-interest 1980s are a reenactment of the Eisenhower 1950s, as the 1950s were a reenactment of the Harding-Coolidge-Hoover 1920s (and the 1920s a reenactment of the Cleveland-McKinley 1890s). In the same fashion, the nation turns at 30-year intervals to public purpose, reform and affirmative government: Theodore Roosevelt ushering in the Progressive period in 1901, Franklin Roosevelt the New Deal in 1933, John Kennedy the New Frontier in 1961.

There is nothing mystical about this 30-year cycle. Thirty years is the span of a generation. People tend to be formed politically by the ideals dominant in the years when they first attain political consciousness: roughly between the ages of 16 and 25. When their own generation's turn in power comes some 30 years later, they are likely to carry forward the ideals they imbibed when they came of political age.

So young people who grew up during the Progressive era when Theodore Roosevelt and Woodrow Wilson were setting the nation's sights—Franklin Roosevelt, Eleanor Roosevelt, Harry Truman—renewed the goals of their youth 30 years after in the New Deal and the Fair Deal. So young people who grew up when FDR was inspiring the country—John Kennedy, Lyndon Johnson, Robert Kennedy—brought the New Deal up to date in the New Frontier and the Great Society. In the same manner, John and Robert Kennedy touched and formed a political generation in the 1960s. If the rhythm holds, that generation's time will arrive in the 1990s.

Nor is there any mystery why the cycle turns and turns again. Each phase runs its natural course. During the seasons of idealism and reform, strong leaders call for active popular involvement in national affairs and enlist government as a means of promoting the general welfare. Such periods eventually leave the electorate exhausted by the process and disenchanted by the results. People then are ready to respond to leaders who tell them to stop worrying themselves about public policy; left to self-interest in a deregulated marketplace, our problems will solve themselves.

The conservative mood runs its course, too. The national batteries recharge. Problems neglected become acute, threaten to become unmanageable, and demand remedy. People grow bored with selfish motives and vistas. They seek some meaning in life beyond self-interest and the fast buck. Materialism turns out not to be enough. They begin finally to ask not what their country can do for them but what they can do for their country.

We have seen the cycle turn 180 degrees in the years since Robert Kennedy lived and died. Unless I am badly mistaken, the rhythm is holding; the cycle is beginning to turn again; we are at the start of the transition from one phase to the next. The nation, after its strange interlude in Reaganland, is ready to return to its nobler ideals and its better self, to return to the old quest to fulfill the promise of American life for all our people. And in this changing climate the life and purpose of Robert Kennedy have a new relevance, a new saliency, a fresh meaning for a new generation.

Twenty years ago this month many of us were working our heads and hearts out to make Robert Kennedy president of the United States. His journey and ours came to a tragic end here in Los Angeles. No one can tell where roads not taken might have led. Yet the probability is that Robert Kennedy would have gone on from his victory in the California primary to win the Democratic nomination for president and that he would have beaten Richard Nixon in the fall election.

A Robert Kennedy presidency would have changed many things. It would have meant the withdrawal of American troops from Vietnam in 1969 rather than in 1972, and many Americans (and many more Vietnamese and Cambodians) killed in those years might be alive today. It would have meant real gains in slowing down the nuclear arms race, the cessation of nuclear testing, and more rational relations with the Soviet Union.

It would have meant a culmination of the reform phase of the political cycle, consolidating and extending the achievements of John Kennedy's New Frontier and Lyndon Johnson's Great Society. We must not forget that the liberal tide of the 1960s was still running strong enough in 1969 to shape even Richard Nixon's domestic program. The Environmental Protection Act, the Occupational Safety and Health Act, the Comprehensive Employment and Training Act with its CETA employment program were all enacted under Nixon. If that strong liberal tide so influenced a conservative administration, what signal opportunities it would have given a reform president!

The confidence that both white and black working-class Americans had in Robert Kennedy created the possibility of continued progress toward racial justice. His appeal to the young might have mitigated some of the under-thirty excesses of the time. And of course the election of Robert Kennedy in 1968 would have delivered the republic from Watergate with its attendant perversion of the Constitution and destruction of faith in government.

Most Americans who remember the 1960s, even those (and there were many) who disliked Robert Kennedy, would very likely agree that he would have made a difference as president. He was a man of passionate conviction carrying a message of change and, for the forlorn and dispossessed of America, a message of hope. He was at the same time a tough and experienced party politician who understood the uses of power and who knew the ways, and byways, of all three branches of the national government. And he was a compelling campaigner with unusual capacity to inform, move, and inspire the electorate and to rally popular support for his policies.

The Robert Kennedy who emerged as the liberal leader in the 1960s could not have been easily predicted by those who knew him in earlier years. I well remember my first encounter with him. In 1954 he sent a letter to the *New York Times* condemning the Yalta agreement. I dispatched a testy reply, describing his letter as "an astonishing mixture of distortion and error." The exchange amused John Kennedy, who told me, "My sisters are very mad at you because of the letter you wrote about Bobby." Bobby was mad too and dashed off a second letter to the *Times*, concluding that he did not "wish to appear critical of Mr. Schlesinger's scholarship for his polemics cover such a wide variety of subjects that he is not always able to read all of the documents he so vigorously discusses." He sent me a carbon with a covering note in which he crisply said that his second letter to the *Times* ought to "clarify the record sufficiently for you to make the necessary public apology." I replied in like spirit; but the *Times*, bored with the argument, did not bother to print the rebuttals and surrebuttals.

I first met him in the 1956 campaign when I was working with Adlai Stevenson. Robert joined the Stevenson party and accompanied the candidate in trips around the country. No one quite knew what he was doing; in fact, he was learning how a national campaign should (or should not) be run. From my own viewpoint on Stevenson's staff, he seemed an alien presence, sullen and rather ominous, saying little, looking grim and exuding an atmosphere of surly disapproval.

One afternoon in October the campaign party found itself in Morgantown, West Virginia. Stevenson was scheduled to speak that evening in New York City. Fog and rain set in, and a single plane was available to fly the candidate out of Morgantown. Eventually buses arrived to take the rest of us to Pittsburgh. Under pelting rain we scrambled aboard, groping for seats in the darkness. I turned to look at my seatmate and found, I am sure to our mutual dismay, Robert Kennedy. For the next several hours we rode through the storm to Pittsburgh. Having no alternative, we fell into reluctant conversation. To my surprise he was altogether pleasant, reasonable, and funny. We became friends at once and remained so for the rest of his life. I could never take seriously thereafter the picture of Robert Kennedy as a bearer of grudges, vindictive and unforgiving.

After the 1960 election, it was Robert Kennedy who first proposed that I come to the White House as a presidential special assistant. In January 1961 the president-elect came to Cambridge for a meeting of the Harvard board of overseers and used my house as his headquarters for the day. In an interval between meetings, he said to me, "Bobby says that you are ready to come to work at the White House." I said, "I am not sure what I would be doing as special assistant, but, if you think I can help, I would like very much to come." He said, "Well, I am not sure what I will be doing as president either, but I am sure there will be enough in the White House to keep us both busy."

During the New Frontier Robert Kennedy assembled a brilliant group in the Department of Justice and, after a hesitant start, became a leader in the struggle for racial justice and equal rights. He rigorously kept politics out of the administration of justice and worked to bring the imperious J. Edgar Hoover and his long untouchable FBI under control. Hoover was then a national idol, and his obsession was the pursuit of communists. Kennedy thought this nonsense. The American Communist Party, he told a newspaperman, "couldn't be more feeble and less of a threat, and besides its membership consists largely of FBI agents." Against Hoover's will, Robert Kennedy forced him to divert FBI agents and budget into two new fields of activity—organized crime and racial justice.

The Department of Justice was only part of Robert Kennedy's work. "Management, in Jack Kennedy's mind," Chester Bowles once said, " . . . consisted largely of calling Bob on the phone and saying 'Here are ten things I want to get done.'" Liberals throughout the administration found the Attorney General the indispensable ally on every sort of issue. The president found him the indispensable adviser, as during the Cuban missile crisis. Robert Kennedy had the wonderful capacity, when faced by complex problems, to ask the questions that penetrate to the heart of a decision. He was, as Winston Churchill said of Franklin Roosevelt's great aide, Harry Hopkins, "Lord Root-of-the-Matter."

What a partnership they made! Under his brother's influence, Robert began to lose his rigidity and intolerance. He grew relaxed and rueful, developed his wry, self-mocking sense of humor, acquired broader and more ironic views of life and soon displayed a personal charm against which newspaper editors routinely warned their reporters. His life was a story of growth, of change, of responsiveness to problems and pressures and hungers and needs. "Most people," as his Harvard classmate Anthony Lewis observed, "acquire certainties as they grow older; he lost his."

Then John Kennedy went to Dallas. The assassination devastated his younger brother. For weeks and months Robert wandered in grief. Yet, in a paradoxical sense, it liberated him too—to become a voice and leader in his own right. He had repressed his inner self since childhood, first to prove himself to his father, then to serve his brother. In 1961 his father was hopelessly disabled by a stroke; in 1963 his brother was murdered. At last Robert Kennedy was on his own.

Two themes absorbed him in these years. One was the quest for peace—first of all, an end to the senseless war in Vietnam. "Can we," he cried in 1968, "ordain to ourselves the awful majesty of God—to decide what cities and villages are to be destroyed, who will live and who will die, and who will join the refugees wandering in a desert of our own creation?" He defined the problem of communism in Latin America in words that still ring today: "If we allow communism to carry the banner of reform, then the ignored and the dispossessed, the insulted and injured, will turn to it as the only way out of their misery." He called for new initiatives to bring the nuclear arms race under control.

The other theme looked homeward. He had an agonized sense that the disparities of power and opportunity in American society were acute and becoming intolerable. And he believed that American society with its abundant wealth and high ideals could reduce these disparities and give the poor and powerless a better chance to help themselves. Present conditions, he would say in speech after speech, were "not acceptable," and we diminished ourselves as a moral community when we accepted them. He identified himself increasingly with the desolate and excluded of America: Indians on reservations, Hispanics picking grapes in California, hungry blacks along the Mississippi delta, migrant workers in filthy camps in upstate New York, despairing families in rat-infested tenements in New York City. "Today in America," he wrote, "we are two worlds."

His aim was to make the two worlds one. Always challenging, always probing, always testing, he sought new ways to empower the people, to foster individual responsibility and community self-reliance and self-development, to work out new structures by which people can sustain their dignity, restore order to their lives, and hope and devise new and workable means of helping themselves. This unrelenting search for new methods and remedies made him the creative political leader of the day.

His was a message of change, bringing hope to some, fear to others. Robert Kennedy was an uncomfortable man. He embodied a rude challenge to the complacencies of American life. But his brusque directness made people listen, even when they did not wish to hear. And he was also a man of gentleness and humor and a contagious sense of the absurdity of existence.

Then came 1968, and the presidential campaign. It was an uproarious campaign, filled with enthusiasm and fun. One newspaperman described it as a "huge, joyous adventure." Some people saw Robert Kennedy as a divisive figure. But he saw himself as on a journey of reconciliation, seeking to bridge the great schisms in American society: between white and nonwhite, between rich and poor, between age and youth, between order and dissent. Born the son of wealth, he died the champion of the outcasts of the world.

The themes of Robert Kennedy's life came to seem exotic amidst the conservatism of the 1980s. We forgot about the poor and the powerless. We hated to think about the humiliated and the dispossessed. Instead of reducing the disparities in American life, we widened them. We swept national anguish under the rug. We asked what our country could do for us, not at all what we could do for our country.

But the cycle is turning. Having achieved the majestic age of 70, I have lived through several of these cyclical alternations, and I believe I can recognize the symptoms of change. The decline of Reaganism was already visible with the midterm elections and the Democratic capture of the Senate of 1986, well before the Iran-*Contra* scandals and the stock market troubles. The scheme to get the Ayatollah to subsidize the *Contras*, which must have been devised by Rube Goldberg, and the mode of execution, which could only have been planned by Inspector Clouseau, only confirm and accelerate the cyclical change already under way.

We can see the renewal of idealism, the revolt against complacency, the revulsion against greed on every side—on college campuses, in trade union halls, in the periodicals, in plays and movies. Reaganism is finished, bankrupt, used up, played out: at last, it is truly bedtime for Bonzo. We stand on the verge of a new political epoch, a new time of idealism, innovation and reform, comparable to the generous energies released after the accession to office of Theodore Roosevelt in 1901, of Franklin Roosevelt in 1933, and of John Kennedy in 1963.

The recent *Rolling Stone* survey showed that young people, when asked to select the two people they most admired who had been active in public life over the last 20 years, chose Martin Luther King, Jr, and Robert Kennedy, "men of courage who challenged the established order, who espoused love and peace and attacked prejudice and inequality."

Robert Kennedy's life comes back to us today with new power, and should infuse us with new purpose. Above all, let us act upon the conviction by which Robert Kennedy lived, the conviction that gave so much hope to the excluded and powerless in America and beyond America: the intense conviction that an individual can make a difference to the life of his times. We have cherished through our lives the great words Robert Kennedy spoke at Capetown in South Africa in 1966, words that will inspire new generations to new boldness and sacrifice in the cause for which he lived and died:

It is from numberless diverse acts of courage and belief that human history is shaped. Each time a man stands up for an ideal, or acts to improve the lot of others, or strikes out against injustice, he sends a tiny ripple of hope, and crossing each other from a million different centers of energy and daring these ripples will build a current which can sweep down the mightiest walls of oppression and resistance.

THE SECRET OF MR. LINCOLN'S GREATNESS[1]

JOHN A. LLOYD[2]

> At 7:21 on the morning of April 15, 1865, Abraham Lincoln died. . . . One hundred twenty-three years after his death, the people, not only of the United States, but of the entire world, study and ponder and explore and venerate Abraham Lincoln.

With these words, John A. Lloyd began his lecture, "The Secret of Mr. Lincoln's Greatness." Mr. Lloyd delivered the address as part of the annual ceremonies commemorating Lincoln's birthday at Lincoln Memorial University in Harrogate, Tennessee, on February 12, 1988.

Lincoln Memorial University was established in 1897 as a living memorial to Abraham Lincoln, his philosophy and ideals. The origin of the university began when Lincoln suggested to a Union general, O. O. Howard, that he start a college in the Cumberland Gap in Tennessee, adjoining North Carolina and Kentucky, to offer an education at inexpensive rates to mountain people in the tri-state area. Thirty years after Lincoln's suggestion, Howard and others were able to purchase the buildings of an abandoned sanitarium and establish the school.

Today, Lincoln Memorial University is a private, nonsectarian liberal arts school with strong professional programs in business, nursing education, and applied sciences, a faculty of more than 100, and an enrollment of approximately 1400. It publishes the *Lincoln Herald*, a scholarly journal devoted to research in Lincolniana and the Civil War, and is the home of the Abraham Lincoln Museum, which has become one of the country's largest collections of Lincoln and Civil War memorabilia.

The activities commemorating Lincoln's birthday included a memorial service in the Elizabeth D. Chinnock Chapel on campus, a musical program by the university's Lincoln Singers, a speech by the president of L.M.U. on Lincoln's frontier philosophy and religion, and the second annual Great Lincoln Debates, in which local high school students participated.

John A. Lloyd was the featured speaker at the Lincoln Day noon lun-

[1]Delivered in the cafeteria of Lincoln Memorial University in Harrogate, Tennessee, at noon on February 12, 1988, as part of the university's annual ceremonies commemorating the birthday of Abraham Lincoln.

[2]For biographical note, see Appendix.

cheon. His address was part of a lecture series established by the university to honor Lincoln artist Lloyd Ostendorf. John A. Lloyd, a business executive and authority on Lincoln, delivered the lecture at a banquet attended by 300 to 350 faculty, staff members, and students in the cafeteria of the Lincoln Memorial University Campus on February 12, 1988.

John A. Lloyd's speech: Ladies and gentlemen:

At 7:21 on the morning of April 15, 1865 Abraham Lincoln died. Secretary of war Edwin Stanton is said to have made one of the following remarks: "Now he belongs to the ages" or "Now he belongs to the Angels." Neither seems as cogent as one made by a bystander who said "Now Abraham Lincoln is immortal."

One hundred twenty-three years after his death, the people, not only of the United States, but of the entire world study and ponder and explore and venerate Abraham Lincoln.

Forty men have occupied the office of the presidency since our republic was founded, but a half dozen seem to stand above the others: Washington, the founding father, defended by Henry Lee in his eloquent eulogy in 1799 as being "First in war, first in peace, first in the hearts of his countrymen"; Jefferson, who is remembered for his political philosophy and for his promotion of the Louisiana Purchase and the Lewis and Clark expedition; Jackson, the swashbuckling commoner who revised the bank of the United States and the country's monetary system; the Roosevelts: Theodore, who consummated the McKinley conquests and made America a world power, and Franklin Roosevelt, who changed completely the sociological and commercial complexion of the country; and the sixth, Abraham Lincoln.

These six are the most written about, the most talked about, the most often portrayed in film, in television, on radio, and on stage. Some persons may wish to delete one or the other of the presidents on my list and substitute or add their own preference, and I would not quibble with them.

But make this test: Ask a score of the men and women you know to write down the names of a half-dozen greatest presidents of the United States, and you will get a variety of answers, but on nearly every list you will find the name of Abraham Lincoln.

Ask your foreign friends to name the ten greatest figures of world history in the last two hundred years, and on nearly every list you will find the name of Abraham Lincoln.

Why have more books been written about Lincoln than any other American, perhaps than any other human being? Why is he so often quoted? Why is he so definitely an influence so long after his death?

Jay Monaghan in his *Lincoln Bibliography*, published back in 1945, listed 3,958 books and pamphlets written about Lincoln up to that time, and the output in the ensuing years has shown no diminution: it probably has more than doubled.

Will we find the answer to "Why Lincoln?" if we mine that great paper mass sheet by sheet—thousands of them—and word by word—millions of them?

So much of this mass of words is legend, told and retold, myth repeated over and over. But remember this, Lincoln the myth and Lincoln the legend would have died the death that fictional and fanciful accounts deserve long, long ago. It is the real, earthy Lincoln who is immortal, not the legendary so-called martyr.

Somewhere in his humble, honest reality, in the breadth of his intellect, in the courage and stamina of his character, and in the deep recesses of his soul lies the answer to the enigmatic question "Why Lincoln?"

So baffled have I been by this question that I have read and searched for the answer and was about to abandon hope of finding it, when suddenly I came across an incident in sacred writing that I believe reveals the secret.

In the story of the calling by Jesus of men to be his disciples, it is told how Peter and James and John and Bartholomew came to be enlisted; then, an entirely different reason for selection flashes across the page when Nathaniel is chosen. This is how it is written: "Jesus saw Nathaniel coming and saith to him; behold an Israelite, indeed, in whom there is no guile!"

My dictionaries define the world "guile" as "craft," "deceit," "cunning," "duplicity," or "treachery."

And the thought came to me: Here I have found the answer to my question, "Why Lincoln?" But to be certain, the search could not be complete until it took another turn. I began deliberately and carefully to try to find in the story of Lincoln's years, in his speeches and in his acts, evidence of guile. And in more than cursory study I can find no act or even a phrase revealing craft, deceit, or hypocrisy, cunning, duplicity, or treachery.

The same threads of truth and honesty and integrity and realism run through his every utterance from youth to death. The pure gold of his integrity is there throughout his life, but he not only never told of it, I doubt if he ever realized it. It was just the way he was.

Lincoln could always be believed, and because people could believe him, they believed him, and they believed in him to this very last day.

Benjamin Thomas in his magnificent biography of Abraham Lincoln writes that,

> Men friendly to the Union cause remembered July and August of 1864 as the darkest days of the war. Earlier setbacks had tried the nation's faith, but the reverses of this hot, dry summer fell with greater oppressiveness because high hopes had been dashed. No joyful tidings came from the army now. Confusion reigned in politics. Peace appeared to be a distant dream.

On June 8th Mr. Lincoln had been nominated for a second term by the National Union Convention held in Baltimore. For some months before that convention the politicians had been predicting that he would not be nominated. However, he received 484 votes out of 506 cast.

After the convention there was a strong feeling that the ticket could not be elected and the president felt the same way about it. On August 23, at a cabinet meeting, he had the members sign without reading it, the back of a memorandum which read:

> This morning as for some days past, it seems extremely probable that this administration will not be re-elected. Then it will be my duty to so cooperate with the President-elect as to save the Union between the election and the inauguration; as he will have secured his election on such ground that he cannot save it afterwards.

But the prophets of doom were wrong about one very important fact: Lincoln was re-elected. He carried every state but Kentucky, New Jersey, and Delaware. The electoral college vote was 212 for Lincoln to 21 for McClellan and the popular majority for Lincoln was nearly a half million.

But, despite the one good sign, Lincoln's renomination, it was true as Thomas wrote, July and August were remembered as "the darkest days of the war." And all during those trying days, President Lincoln's mind and heart were fastened upon the war and upon the Union which he was determined to preserve.

On the 22nd of August, an event occurred that Mr. Lincoln's secretaries, John Nicolay and John Hay, considered so important that they gave it full treatment in their description of the President's appointments on that day; and the *Washington Star*, in its issue of August 23, 1864, carried a special item about it.

On that day President Lincoln defined America.

This is what took place. The 166th Ohio regiment, on its way home after completing its term of service, paraded to the executive mansion to pay its respects to its commander-in-chief and he took the time out from his busy and oppressive schedule to express his thanks to them for their service. In doing so, he said:

> I suppose you are going home to see your families and friends. For the services you have done in this great struggle in which we are all engaged, I present you sincere thanks for myself and the country.
> I almost always feel inclined when I happen to say anything to soldiers, to impress upon them, in a few brief remarks, the importance of success in this contest. It is not merely for today, but for all time to come that we should perpetuate for our children's children that great and free government which we have enjoyed all our lives. I beg you to remember this, not merely for my sake, but for yours.
> I happen, temporarily, to occupy this big white house. I am a living witness that any one of your children may look to come here as my father's child has.
> It is in order that each one of you may have, through this free government which we have enjoyed, an open field and a fair chance for your industry, enterprise and intelligence; that you may all have equal privileges in the race for life, with all its desirable human aspirations; it is for this that the struggle should be maintained, that we may not lose our birthright. The nation is worth fighting for, to secure such an inestimable jewel.

And there you have it; the most succinct, down-to-earth definition of what America is all about that I have been able to find anywhere.

In that short address to those fighting men of the grand army, Lincoln defined America, he described the American dream, he illuminated the tapestry of freedom for all to see its grandeur.

Hear him again as we diagram the thoughts revealed in those sentences of August 27, 1864. What is it that he says we have? "Free government where every man has rights." And what are the rights of men under this free government? They constitute, he says "Our birthright." What are they?

He lists three:

> First: "Every man has a right to be equal with every other man."
> Second: "An open field and a fair chance for your industry, enterprise and intelligence."
> Third: "Equal privilege in the race of life with all its desirable human aspirations."

This is what America is all about, told simply by one who understood the American dream because he had made it come true for himself and could describe it for every American then and now and forever.

And indeed, as he said it: "The nation is worth fighting for to secure such an inestimable jewel."

Under this original American concept man is to be secure in his right to "an open field and a fair chance" for his "industry, enterprise and intelligence." And here, indeed, is the glory of the American dream: a fair chance for every man's industry, enterprise and intelligence. It is exactly because Americans in days gone by have grasped this chance that the American dream has come true. But in our day we discern the point of danger: that government turns its overpowers into tyranny and attempts to control and to regulate and to circumscribe man's "industry, enterprise and intelligence." For over-government—such as we now have—stifles these attributes so necessary to the greatness of a people and their nation.

Finally is the right "that you may all have equal privileges in the race of life with all its desirable human aspirations," not a government-conferred victory in the race of life, but "equal privileges in the race," that is one of the meanings of freedom. Such, Lincoln said, is freedom. Such is the purpose of America. "The nation is worth fighting for," he concluded, "to secure such an inestimable jewel."

And in that sentence he puts the cap sheaf on his definition of American by giving us the challenge of the citizen's duty: to be willing to fight to make secure such an inestimable jewel.

And fight we must, or the robbers will take the jewel.

In this connection let me point out that Mr. Lincoln was telling all the generation to which he was speaking and all generations of Americans who will come after them, that protection (he used the words "to secure" and I think he meant to make secure) of the American dream is the challenge to each of us; no one is excused from this duty.

He expressed it in another way in 1863. The new treasury building across the street from the president's house had just been completed and President Lincoln was asked to raise the flag at the ceremonies marking the event.

This he did and, in doing it, he made what has become famous as his "one sentence speech." As he grasped the halyard, this is what he said: and in saying it then, he also said it to us, today: "The part assigned to me is to raise the flag, which, if there be no fault in the machinery, I will do and "*when up, it will be for the people to keep it up*."

Remember now this: *We are the people*. Only the people can keep the flag and all it stands for flying, proudly flying.

And this is the most important task, *we the people*, have had in all our history or ever will have.

We are American citizens, God help us to do our duty as such.

APPENDIX

Biographical Notes

Bennett, William John (1943-). Born Brooklyn, New York; B.A., Williams College, 1965; Ph.D., University of Texas, 1970; J.D., Harvard University, 1971; Litt. D., Gonzaga University, 1982; H.H.D., Franklin College, 1982; L.H.D., University of New Hampshire, 1982; LL.D., Williams College, 1983; assistant to president, Boston University, 1972-76; executive director, National Humanities Center, 1976-79; associate professor, North Carolina State University, Raleigh, 1979-81; chairman, National Endowment for the Humanities, 1981-85; secretary, United States Department of Education, 1985-87; Director, National Drug Control Policy Office, 1989- . (See also *Current Biography*, 1985.)

Boaz, David Douglas (1953-). Born, Mayfield, Kentucky; B.A., Vanderbilt University, 1975; executive director, Young Americans Foundation, 1975-76; editor, *New Guard* magazine, 1976-78; executive director, Council for a Competitive Economy, 1978-80; vice president, Cato Institute, 1981- ; co-editor, *Beyond the Status Quo*, 1985; editor, *Left, Right, and Babyboom*, 1986; author, *Assessing the Reagan Years*, 1988, *An American Vision: Policy for the '90s*, 1989.

Bush, George Herbert Walker (1924-). Born, Milton, Massachusetts; B.A., Yale University, 1948; honorary degrees, Adelphi University, Austin College, Northern Michigan University, Franklin Pierce College, Allegheny College, Beaver College; co-founder, director, Zapata Petroleum Corporation, 1953-59; president, Zapata Off Shore Company, 1956-64, chairman of the board, 1964-66; member of 90th-91st U.S. Congresses, 7th district of Texas; U.S. ambassador to the United Nations, 1971-72; chairman, Republican National Committee, 1973-74; chief, U.S. Liaison Office, Peking, People's Republic of China, 1974-75; director of Central Intelligence Agency, 1976-77; vice president of the United States, 1981-89; president of the United States, 1989- ; director, 1st International Bank, Ltd., London, 1st International Bank, Houston, Eli Lilly Corporation, Texasgulf, Purolator; chairman, Heart Fund; trustee, Trinity University, Baylor College of Medicine, Phillips Academy; chairman, Republican Party of Harris County, 1963-64; delegate to Republican National Convention, 1964, 1970; served as lieutenent (j.g.), pilot, U.S. Naval Reserve, World War II; decorated, D.F.C., air medals. (See also *Current Biography*, 1983).

Franklin, John Hope (1915-). Born, Rentiesville, Oklahoma; A.B., Fisk University, 1935; A.M., Harvard University, 1936, Ph.D., 1941; honorary degrees, seventy-four institutions; instructor, Fisk University, 1936-37; professor, St. Augustine's College, 1939-43; professor, North Carolina College at Durham, 1943-47; professor, Howard University,

1947-56; chairman, department of history, Brooklyn College, 1956-64; professor of American history, University of Chicago, 1964-82, chairman, department of history, 1967-70; James B. Duke professor of history, Duke University, 1982-85; professor of legal history, Duke University Law School, 1985- ; chairman, Board of Foreign Scholarships, 1966-69; member, National Council on Humanities, 1976-79; director, Illinois Bell Telephone Company, 1972-80; member, editorial board, American Scholar, 1972-76; board of directors, Salzburg Seminar, Museum of Science and Industry, 1968-80, DeSable Museum, 1970- ; trustee, Chicago Symphony, 1976-80, Fisk University, 1947-80; president, American Historical Association, 1970-71; member, Association for Study of Negro Life and History, Phi Beta Kappa, Phi Alpha Theta, American Philosophical Society; Edward Austin Fellow, 1937-38; Rosenwald Fellow, 1937-39; Guggenheim fellow, 1950-51, 1973-74; President's fellow, brown University, 1952-53; Center for Advanced Study in behavioral Science fellow, 1973-74; Sr. Mellon fellow, National Humanities Center, 1980-82; Fulbright professor, Australia, 1960; Jefferson lecturer in the humanities, 1976; named to Oklahoma Hall of Fame, 1978; Fulbright Distinguishing lecturer, Zimbabwe, 1986; Fellow American Academy of Arts and Sciences; author, *Free Negro in North Carolina*, 1943, *Militant South*, 1956, *Reconstruction After the Civil War*, 1961, *The Emancipation Proclamation*, 1963, *Land of the Free* (with others), 1966, *Racial Equality in America*, 1976, *A Southern Odyssey*, 1976, *George Washington Williams: A Biography*, 1985, *Illustrated History of Black Americans*, 1970, *From Slavery to Freedom: A History of Negro Americans*, 6th edition, 1987; editor, *Civil War Diary of James T. Ayers*, 1947, *A Fool's Errand by Albion Tourgee*, 1961, *Army Life in a Black Regiment by Thomas Higginson*, 1962, *Color and Race*, 1968, *Reminiscences of an Active Life* by John R. Lynch, 1970; editor (with August Meier), *Black Leaders in the Twentieth Century*, 1982; editor (with Harlan Abraham Eisenstadt), *Harlan Davidson's American History Series*.

HOLLAND, JEFFREY R. (1940-). Born, St. George, Utah; A.S., Dixie College, 1963; B.S., Brigham Young University, 1965, M.A., 1966; M. Phil., Yale University, 1972, Ph.D., 1973; dean, religious instruction, Brigham Young University, 1974-76, president, 1980- ; teacher, Latter-day Saints Church Educational System, 1965-74; commissioner of education, Church of Jesus Christ of Latter-day Saints, 1976-80; board of governors, Latter-day Saints Hospital, Salt Lake City; board of directors, Polynesian Cultural Center, Laie, Hawaii; member, advisory board, National Multiple Sclerosis Read-a-Thon Commission; contributor of numerous articles to professional journals.

HUNTER-GAULT, CHARLAYNE (1942-). Born, Due West, South Carolina; student, Wayne State University, 1959-61; B.A., University of Georgia, 1963; staffwriter, *New Yorker*, 1963-67, *Trans-Action*, 1967-68, *New York Times*, 1968-77; correspondent, Public Broadcasting System, *MacNeil/Lehrer Report*, 1978-82; national correspondent, MacNeil/Lehrer NewsHour, 1983- ; board of directors, Committee to Protect Journalists, Center for Communication, Foundation for Child Development; Russell Sage Fellowship, Washington University, 1967; recipient (with Joseph Lelyveld), *New York Times* Publishers Award, 1970, 1974, 1976; National News and Documentary Emmy Award, 1983, 1985;

George Foster Peabody Award, 1986; Newswomen's Club of New York Front Page Award; Good Housekeeping Broadcast Personality of the Year Award; American Women in Radio and Television Award; Atlanta Women in Communciations Award for Excellence in Journalism; Woman of Achievement Award, New York chapter, American Society for University Women. (See also *Current Biography*, 1987.)

KENNEDY, DONALD (1931-). Born, New York City; A.B., Harvard University, 1952, A.M., Ph.D., 1956; faculty member, Syracuse University, 1956-60; faculty member, Stanford University, 1960-77, professor of biological sciences, 1965-77, chairman of the department, 1965-72; senior consultant, Office of Scientific and Technological Policy, Executive Office of the President, 1976; commissioner, Federal Drug Administration, 1977-79; vice president and provost, Stanford University, 1979-80, president, 1980- ; board of overseers, Harvard University, 1970-76; fellow, American Academy of Arts and Sciences; member, National Academy of Sciences, American Physiology Society, Society of General Physiologists, American Society of Zoologists, Society of Experimental Biology (U.K.); author (with W. H. Telfer), *The Biology of Organisms*, 1965; editor, *The Living Cell*, 1966, *From Cell to Organism*, 1967; editorial board, *Journal of Experimental Zoology*, 1965-71, *Journal of Comparative Physiology*, 1965-76, *Journal of Neurophysiology*, 1969-75, *Science*, 1973-77. (See also *Current Biography*, 1984.)

KOVALCHECK, KASSIAN A. (1943-). Born, Pittsburgh, Pennsylvania; B.A., Wabash College, 1965, M.A., Indiana University, 1967, Ph.D., 1972; instructor, Vanderbilt University, 1969, assistant professor, 1972, associate professor of communication studies and director of forensics, 1975- ; Ellen Gregg Ingalls Award for Classroom Teaching, Vanderbilt University, 1987, Ernest Jones Award for Undergraduate Advising, Vanderbilt University, 1987; past president of the Tennessee Speech Association, and author of more than 26 articles primarily concerned with argumentation and debate.

LEWIS, ANTHONY (1927-). Born, New York City; A.B., Harvard University, 1948; deskman Sunday department of *New York Times*, 1948-52; Staff of the Democratic National Committee, 1952; reporter of the *Washington Daily News*, 1952-55; Washington bureau of the *New York Times*, 1965-72; editorial columnist, 1969- ; lecturer on law at Harvard University, 1974- ; James Madison visiting professor at Columbia University, 1983- ; Heywood Broun award, 1955; Pulitzer for national reporting, 1955 and 1963; Nieman fellowship, 1955-57; author, *Gideon's Trumpet*, 1964 (awarded best fact-crime book by Mystery Writer American), *Portrait of a Decade:The Second American Revolution*, 1964.

LLOYD, JOHN A. (1901-).Born, Jackson, Ohio; L.L.D., of Commercial Science, University of Cincinnati, 1970; elected member, Ohio State Senate, 1930-36; Ohio Superintendent of Insurance, 1939-43; vice president of Union Central Life Insurance Company, 1943-56; president and chief executive officer, 1956-77; chief executive officer of Lloyd and Company, 1978- ; trustee of the Ohio Historical Society; president of Cincinnati Chamber of Commerce, 1950-53; trustee of Cincinnati Symphony Orchestra; president of American Life Convention, 1963-66; member of Abraham Lincoln Museum Board of Visitors; author, *Vignettes of Lincoln*, 1974, *Snowbound with Mr. Lincoln*, 1977.

Loucks, Vernon Reece, Jr. (1934-). Born, Kenilworth, Illinois; B.A., Yale University, 1957; M.B.A., Harvard University, 1963; United States Marine Corps, first lieutenant, 1957-60; senior management consultant of George Fryand associates, 1963-65; senior management consultant, Baxter Travenol Laboratories, 1966- , executive vice president, 1973-76, director, 1975- , president and chief executive officer, 1976- ; member of several boards of directors of businesses and foundations.

Moyers, Bill (Billy Don) (1934-). Born, Hugo, Oklahoma; B.A. Journalism, University of Texas, 1956; (with honors) graduate student at University of Edinburgh, 1956-57; B.D., Southwestern Baptist Theological Seminary, 1959; Personal assistant to Senator Lyndon B. Johnson, 1960; associate director of Peace Corps, 1961-62, department director, 1963; special assistant to President Johnson, 1963-67; White House press secretary, 1965-67; publisher of *Newsday*, 1967-70; editor-in-chief of *Bill Moyers Journal*, 1971-76, 1978-81; editor and chief correspondent of CBS Reports, CBS-TV, 1976-78; Senior news analyst of CBS News, 1981-86; executive editor of Public Affairs TV, 1987- ; contributing editor to *Newsweek*, 1974-75; Emmy award, 1983, 1984, 1985; National Academy of TV Arts and Sciences, 1975, 1978, 1980, 1982, 1983, 1984, 1985, 1986, 1987; Ralph Lowell medal for contribution to Public Television; Silver Gavel award, American Bar Association; Arthur Morse fellow, Aspen Institute of Humanistic Studies; George Peabody award, 1976, 1980, 1985, 1986; DuPont Columbia award, 1979, 1986; George Polk award, 1981, 1986; author, *Listening to America*, 1971.

Reagan, Ronald Wilson (1911-). Born, Tampico, Illinois; B.A., Eureka College (Illinois), 1932; sports announcer, radio station WHO, Des Moines, Iowa, 1932-37; motion picture and television actor, 1937-66; program supervisor, General Electric Theater; president, Screen Actors Guild, 1947-52, 1959; captain, U.S. Air Force, 1942-45; governor, California, 1967-74; unsuccessful candidate for Republican presidential nomination, 1976; U.S. President, 1981-89; author, *Where's the Rest of Me*, 1965 (reprint 1981 as *My Early Life*), *Abortion and the Conscience of the Nation*, 1984. (See also *Current Biography*, 1982.)

Reed, Charles Bass (1941-). Born, Harrisburg, Pennsylvania; B.S., George Washington University, 1963, M.A., 1964, Ed.D., 1970; assistant associate professor, George Washington University, 1963-70; assistant director of National Performance-Based Teachers Education Project, American Association of Colleges for Teacher Education, 1970-71; coordinator of research and development in teacher education in Florida Department of Education, 1971-72; associate for planning and coordination Florida Department of Education, 1972-75; director of office of educational planning, budgeting, and evaluation, 1975-79; education policy coordinator Executive Office of Governor of Florida, 1979-80; director of legislative affairs, Executive Office of Governor, 1981-82, department chief of staff, 1982-84, chief of staff, 1984-85; chancellor Florida State University System, 1985- ; Member of Education Commission of the States (executive committee, 1984-) (Distinguished Service award, 1982.)

RIFKIN, JEREMY (1945-). Born, Chicago, Illinois; B.S., University of Pennsylvania, M.A., Tufts University; founder, People's Bicentennial Commission, 1971-76; founder and codirector, People's Business Commission, 1976-77; founder and president of the Foundation on Emerging Technologies, 1977- ; author, *How to Commit Revolution American Style* (with John Rossen), 1972, *Own Your Own Job*, 1977, *Who Should Play God* (with Ted Howard) 1977, *The North Will Rise Again: Pension, Politics, and Power in the 1980s* (with Randy Barber), 1978, *The Emerging Order: God in the Age of Scarcity* (with Ted Howard), 1980, *Algeny* (with Nicanor Perlas), 1983, *Declaration of a Heretic*, 1985.

SAGAN, CARL EDWARD (1934-). Born, New York City; B.A., University of Chicago, 1954, B.S., 1955, M.S., 1956, Ph.D, 1960; D.Sc. (honorary), Rensselaer Polytechnic Institute, 1975, Denison University, 1976, Clarkson College, 1977; D.H.L. (honorary), Skidmore College, 1976; research fellow, University of California, Berkeley, 1960-62; visiting assistant professor, Stanford Medical School, 1962-63; Smithsonian Astrophysics Observatory, 1962-68; lecturer and then assistant professor, Harvard University, 1962-68; member of faculty, Cornell University, 1967- , professor 1970- , David Duncan professor of physical sciences, 1976- , director of Laboratory of Planetary Studies, 1968- , visiting professor and guest lecturer, various colleges and universities; lecturer for the Apollo flight crews of NASA, 1969-72; narrator, BBC/PBL television production, "The Violent Universe," 1969; recipient, Smith Prize, Harvard, 1964, NASA medal for scientific achievement, 1972, Prix Galabert, 1973, John Campbell Award, 1974, Klumpke-Roberts Prize, 1974, Priestley Award, 1975, NASA Award for Public Service, 1977, Pulitzer Prize for *The Dragons of Eden*, 1978; National Science fellow, 1955-60, Sloan Research fellow, 1963-67; author *Atmospheres of Mars and Venus*, 1961, *Planets*, 1966, *Intelligent Life in the Universe*, 1966, *Planetary Exploration*, 1970, *Mars and the Mind of Man*, 1973, *The Cosmic Connecticut*, 1973, *Other Worlds*, 1975, *The Dragons of Eden*, 1977, *Murmurs of Earth: The Voyager Interstellar Record*, 1978, *Broca's Brain*, 1979, *Cosmos*, 1980, *Contact*, 1985, *Comet*, 1985; editor and author of various articles in scientific and astronomy journals. (See also *Current Biography*, 1970.)

SCHLESINGER, ARTHUR, JR. (1917-). Born, Columbus, Ohio; A.B., *summa cum laude*, Harvard University, 1938; member, Society of Fellows, 1939-42; Doctor of Letters, Muhlenberg College, 1950; associate professor, Harvard University, 1946-54, professor, 1954-61; member, Adlai Stevenson campaign staff, 1952, 1956; special assistant to President of the United States, 1961-64; Albert Schweitzer Chair in the Humanities, City University of New York, 1967- ; member, Board of Trustees, American Film Institute; trustee, Twentieth Century Fund; awards, Pulitzer Prize for history, 1945, Guggenheim fellowship, 1946, American Academy of Arts and Letters grant, 1946, Pulitzer Prize for biography, 1965, National Book Award, 1965; author, *The Age of Jackson*, 1945, *The Coming of the*

New Deal, 1958, *Kennedy or Nixon*, 1960, *A Thousand Days: John F. Kennedy in the White House*, 1965, *The Bitter Heritage*, 1967, *The Crisis of Confidence*, 1969, *The Imperial Presidency*, 1973, *Robert F. Kennedy and His Times*, 1978, and other works. (See also *Current Biography*, 1976.)

SPETH, GUS (JAMES GUSTAVE) (1942-). Born, Orangeburg, South Carolina, B.A. *summa cum laude*, Yale University, 1964; B. Littlk Balliol College, Oxford University, 1966; LL.B., Yale University, 1969; admitted, Washingotn, D.C. bar, 1969; law clerk to Justice Hugo L. Black, U.S. Supreme Court, 1969-70; senior attorney, Natural Resources Defense Council, 1970-77; member, Council on Environmental Quality, 1977-79, chairman, 1979-81; professor of law, Georgetown University Law Center, 1981-82; president, World Resources Institute, 1982- ; chairman, President's Task Force on Global Resources and Environment, 1980; board of directors, Natural Resources Defense Council, 1981-82, Environmental Law Institute, Workplace Health Fund, Global Tomorrow Coalition; vice-chairman, board of Environmental and Energy Study Institute; member, Council on Foreign Relations; recipient, National Wildlife Federation's Resources Defense Award, 1976; Rhodes Scholar, 1964-66; Global 500 Honor Roll, United Nations Environment Programme, 1988; honorary fellow, China Environmental Strategy Center, 1988; contributor, articles to professsional journals.

STEWART, DONALD M. (1938-). Born, Chicago, Illinois; B.A., Grinnell College, 1959; M.A., Yale University, 1962; M.P.A., Harvard University, 1969; postgraduate work at Harvard University, 1975; assistant to representative for West Africa Ford Foundation, 1962-64; program assistant of Middle East Africa Project, 1964-66; assistant representative Cairo, 1966-67; program officer Middle East Africa Program, 1968-70; executive assistant to president of University of Pennsylvania, 1970-72; researcher Ford Foundation Study Award, 1972-73; director Community Leadership Seminar Program, 1973-74; Continuing Education, 1973-74; Higher Education Research, 1973-74; instructor, City Planning and Public Policy Analysis, 1973-74; president, Spelman College, 1976-86; president and treasurer of Atlanta Symphony Orchestra; member of governing board of Grinnel College; member of Council on Foreign Relations; board of directors of Commission for Economic Development; president of Commission on Arts and Humanities; Member of National Academy of Public Administrators.

CUMULATIVE SPEAKER INDEX

1980-1989

A cumulative author index to the volumes of *Representative American Speeches* for the years 1937-1938 through 1959-1960 appears in the 1959-1960 volume, for the years 1960-1961 through 1969-1970 in the 1979-1970 volume, and for 1970-1971 through 1979-1980, in the 1979-1980 volume.

Haiman, F. S. 1984-85, 42-58, How fares the First Amendment?

Harriman, P. C. 1986-87, 22-31, "The sinews of peace": remarks commemorating the 40th anniversary of Winston Churchill's 'Iron Curtain' speech; 1987-88, 85-96, The President and Congress in U.S. foreign policy: where is the water's edge?

Harris, P. R. 1980-81, 35-48, Political pluralism and religious absolutism

Hart, Gary. 1982-83, 55-62, A time for economic reform

Holland, J. R. 1984-85, 79-95, A "notion" at risk: the greater crisis in American education; 1988-89, 123-34, Whose children are these?

Hook, Sidney. 1984-85, 107-21, The humanities and the defense of a free society

Hooks, B. L. 1983-84, 81-91, Struggle on

Hunter-Gault, Charlayne. 1988-89, 172-76, Georgia—of 25 years ago—on my mind

Ilchman, A. S. 1981-82, 102-11, The public purposes of private colleges

Jacob, J. E. 1981-82, 145-50, The state of black America; 1986-87, 86-93, Two challenges: South Africa and urban education

Jacobs, H. C. 1985-86, 149-55, Readers: an endangered species?

Jordan, V. E., Jr. 1980-81, 210-18, To build a more equal society; 1985-86, 33-40, Let us finish the task

Keller, Albert, Jr. 1982-83, 171-73, A memorial to American Vietnam War veterans

Kennedy, Donald. 1983-84, 63-75, The long-term worldwide biological consequences of nuclear war; 1985-86, 156-66, "Can we help?": public service and the young; 1986-87, 150-59, Investing in the young; 1988-89, 35-46, Science and the American future

Kennedy, E. M. 1980-81, 25-35, The dream shall never die: speech to the Democratic National Convention; 1983-84, 52-63, Tolerance and truth in America; 1986-87, 43-49, The worsening crisis in health care; 1987-88, 55-64, Beyond entertainment tonight: the press and the 1988 campaign

Kirkland, J. L. 1981-82, 150-60, Solidarity, indispensable key to the future

Kirkpatrick, J. J. 1982-83, 161-70, Promoting free elections

Knapp, D. C. 1980-81, 186-95, Education in the '80s

Koop, C. E. 1982-83, 207-18, Violence and public health; 1983-84, 164-75, An epidemic of violence; 1986-87, 49-58, Educating our children about AIDS

Koppel, Ted. 1987-88, 49-55, The vannatizing of America

Kovalcheck, K. A., Jr. 1988-89, 59-73, Eternal vigilance is still the price of liberty

Laingen, L. B. 1980-81, 81-83, Welcome home

INDEX TO VOLUME 61 (1989) BY SUBJECT

The Palestinian Problem (61:1)
Ethics in Politics and Government (61:2)
The Welfare Debate (61:3)
Energy and Conservation (61:4)
Political Change in Southeast Asia (61:5)
Representative American Speeches 1988–1989 (61:6)

America" sponsored by the Harvard-Radcliffe Black Students Association at Harvard University, Cambridge, Massachusetts. F. 4, '89. **61:6**

Integration in Education

Georgia—of 25 years ago—on my mind. Charlayne Hunter-Gault. Speech delivered at the commencement exercises of the University of Georgia, Athens, Georgia. Je. 11, '88. **61:6**

BUSINESS MANAGEMENT

A reclamation of leadership. Vernon R. Loucks, Jr. *Vital Speeches of the Day* N. 15, '88. **61:6**

CAMBODIA

Foreign Relations

Vietnam

Efforts toward a Cambodian settlement. Vernon A. Walters. *Department of State Bulletin* F. '89. **61:5**

Politics and Government

Efforts toward a Cambodian settlement. Vernon A. Walters. *Department of State Bulletin* F. '89. **61:5**

The endless war: the return of the Khmer Rouge. Steven Erlanger. *New York Times Magazine* Mr. 5, '89. **61:5**

CHARACTER

Individual character and political ethics. Nicholas Xenos. *Grand Street* 7. Summer '88. **61:2**

CHERNOBYL NUCLEAR DISASTER, 1986

Nuclear power's burdened future. Christopher Flavin. *The Bulletin of the Atomic Scientists* Jl./Ag. '87. **61:4**

CHILD WELFARE

The hollow promise. David Whitman. *U. S. News & World Report* N. 7, '88. **61:3**

A right to the tree of life. Michael Robin. *The Nation* Je. 9, '84. **61:3**

Who will protect the children? Marian Wright Edelman. *USA Today Magazine* Mr. '86. **61:3**

New York (N.Y.)

Children of poverty. Andrew Stein. *New York Times Magazine* Je. 8, '86. **61:3**

Children of the night. Dinitia Smith. *New York* D. 1, '86. **61:3**

CONFLICT OF INTERESTS (PUBLIC OFFICE)

Tainted saint. Brooks Jackson. Adapted from *Honest Graft: Big Money and the American Political Process*. S./O. '88. **61:2**

CORRUPTION

Politics and Government

United States

Deregulation by sleaze. Frank Donner and James Ledbetter. *The Nation* F. 6, '88. **61:2**

Executive summary of the report of the congressional committees investigating the Iran-Contra affair. 100th Congress, 1st Session, H. Rept. No. 100-433, S. Rept. No. 100-216. '87. **61:2**

Political imperfections: scandal time in Washington. Suzanne Garment. *Public Opinion* 10:1. '87. **61:2**

DAMS

Low-head hydropower for local use. Peter Kakela, Gary Chilson, and William Patric. *Environment* Ja./F. '85. **61:4**

DISARMAMENT

Thoughts on the 125th anniversary of the Battle of Gettysburg. Carl Sagan. Speech delivered at the 125th celebration of the Battle of Gettysburg and the rededication ceremonies of the Eternal Light Peace Memorial at Gettysburg National Military Park, Pennsylvania. Jl. 3, '88. **61:6**

DRUGS

Drugs and Youth

The war against drugs: where we stand. William J. Bennett. Speech delivered at the White House Conference for a Drug-Free America. Mr. 2, '88. **61:6**

United States

The legalization of drugs. David Boaz. *Vital Speeches of the Day* Ag. 15, '88. **61:6**

ELECTRIC PLANTS

Environmental Aspects

Scrubber scrapper. Edward C. Baig. *Fortune* Ap. 14, '86. **61:4**

Energy Usage

Coal-fired power plants for the future. Richard E. Balzhiser and Kurt E. Yeager. *Scientific American* S. '87. **61:4**

GAS SUPPLY

America's plentiful energy resource. David Osborne. *The Atlantic Monthly* Mr. '84. **61:4**

GASOLINE

Taxation

Oil drip. *The New Republic* Ap. 28, '86. **61:4**

GENETIC ENGINEERING

Social Aspects

Biotechnology at a crossroads. Jeremy Rifkin. Speech delivered at the United States Agricultural Communicators Congress in Washington, D.C. Jl. 12, '88. **61:6**

GOVERNMENT ETHICS

The glass house. Paul Simon. From *The Glass House: Politics and Morality in the Nation's Capital.* © '84. **61:2**

Lobbying and legislative ethics. Jay H. Hedlund. From Bruce Jennings and Daniel Callahan, eds., *Representation and Responsibility: Exploring Legislative Ethics.* '85. **61:2**

The need for people of virtue. Lee H. Hamilton. From *Ethics: Easier Said Than Done.* Spring/Summer '88. **61:2**

We need more leadership in ethics. Ted Stevens. From *Ethics: Easier Said Than Done.* Spring/Summer '88. **61:2**

When the government tells lies. Anthony Marro. *Columbia Journalism Review* Ap./Mr. '85. **61:2**

White House ethics. Robert N. Roberts. From *White House Ethics: The History of the Politics of Conflict of Interest Legislation.* © '88. **61:2**

Laws and Regulations

Ethics in government laws. Alfred S. Neely IV. From *Ethics-in-Government Laws: Are They Too Ethical?* © '84. **61:2**

The Office of Government Ethics: vigilant watchdog or toothless terrier? W. John Moore. *Government Executive* O. '87. **61:2**

Legislative Bodies

Ethics in the legislative process: an overview. Daniel Callahan and Bruce Jennings. From *Ethics: Easier Said Than Done.* Spring/Summer '88. **61:2**

GREENHOUSE EFFECT

Can the world be saved? Gus Speth. Speech delivered to the United States Environmental Protection Agency seminar in Washington, D.C. Je. 21, '88. **61:6**

Israel's 40-year quandary. Joseph M. Hochstein. *Editorial Research Reports* 1:14. Ap. 15, '88. **61:1**

A small peaceful village. Yitshaq Ben-Ami. From *Years of Wrath, Days of Glory: Memoirs from the Irgun*. © '82. **61:1**

Jewish-Arab Relations

The future. Henry Cattan. From *The Palestine Question*. '88. **61:1**

Israel's Arab minority: the beginning of a tragedy. Hal Draper. From *Zionism, Israel, & the Arabs: The Historical Background of the Middle East Tragedy*. © '67. **61:1**

The United Nations and the national rights of the people of Palestine. W. Thomas Mallison. From *The United Nations and the Question of Palestine: A Compilation of Essays, 1980–1982*. '80. **61:1**

ISRAEL-ARAB WARS, 1967–

Territorial Questions

Israel's 40-year quandary. Joseph M. Hochstein. *Editorial Research Reports* 1:14. Ap. 15, '88. **61:1**

JEWISH-ARAB RELATIONS

Public Opinion

United States

The formation of American public opinion and the question of Palestine. Edward W. Said. From *Ibrahim Abu-Lughod, ed., Palestinian Rights: Affirmation and Denial*. '82. **61:1**

JEWS

Nationalism

The Jewish case, put before the Palestine Royal Commission. Chaim Weizmann. From Barnet Litvinoff, ed., *Israel: A Chronology and Fact Book, 2500 B.C.–1972*. '74. **61:1**

KHMER ROUGE

The endless war: the return of the Khmer Rouge. Steven Erlanger. *New York Times Magazine* Mr. 5, '89. **61:5**

KOREA (SOUTH)

Foreign Relations

Korea (North)

It's time to reassess the U.S.-Korea defense treaty. Doug Bandow. *USA Today Magazine* Jl. '88. **61:5**

MILITARY ASSISTANCE, AMERICAN

Developing Countries

Morality and the Reagan Doctrine. Charles Krauthammer. *The New Republic* S. 8, '86. **61:2**

NATIONAL LIBERATION MOVEMENTS

Morality and the Reagan Doctrine. Charles Krauthammer. *The New Republic* S. 8, '86. **61:2**

NATURAL GAS

Prices

America's plentiful energy resource. David Osborne. *The Atlantic Monthly* Mr. '84. **61:4**

NUCLEAR ENERGY

Dim hopes for nuclear power. Daniel Kirshner. *Environment* Jl./Ag. '85. **61:4**

The future of nuclear power. Russ Manning. *Environment* My. '85. **61:4**

U. S. nuclear power in the next twenty years. Bernard I. Spinrad. *Science* F. 12, '88. **61:4**

Environmental Aspects

Nuclear power's burdened future. Christopher Flavin. *The Bulletin of the Atomic Scientists* Jl./Ag. '87. **61:4**

International Aspects

Nuclear power's burdened future. Christopher Flavin. *The Bulletin of the Atomic Scientists* Jl./Ag. '87. **61:4**

NUCLEAR FUSION

Fusion: fuel for the future? *The Futurist* Mr./Ap. '88. **61:4**

NUCLEAR POWER PLANTS

Decommissioning

As Shoreham goes. *The Nation* Je. 11, '88. **61:4**

Environmental Aspects

Dim hopes for nuclear power. Daniel Kirshner. *Environment* Jl./Ag. '85. **61:4**

The future of nuclear power. Russ Manning. *Environment* My. '85. **61:4**

NUCLEAR WARFARE

Prevention

Thoughts on the 125th anniversary of the Battle of Gettysburg. Carl Sagan. Speech delivered at the 125th celebration of the Battle of Gettysburg and the rededication ceremonies of the Eternal Light Peace Memorial at Gettysburg National Military Park, Pennsylvania. Jl. 3, '88. **61:6**

PETROLEUM

Prices

Get ready for the coming oil crisis. John Paul Newport, Jr. *Fortune* Mr. 16, '87. **61:4**

Lower oil prices fuel concern. James J. MacKenzie. *Technology Review* Ag./S. '86. **61:4**

Oil drip. *The New Republic* Ap. 28, '86. **61:4**

PETROLEUM INDUSTRY

Finance

The great Texas oil bust. Daniel Pedersen and Daniel Shapiro. *Newsweek* Mr. 31, '86. **61:4**

PETROLEUM SUPPLY

Get ready for the coming oil crisis. John Paul Newport, Jr. *Fortune* Mr. 16, '87. **61:4**

Lower oil prices fuel concern. James J. MacKenzie. *Technology Review* Ag./S. '86. **61:4**

The next oil crisis. *Commonweal* Mr. 13, '87. **61:4**

PHILIPPINES

Politics and Government

Aquino's Philippines: the center holds. Sandra Burton. *Foreign Affairs* 65. '87. **61:5**

Democracy in the Philippines. Belinda A. Aquino. *Current History* Ap. '89. **61:5**

"Total war" in the Philippines. Ninotchka Rosca. *The Nation* Je. 19, '89. **61:5**

POLITICAL ETHICS

Individual character and political ethics. Nicholas Xenos. *Grand Street* 7. Summer '88. **61:2**

POOR

Distancing the homeless. Jonathan Kozol. *Yale Review* Winter '88. **61:3**

Forgotten Americans: the "working poor." Tom Joe. *USA Today Magazine* Mr. '84. **61:3**

Housing

"Is the next step Penn Station?" Richard J. Margolis. *The New Leader* F. 10, '86. **61:3**

Massachusetts

The greatest welfare reform: REAL JOBS. Michael S. Dukakis. *USA Today Magazine* Mr. '88. **61:3**

Single-Parent Families

Government Policy

Getting rough on the poor. Andrew Hacker. *New York Review of Books* O. 13, '88. **61:3**

REFUGEES

Cambodian

The endless war: the return of the Khmer Rouge. Steven Erlanger. *New York Times Magazine* Mr. 5, '89. **61:5**

Palestinian Arabs

Conclusion. Benny Morris. From *The Birth of the Palestinian Refugee Problem, 1947–1949.* © '87. **61:1**

Preface. Fawaz Turki. From *The Disinherited: Journal of a Palestinian Exile.* © '72. **61:1**

REGULATORY AGENCIES

United States

Deregulation by sleaze. Frank Donner and James Ledbetter. *The Nation* F. 6, '88. **61:2**

RELIGION AND POLITICS

Exorcising Wilson's ghost: morality and foreign policy in America's third century. George Weigel. *The Washington Quarterly* 10:4. Autumn '87. **61:2**

SCHOOL AND THE HOME

Whose children are these? Jeffrey R. Holland. *Vital Speeches of the Day* Jl. 1, '88. **61:6**

SCIENCE AND STATE

United States

Science and the American future. Donald Kennedy. Speech delivered at the 155th meeting of the American Association for the Advancement of Science, San Francisco, California. Ja. 14, '89. **61:6**

SCIENTIFIC RESEARCH

Finance

Science and the American future. Donald Kennedy. Speech delivered at

Sri Lanka's ethnic conflict: the Indo-Lanka peace accord. Ralph R. Premdas and S. W. R. de A. Samarasinghe. *Asian Survey* Je. '88. **61:5**

Tension and conflict in Sri Lanka. Robert N. Kearney. *Current History* Mr. '86. **61:5**

TAMILS

Resolving the Sri Lankan conflict. Robert A. Peck. *Department of State Bulletin* My. '87. **61:5**

The roots of conflict in Sri Lanka. Victoria A. Rebeck. *The Christian Century* S. 23, '87. **61:5**

Tension and conflict in Sri Lanka. Robert N. Kearney. *Current History* Mr. '86. **61:5**

Sri Lanka

Political Activities

Sri Lanka's ethnic conflict: the Indo-Lanka peace accord. Ralph R. Premdas and S. W. R. de A. Samarasinghe. *Asian Survey* Je. '88. **61:5**

TERRORISM

Sri Lanka

Resolving the Sri Lankan conflict. Robert A. Peck. *Department of State Bulletin* My. '87. **61:5**

TEXAS

Economic Conditions

The great Texas oil bust. Daniel Pedersen and Daniel Shapiro. *Newsweek* Mr. 31, '86. **61:4**

THIN FILMS

A bright spot on the solar scene. Robert Pool. *Science* Ag. 19, '88. **61:4**

UNITED STATES

Armed Forces

Forces in Korea

It's time to reassess the U.S.-Korea defense treaty. Doug Bandow. *USA Today Magazine* Jl. '88. **61:5**

Commerce

Canada

An old favorite returns. John DeMont. *Maclean's* Ja. 9, '89. **61:4**

Foreign Relations

Exorcising Wilson's ghost: morality and foreign policy in America's third

century. George Weigel. *The Washington Quarterly* 10:4. Autumn '87. **61:2**

Morality and foreign policy. George Kennan. *Foreign Affairs* 64:2. '85–'86. **61:2**

Anti-Communist Measures

Morality and the Reagan Doctrine. Charles Krauthammer. *The New Republic* S. 8, '86. **61:2**

Asia

When ideology bows to economics. Douglas Stanglin with Dusko Doder and Mike Tharp. *U. S. News & World Report* F. 6, '89. **61:5**

Cambodia

Efforts toward a Cambodian settlement. Vernon A. Walters. *Department of State Bulletin* F. '89. **61:5**

Korea (South)

It's time to reassess the U.S.-Korea defense treaty. Doug Bandow. *USA Today Magazine* Jl. '88. **61:5**

Malaysia

Developments in Malaysia. David F. Lambertson. *Department of State Bulletin* N. '88. **61:5**

Philippines

Aquino's Philippines: the center holds. Sandra Burton. *Foreign Affairs* 65. '87. **61:5**

Southeast Asia

The voting fields. *The New Republic* Ag. 10–17, '87. **61:5**

Politics and Government

Farewell address. Ronald W. Reagan. *Vital Speeches of the Day* F. 1, '89. **61:6**

Inaugural address. George H. W. Bush. *Department of State Bulletin* Ap. '89. **61:6**

Robert F. Kennedy remembered. Arthur Schlesinger, Jr. Speech delivered at a special retrospective conference on the theme "R.F.K. Remembered" at Loyola Marymount University, Los Angeles, California. Ap. 23, '88. **61:6**

The secret of Mr. Lincoln's greatness. John A. Lloyd. Speech delivered as part of Lincoln Memorial University's annual ceremonies commemorating the birthday of Abraham Lincoln, Harrogate, Tennessee. F. 12, '88. **61:6**

Social Conditions

These things we know. John Hope Franklin. Speech delivered at the

207th commencement exercises of Louisiana State University, Baton Rouge, Louisiana. My. 18, '88. **61:6**

Social Policy

Forgotten Americans: the "working poor." Tom Joe. *USA Today Magazine* Mr. '84. **61:3**

WORKFARE

From welfare to workfare. Jacob V. Lamar, Jr. *Time* F. 3, '86. **61:3**

The greatest welfare reform: REAL JOBS. Michael S. Dukakis. *USA Today Magazine* Mr. '88. **61:3**

Is it hype or true reform? Mickey Kaus. *Newsweek* Je. 13, '88. **61:3**

The key to welfare reform. David Whitman. *Atlantic* Je. '87. **61:3**

Welfare reform may finally be in the works. Susan B. Garland. *Business Week* N. 2, '87. **61:3**

Why welfare reform is a sham. Mimi Abramovitz. *The Nation* S. 26, '88. **61:3**

Workfare. Laurie Udesky. *Progressive* Ag. '87. **61:3**

Single-Parent Families

Government Policy

Getting rough on the poor. Andrew Hacker. *New York Review of Books* O. 13, '88. **61:3**

ZIONISM

Israel

In place of a summary. Simha Flapan. From *Zionism and the Palestinians.* © '79. **61:1**